INTERACTIVE PUBLISHERS HANDBOOK

Sponsored by
Apple Computer's **"MASTERS OF MEDIA"** program
and the **APPLE MEDIA PROGRAM (AMP)**

INTERACTIVE PUBLISHERS HANDBOOK

by
PAUL PALUMBO

CARRONADE GROUP

Masters of Media.
INTERACTIVE PUBLISHERS HANDBOOK
Sponsored by
Apple Computer's **"MASTERS OF MEDIA"** program
and the **APPLE MEDIA PROGRAM (AMP)**

Interactive Publishers Handbook
© 1996 Paul Palumbo
All rights reserved, including the right of reproduction in whole or in part in any form.

ISBN#: 1-885452-07-1
Printed and bound in the United States of America
Cover Design by Tim Neil
Edited by Clancy Fort and Jon Samsel

Published by The Carronade Group
An Imprint of Liquid Mercury, Inc.
2355 Francisco Street, Suite 6, San Francisco, CA 94123
(800) 529-3501, (415) 474-3500
http://www.carronade.com

Acknowledgement is made to the following for permission to reproduce the material indicated:

Thomas J. Cervantez of the law firm Pillsbury, Madison & Sutro, LLP for two sample contracts— "Software Developer and Publishing Agreement" and "Affiliated Label Agreement," ©1996; Allen S. Melser and Becky L. Troutman of the law firm Popham, Haik, Schnobrich & Kaufman for the work— "Intellectual Property Rights Affecting Multimedia Projects," ©1996, Allen S. Melser for the work— "Patents and Corporate Litigation: Practical Observations," ©1996.

A special thanks to Multimedia Daily, for granting permission to re-purpose portions of author's previously published market analysus and data.

Limits of Liability and Disclaimer of Warranty: The author and publisher of this book have used their best efforts in preparing this book and the programs contained in it. These efforts include the development, research, and testing of the theories and procedures to determine their effectiveness. THE AUTHOR AND PUBLISHER MAKE NO WARRANTY OF ANY KIND, EXPRESSED OR IMPLIED, WITH REGARD TO THESE PROGRAMS OR THE DOCUMENTATION CONTAINED IN THIS BOOK. THE AUTHOR AND PUBLISHER SPECIFICALLY DISCLAIM ANY WARRANTIES OF MERCHANTABILITY OR FITNESS FOR A PARTICULAR PURPOSE. THE AUTHOR AND PUBLISHER SHALL NOT BE LIABLE IN ANY EVENT FOR INCIDENTAL OR CONSEQUENTIAL DAMAGES IN CONNECTION WITH, OR ARISING OUT OF, THE FURNISHING, PERFORMANCE, OR USE OF THESE PROGRAMS.

TABLE OF CONTENTS

Dedication
About the Author
Introduction

Chapter 1 - The Market   19
Chapter 2 - The Customers   37
Chapter 3 - Financing   53
Chapter 4 - The Product   69
Chapter 5 - Marketing and Public Relations   111
Chapter 6 - Distribution   149
Chapter 7 - Online Network Franchise   179
Chapter 8 - Merchandising   199

Appendix

Case Studies   206
Patents and Corporate Litigation: Practical Considerations   215
Software Development and Publishing Agreement   225
Intellectual Property Rights Affecting Multimedia Projects   249
Affiliated Label Agreement   269
Distributor Directory   283
Law Firm Directory   295
Venture Capital Directory   301
Replication & Packaging Directory   307

DEDICATION

In 1994, Steve Hollis entered our lives like a jolt of adrenaline. As a sales rep for Computer Currents magazine, we watched a positive, charismatic showman work a convention crowd like no other. We were in awe.

Over time (and a few beers, lobster tails & good cheer) we learned that Steve was also a good person. Someone whose suave English charm never failed to light up a room. As a courageous entrepreneur— Steve was always planting the seeds for some new business endeavor. His greatest triumph was perhaps Multimedia Live!, a multimedia conference and expo which broke new ground as a showcase for state-of-the-art multimedia product.

In January 1996, just a few days after his 40th birthday, Steve Hollis left our lives forever. His death was a tragic loss to those who knew and loved him. In our grief, we are comforted by the thought that great men don't leave this world quietly. On foggy nights, we sometimes hear distant voices drifting in off the Bay, encouraging us to go on— to work harder— to dig in. We swear it's Steve.

We're still working hard to achieve our dreams in an industry that doesn't always pause long enough to applaud its own accomplishments. We'd like to pause long enough to salute our friend, Steve Hollis. You're dreams live on in all of us. We will never forget you.

— **Jon Samsel & Clancy Fort**
Publishers

ABOUT THE AUTHOR

Paul A. Palumbo is an entertainment analyst and writer based in Seaside, California. Mr. Palumbo began his career with Paul Kagan Associates, Carmel, CA., in early 1991, as an M & A writer and analyst covering global media and multimedia deal making. In 1994 Mr. Palumbo joined Adams Media Research as an analyst, and worked closely with Tom Adams, one of the entertainment industry's premiere consultants and senior analysts. In 1995, Mr. Palumbo began working as a freelance analyst and writer, and regularly contributes to such newsletters as Variety Deal Memo, New Media Stragegist, Multimedia Daily and Electronic Gaming News.

Mr. Palumbo has also written two emerging media special reports: Broadband Television Strategies: Content and Distribution Paradigms for the Digital Era for Simba Information, Wilton, CT., and New Media 100 for Baskerville Communications, Thousand Oaks, CA., which is an in-depth finanacial analysis of the top 100 media, multimedia, distribution and telecommunications companies in the United States.

SPONSORS

The **APPLE MEDIA PROGRAM (AMP)** is the Online media infomation source for technology, tools, resources and the new media developer community. Designed for content developers and the creative community, AMP offers a breadth of resources and information to keep new media developers up-to-date on Apple's offerings for authoring and playback. AMP gives you access to some of the best minds and most successful members of the Interactive Media Community. Program features include the AMP Web Site and Members Only Area, Market Research Reports & Guidebooks, Apple Multimedia Information Mailing, Co-marketing Opportunities, Development Hardware Purchasing Priviliges, Multimedia Events and Training Discounts, and Apple's Interactive Music Track.

Apple Media Program
Apple Computer, Inc.
One Infinite Loop
Cupertino, CA 95014

Voice: 408-974-4897
www: http://www.amp.apple.com

Apple Computer's **"MASTERS OF MEDIA"** program educates customers on how to make and save money by leveraging their investment in their intellectual property, and by managing the technology to more effectively communicate their ideas. For the creative or publisher, the equity is their content, for the production or pre-press company, color production and color fidelity, and for the corporation the equity is their brand. "Masters of Media" is a comprehensive program for artists, designers, musicians, publishers, webmasters, advertising agencies, entertainment companies, and corporate communicators, providing the means to move and expand their content from one media to all media. Communications no longer have to be media-specific, but can now become media universal. Macintosh technologies allow everyone the power to visualize their ideas more easily, whether they want to communicate across multiple media, in multiple languages, with consistent color, in 3D, on the Internet, in virtual reality, or to automate the repetitive tasks of media creation. "Master The Media"

"Masters of Media"
Apple Computer, Inc.
One Infinite Loop
Cupertino, CA 95014

Voice: 1-800-776-2333
       408-996-1010
www: http://www.masters.media.apple.com
     http://www.apple.com

INTRODUCTION

Interactive title development is a fascinating growth and innovation-driven industry. As a result, it has also attracted some of the brightest entrepreneurial minds in the world, as well some of the most creative talent drawn from the entertainment business. The purpose of this book is to tap into that existing information and knowledge base and to present new and established developers a real-world view of the interactive business from an insider's perspective.

The executives and analysts that chose to share their interactive insight with the Carronade Group during the research phase of this book not only have years of hands-on experience in interactive entertainment, but the battle scars to prove it. Nowadays, interactive title development is very similar to any other entertainment genre, including film, TV production, made-for-video or publishing: It's very difficult to predict what the "hits" are going to be, and wrong development decisions are very expensive.

Enter the *Interactive Publishers Handbook*. This book is designed as a one-stop easy reference manual. It's laced with dozens of examples and models cut from today's market that will help developers make better business decisions about where and when to invest scare capital, and how to avoid costly mistakes. This book will provide readers with the valuable, hard-won, accumulated knowledge of some of the most recognizable and successful players in the business today, augmented and enhanced with key analysis provided by the Carronade Group. In addition, this handbook contains views, opinions and numerous specific interactive title development case studies drawn from a broad array of successful publishers.

Introduction

These publishers and executives have chosen to share their years of interactive experience with a broader audience. That decision was made in an effort to better educate title developers about the realities of today's business model and also to shed light on the entire enrichment chain— from document design to retail distribution— of the interactive software industry. The *Interactive Publishers Handbook* was created to assist all interested parties in making sound business and development decisions.

Reality Check

The problem for developers chasing profits in the interactive business is that publishing markets for CD-ROM and other packaged media products have been extremely volatile over the past four years. It's a fact that very few interactive publishers and developers are making money today. Most analysts and industry observers believe there will be substantial markets and revenue upside as the hardware base of advanced platform machines grows and network (i.e. Internet) distribution and product exploitation become commonplace, sometime around the year 2000.

In other words, development of an interactive product is not a short-term, get-rich- quick investment play. While today's market is uncertain and chaotic, there are plenty of opportunities. Platform and delivery transition, particularly those driven by innovation and the finicky tastes of consumers, at once provide interactive title developers and publishers with extraordinary latitude to find success, as well as an inverse level of failure.

Both those outcomes are a function of adept (or not) business decisions, intelligent alliance building, successful and affordable access to marketable development concepts and steady access to cash. In fact, the decisions necessary to produce a successful interactive title are typically exquisite in detail and are made long in advance (nine months to two years) of any particular title's debut at retail.

The Interactive Players

A **developer**, as defined in this book, is a company which produces interactive content through third-party, affiliated label or co-publishing deals.

Its key people assets include artists, authors, computer programmers and management. Examples of developers include Cyan (producer of Myst), Vortex Media Arts (producer of Madeline and the Magnificent Puppet Show), and Mondo Media (producer of the Daedalus Encounter).

A **publisher,** as defined in this book, is a company which finances, markets, promotes and distributes interactive media into any market. At this time, most interactive publishers are also developers. Examples of publishers include Broderbund, Electronic Arts, Virgin Interactive, Davidson & Associates and Mindscape.

The two groups are brought together by means of a development deal, a formal business relationship created to bring a proposed new product to market. A typical development deal will guarantee the developer a fee for the cost of producing a marketable title, but can also include a minimum backend (or royalty) participation once certain retail sales milestones are met.

Publishers typically collect anywhere from 30% to 35% of wholesale price in return for assuming the risk of upfront development costs. Those can range from $250,000 to $500,000 at the lower end of the development scale (education, reference, strategy/simulation fare), all the way up to $750,000 to $1,500,000 (and far beyond) for super high-tech action titles with glitzy Hollywood production values.

Wholesale price is defined as the price at which a product is sold into the distribution channel. Wholesale prices range from 45% to 55% of retail price.

The Decision Sets

There are many requirements that go into a production decision. In order to even have a chance at achieving market success, product decision sets require sound knowledge of the publishing business, the packaged media business, technology, talent evaluation, managing/acquiring resources, pre-planning, planning, post-production, storytelling insight, distribution, tight-fisted fiscal control and creative vision.

Introduction

The scope and mission of your business plan and the positioning of a particular title involves questions such as: Are you a developer? A publisher? Are you both? Do you license franchises that have already found an audience, like EA's huge pro-football sports franchise with John Madden, and if so, how? These are fundamental questions that must be answered everyday by every interactive entity in order to build a successful and sustainable business.

Market Intelligence

The interactive publishing industry is just now coming to grips with the reasons consumers make product purchase decisions, not to mention the length of channel selling cycles and depth of buy-ins at retail. That information provides publishers a means to develop models and scenarios that can help to accurately predict profitability.

Those types of cost/revenue analyses can then be used to justify "green-lighting" an in-house project, or to convince an outside publisher(s) to risk an upfront development investment that moves the process to the next level.

Every business is basically concerned with where the cash (i.e. investment capital) is, and where the influx of money (return on investment—or ROI) comes from. For the most part, the publishing community controls the purse strings in interactive nowadays, and in many cases the content as well.

Thus, many of the winners in the this business are going to be allied with publishing companies or large entertainment combines (like Disney/ABC, Viacom and Time Warner) somewhere in the enrichment chain because they already have ready access to cash (at least $300 million to $500 million per year in gross revenue) and an abundance of marketable properties (a.k.a. content).

Two years ago, every developer's dream was to become a publisher. Today, developers are smarter and have discovered that the interactive publishing business is extremely capital intensive. That implies a corresponding—some say "crushing"—level of company specific risk as pub-

Paul Palumbo

lishers roll the investment dice on what consumers will ultimately pay for.

In addition, large publishing houses are not immune from bad business decisions either, nor can they necessarily withstand the consolidation forces now rippling through the industry as major Hollywood studios and software companies (Microsoft, Disney and DreamWorks SKG) strike for greater market share.

While the ultimate goal of any development venture or partnership is to get compelling content to the consumer, the process by which publishers and developers accomplish that feat is what this book is all about.

Furthermore, the purpose of this book is to focus on two major development strategies: 1) Finding ways of generating sufficient royalties to keep creative staff employed and working while building a library of titles; and 2) Migrating the business toward a "creation model," where proprietary interactive assets can become franchise properties. Those type of properties pay off like annuities, and can include ancillary merchandising windows that Hollywood studios are so fond of exploiting.

This book provides timely information about how, and where to access financial support to create in-house franchise as well as contract titles. In the case of contract titles, alliances with larger publishers will permit a new developer to set up and benefit from royalty income streams.

On the other hand, franchise property creation will allow the developer to exploit those marketable goods through multiple entertainment and merchandising windows. In both cases, that is where the long-term flow of cash is going to come from.

Developer Longevity

From a business standpoint, the aim of any developer should be to:

- Secure a good deal from the publisher
- Get a better product to the consumer faster than competitors

xv

Introduction

- Make the publisher happy in the process
- Ensure there is sufficient information factored into the development mix upfront , so everybody makes money.

In today's crowded and increasingly competitive marketplace, developers need to control several key aspects of their business:

- Story-telling talent.
- A strong stand-alone technical team
- Critical mass as a publisher ($500 million in yearly revenues), or a partnership with such an entity
- Operating capital (from venture capitalists or poker partners).
- An ability (some say "sixth sense") to anticipate consumer tastes.
- Access to retail shelf space.
- An understanding of alternative (i.e. online) sources of distribution to maximize the value of franchise properties.

All of those competitive elements need to be built into one business plan and fortressed under a corporate banner, or bridged via partnerships, alliances or straight output deals with larger entities. In that regard, what works in favor of developers is that content creation is a shared experience, and that is difficult for larger publishers to emulate.

In sum, that leaves considerable room for smaller developers to carve out a place at the interactive market share table. With rapid improvements in authoring suites and hardware development platforms, the skill sets needed to create quality work still reside in a relatively small talent pool. And those types of assets are typically found in small developer shops, where valuable people "assets" walk home each and every night, and the overhead is modest.

This book contains material derived from dozens of conversations

Paul Palumbo

with venture capitalists, publishers, developers, business analysts, marketing specialists, distribution experts, advertising agencies and major entertainment companies.

To help the reader understand the basis of the content developed for this book, here is a listing of the executives interviewed and quoted frequently. This is not a comprehensive list, but it will provide some insight as to who these executives are and what they do.

Ken Goldstein: Executive Publisher, Broderbund Software

Executive publishers are responsible for setting out and executing broad company strategies and acquiring the assets to complete that vision. Executive publishers are also responsible for setting up budgets, running profitability models and making a case for the success of any one project under consideration.

Michael Pole: Executive Producer, Electronic Arts

Executive producers shepherd interactive projects from concept to the so-called "gold master." They are responsible for delivering product on budget and on time to the publisher. A typical executive producer picks projects, analyzes development companies, sets milestones and manages the overall process in conjunction with internal and external developers.

Mason Woodbury: VP of Marketing Services, Broderbund Software

VPs of marketing become involved in the process at the conceptual stage, along with the executive producer. They typically define the product genre, user market, market potential (i.e. sales), product sell-through cycles, technical support costs, marketing resources necessary for the product to reach payback and beyond that, profitability. It's at this very early stage that the marketing strategy begins to take shape. Titles are not produced in a vacuum.

Kelly Conway: VP of Marketing, Multicom Publishing

Gary Hare: President and CEO, Fathom Pictures

xvii

Introduction

Executives and CEOs for development companies are in charge of setting strategic imperatives. That can include relationship management with publishers, managing company assets and acting as the company's chief evangelist.

CEOs of publishing companies also set strategic imperatives, but typically preside over a much broader tapestry of assets than developers.

Brian Farrell: President and CEO, T*HQ

Andrew Maltin: President, Insights Software

Kip Konwiser: VP of Entertainment, Graphix Zone

VPs of entertainment and business development are usually responsible for developing relationships with content providers and for securing the rights to that content. Examples include securing interactive rights to a major motion picture such as Batman Forever, or licensing the rights into a theatrical window (i.e. Mortal Kombat).

CHAPTER 1
the market

Developers have a strategic and developmental imperative to understand their particular markets because that information is crucial to making profitable publishing decisions and contract deals. The first step in that process is for developers to stick very close to their core audience and know it better than anybody else. That "bottom-up" relationship with users (via Web sites, online forums, consumer surveys, beta testing, focus groups, previous published titles, etc.) yields *data* that can be profiled into consumer wants, needs and desires—and therefore, more marketable titles.

Creating a successful title at retail in today's tough marketplace is the nexus of four key elements:

- Profiling consumer needs that provide developers with upfront market intelligence

- Finding ways of exploiting content that already exists (i.e. re-purposing—whether a motion picture (*Batman*), comic book (*Spiderman*, *X-Men*, etc.), animated TV character (*Bugs Bunny*), TV show (*Star Trek*, *Monty Python*, etc.) or something from the magazine rack (*Better Homes & Gardens*, *Skiing*, *Cycling*, etc.) and has already found a *"community of interest"* or *"audience"*

- Building alliances with publishers that have access to shelf space and development capital

- Allocating creative resources to begin building a library of proprietary media assets.

Market *data* and access to licensed or proprietary content are valuable currencies for developers because it's precisely those type of assets that compel publishers to make third-party deals. Publishers are interested in working with developers for any number of reasons, but two good ones are to undertake a viable project that can't be done more cost effectively by an in-house creative staff, and to leverage assets into a market that is well-known and understood by the developer.

Understanding a particular market allows developers to better examine the risk/reward matrix of interactive title development (insert gr1 here). For example, the risk for high-end game titles like *Wing Commander IV* is much more acute for an average developer than investing in an educational title like Davidson's *Math Blaster* series or a business-related project such as Insights Software's *Pure Motivation*.

On the other hand, a high-end game has multiple opportunities (in the form of multiple exploitation windows) to rack up big sales in the marketplace. Consider LucasArts *Rebel Assault* franchise, a family of titles that averages well over $1 million in sales per title iteration.

Distribution Channels vs. Product Genre

Matching distribution with end-user or target market is a decision that must be made early in the development process. For example, it would not be appropriate to distribute *Where In The World Is Carmen Sandiego* in an arcade venue. Similarly, *Mortal Kombat I, II, and III* would not typically be found in school book fairs or Home Depot (see table 1).

While there is often some overlap in these discrete areas of the retail and wholesale channels, it is important to emphasize that a title must find its way onto a store shelf or other retail environment where a particular community of interest can not only find it, but once observed, feel compelled to make a purchase.

The Market

INTERACTIVE TITLE DISTRIBUTION CHANNELS

Genre	Title Types	Retail Outlet Types
Personal Growth	Cookbooks Home/Garden Wealth building Personal growth	Home Depot Direct Catalog WWW Book Stores
Kids	Education Entertainment Edutainment	Computer Stores Mass Merchants Toy Stores Book Stores Book Fairs Teachers'
Associations		Direct Catalog
Games	Strategy Action/adventure Adrenaline Multiplayer Exploration Role-Playing	Arcades Specialty Video Specialty Software Toy Stores Mass Merchants Catalog Direct WWW

Source: Carronade Group, Inc.

Chapter 1

Interactive Development and "The Hollywood Model"

Hollywood and interactive entertainment are "hits" driven businesses that often require production and distribution to be fortressed under one brand to maximize the most efficient use of capital and to generate the greatest return on that investment (ROI). Nevertheless, compared to the film business, which has the benefit of 75 more years worth of hindsight (i.e. mistakes and market and business experience), or television, which was commercialized back in the early 1950s, interactive title development is a relatively new form of entertainment that has not yet found its final form, let alone formula.

At present, close to 70 cents of each dollar generated by a Hollywood studio comes from aftermarket windows (video, PPV, premium cable TV, basic cable TV and broadcast). In addition, international markets now make up close to 50% of the gross revenue of a typical theatrical release.

Interactive has, at this juncture, very limited exploitation windows and consists primarily of retail sales through established mass merchants for specialty software stores, catalogs and limited online opportunities. In the case of mega hit titles like *Super Mario Bros.* or *Mortal Kombat*, a film deal could get cut, or character licensing going back up the entertainment chain might be an option.

Beyond that, interactive title publishing, unlike the motion picture industry, television or traditional pulp-based media, is a two-way entertainment experience whose development process actually begins where the end-user is engaged. The more senses that are courted—auditory, visual, tactile—the more compelling the overall entertainment experience. And that drives sales.

The real hook for interactive as a medium is it satisfies a culture which has a demand for highly stimulated entertainment. Witness the fact that 20 years ago, three channels of television were considered sufficient, and nobody thought viewers would actually pay for more. In the 1990s, that benchmark has grown to over 175 channels with the advent of DirecTv.

The Market

There are huge differences, however, between movies, TV and CD-ROM entertainment. As opposed to mass audiences necessary to support theatrical releases and TV, CD-ROM is a delivery platform basically aimed at an "audience" of one. But, similar to other forms of packaged media (i.e. films, video tapes and TV shows), CD-ROM success is defined by cumulative sales designed to reach common communities of interest.

But, despite the difficulty in reaching profitability on title development, interactive publishing is fast becoming a mass market medium as the installed base of ROM drives surges, and more households purchase game boxes or PCs. That fact offers developers huge revenue opportunities if they can align the necessary assets to correctly produce, promote and position a particular title.

Consider Hollywood's main aftermarket, home video. In the case of home video, Hollywood releases about 400 films per year, and those titles (as well as catalog product) are shipped to a specialty retail universe of about 26,000 storefronts. That does not include mass merchants, grocery stores, direct mail operations and discount clubs like Costco. Even with that level of distribution sophistication, many independently produced titles still can't find shelf space, and many that do are not profitable.

Considering the crush of interactive titles out there (see detailed section below) and the scarcity of shelf space—not to mention channel immaturity, it's not surprising that many publishers and title developers aren't making money in today's marketplace.

And lastly, the comparison of Hollywood and interactive models comes down to the revenue splits relative to each participant in each industry and to how talent is paid. Given that Hollywood and the record industry have detailed accounting procedures to track SKU dollars and usage of products, the royalty structure is in place to pay artists and producers based on a real- world evaluation of contribution.

Due to the relative infancy of the interactive business, these royalty mechanisms are not yet fully developed, and the lack of reporting product usage further complicates the relationship between publishers and developers.

23

Chapter 1

Interactive Market Stats

Software sales are in direct correlation to the installed base of a particular platform, whether dedicated game consoles or PC boxes. From 1993-1995, the market expanded at about 140% per year, according to a market research study conducted by Infotech.

Those millions of installed units are the playback platform against which interactive title developers must leverage investments, with returns predicated on capturing a forecast share of that hardware base. The total size of a developer or publisher's market is always going to equal the installed base for the particular hardware platform supported. An analogy would be the sales of video tapes against a VCR universe of 80 million TV households.

WORLDWIDE SALES OF CD-ROM DRIVES			
Year	1994	1995	1996E
	(Mil.)	(Mil.)	(Mil.)
Units Sold	16.1	38.7	40.6
Source: Infotech and industry estimates.			

Infotech estimates the total worldwide installed base of CD-ROM drives at the end of 1995 was 65 million units, and it has been forecasted to grow to more than 100 million units by the end of 1996.

The PC was the single greatest contributor to that growth rate, with Original Equipment Manufacturers (or OEM optical disk drive suppliers like Plextor, NEC, Hewlett Packard and Creative Labs) sales accounting for almost 70% of total CD ROM units shipped in 1995. By contrast, CD-ROM based interactive set-top boxes totaled about 5.9 million units in 1995, says Infotech.

The Market

WORLDWIDE SHIPMENTS OF CD-ROM SOFTWARE

Year	1993 (Mil.)	1994 (Mil.)	1995E (Mil.)
Units Shipped	16.5	53.9	70.1

"E" = estimates.

INSTALLED BASE OF INTERACTIVE PCs

U.S. Figures Only—In Millions of Units

Year	1993	1994	1995	1996	1997
Installed Base	4.3	9.0	14.2	21.0	30.5

INSTALLED BASE OF ADVANCED GAME BOXES

U.S. Figures Only—In Millions of Units

Year	1993	1994	1995	1996	1997
Installed Base	0.2	1.0	2.0	6.9	14.0

Source: Forrester Research, Inc. Cambridge, Mass.

Chapter 1

CD-ROM SOFTWARE UNIT SALES AND GROWTH Comparison Of First Half 1994 And 1995—By Category			
Category	1995 (000)	1994 (000)	% Change
Games And Home Creativity	4,140	1,430	189.5%
Home Education	3,629	1,402	158.8%
Content	3,336	1,555	114.5%
Business	413	81	409.9%
All Other Products	2,616	614	326.1%
Totals:	14,134	5,082	178.1%
Source: Software Publishers Association.			

A Limited Installed Base

According to *The CD-ROM Directory*, the number of CD-ROM titles in the global marketplace rose from 5,379 in 1994, to 9,691 in 1995. While that is close to 100% growth, a more sober statistic to consider for 1994 (and beyond) is that even though 53.9 million units were shipped, the per-title average was still a relatively modest 12,500 units.

That puts a lot of pressure on developers who don't have the financial staying power to build a library of product (or media assets) that can begin to pay off long-term. Larger companies such as Microsoft and Electronic Arts can amortize development costs (and losses) over a much larger revenue base, offer retailers greater incentives to carry their product, and strike alliances with new sources of distribution to create additional market positions for product.

A word of caution about statistics and numbers. We are presenting numbers for the purposes of comparison, based on the best information available from the most reliable research firms in the country. A useful formula for calculating market estimates is to take available data, throw out the highest and lowest numbers, then add and divide the remaining sets of figures.

The Carronade Group does not, however, believe there is one set of accurate numbers, except those from the publishers themselves. Those numbers should be referenced as "net" sales, which is units shipped minus any returns. This is particularly tough now with so much 16-bit product flowing back up the channel as that market segment continues to atrophy.

Until artists with "gross royalty deals" and developers begin to demand accurate weekly (or monthly) SKU reports, all reported numbers will tend to be approximations, and in some cases, not necessarily valid ones. The book channel, for example, requires ISBN coding on each product to accurately track retail sales, and a similar system for interactive titles would end a lot of "numbers-related" confusion.

Educational Segment

Educational publishers are the beneficiaries of two strong macro-market fundamentals working on their col,ective behalf: 1) They reside in a high-growth market ($600 million in wholesale revenue forecast for 1995—and projected to grow annually at a 35% clip through the turn of the century); and 2) Their business model more closely resembles the classic book (pulp/print) model, where titles have a much longer shelf-life, and development costs are relatively low when compared to their game counterparts.

Educational title developers list seven competitive bases that they contend must be covered in order to have a chance at retail success, both as a company and in seeding an individual product into the marketplace:

- Quality content.
- Access to key influencer groups (teachers, school districts and parents).

Chapter 1

- Substantial upfront R & D investment.
- Branded portfolio of titles.
- Strong distribution (proprietary or partners).
- Brand equity built with in-house talent.
- Strong creative studio.

While educational publishers are plowing big bucks into R & D (The Learning Company has invested 22% of revenue into new product development for the 1995 fiscal year, and Davidson & Associates, about $20 milion in 1995 R & D). Per-title costs are averaging about $300,000 for the industry as a whole.

That's far below the "technology-driven" game business where production costs can range from $500,000 to $1.5 million per title. Edmark CFO Paul Bialek says the chief difference between the two software categories is technology. He notes, "Educational publishers are technology-enabled but don't celebrate it."

Longer shelf-life for educational titles translate into less critical payback windows and allows products to perform more "like annuities," according to Bialek. While a game title is subject to being "pulled" by a retailer if it doesn't "pop" right away, many educational titles are on store shelves for years. At the same time, many titles and brands enjoy support from key influencer groups like teachers and educators.

Product life cycles can be further extended and enhanced by updates or modifications, while maintaining the focus of the product: core curriculum enhancement and home education. Nevertheless, industry data suggests 25% of the top educational titles still generate about 80% of the revenue, with the remaining 75% left to scratch out positive payback from 20% of the market.

Many educational software publishers (witness Davidson) have been releasing titles since the '80s and have built up strong relationships with distributors and retailers. One of the reasons that both Broderbund and Electronic Arts have been so successful is they have virtually "owned" retail relationships (with firms like Software Etc., Babbages and Egghead) because the two business segments grew up together.

The real concern for small-to-medium-sized publishers nowadays is that established retail relationships may change now that huge conglomerates, like Disney and Microsoft, are getting into the market--two giants that could theoretically throw a lot of cash and product into the channel.

Educational publishers maintain that the corner stone of their long-term strategy to maintain viability—even in a crowded marketplace—is to emphasize development of products that have unique characters and tell good stories.

The Game Segment

The real story behind bullish game developer expectations is the generally accepted notion that software sales tend to spike in correlation to the maturation (i.e. penetration) of its complimentary installed hardware base. In this case, however, the market has to factor in the additional likelihood that there could be multiple (fragmented) installed bases. This suggests investors are hedging their bets and are willing to ride along with a number of developers.

Most analysts believe there is a substantial (latent) market demand for advanced game software, which should spike once an installed hardware base finally makes penetration inroads. According to Lee Isgur, interactive and game analyst with Jeffries & Co., the market is currently "focused on the amount of business these companies are doing right now." And Isgur says in that regard "they are overvalued." But he goes on to say, "Based on the potential business they will probably do before the turn of the century, they are undervalued."

As for the market's current hardware preferences, Sony was the hardware champ in the U.S. in 1995, and Sega took that honor in Japan last year.

As for the revenue prospects for multiplayer online games, Isgur says, "Despite all the market excitement, very few users are playing online

Chapter 1

games. Psychologically, it should be more attractive to play against another person (or persons) than against a machine. On the other hand, it still means that you will have to find the appropriate level player to play with, at the time you want to play."

It's been a rough ride for game developers whose businesses grew up around the 16-bit market and were slow to embrace CD-ROM as the next-generation delivery medium. For example, Acclaim Entertainment is without question one of the premiere game developers in the world. Moreover, the company owns a huge proprietary distribution machine, state-of-the-art creative studio facilities and has access to capital.

Nevertheless, it's reliance on 16-bit systems, and the fact that it's large revenue base will have to be replaced with next generation software sales, has hurt the company.

Short-term, Acclaim is hoping to break with big budget titles co-released with movies. In the long-term, Acclaim has been on a content licensing binge and plans to release most of its new slate on titles for multiple platforms (Sega, Sony) as well as for the PC CD-ROM platform.

Activision is another example. It made a name for itself during the cartridge heyday but had to reorganize after that market matured. With Bobby Kotick at the helm, Activision is now exclusively focused on PC CD-ROM.

Game company "Profit & Loss" (P&L) will always be exposed to excessive market volatility as hardware adoption cycles ebb and flow. Many developers have had to endure two-year's worth of inventory write-downs and declining sales as the 16-bit market decayed, and successor platforms were slow to reach the marketplace.

Despite strong sales for Sony's PlayStation 32-bit platform (about 800,000 U.S. units sold-through), a clear "advanced platform winner" probably won't emerge for another 18 months to two years. And markets in transition are ripe with opportunity, particularly for small firms.

It's a chance to break into the earnings "black" in a big way with one or two titles that "hit" on a hot platform. The downside is that developing for multiple platforms is expensive and risky. That's why many software companies have been willing to hedge their upfront development bets that the PC is indeed going to capture a substantial share of the marke which most analysts expect to be huge.

While the PC has been generally criticized for its lack of "plug-n-play" capability and slow game play, the platform is driving toward market critical mass (approaching 30% penetration of U.S. households), and most of the computers that sell into the consumer channel nowadays have CD-ROM drives pre-installed.

For companies that like Graphix Zone, 7th Level, Spectrum Holobyte and Broderbund that began PC CD-ROM development early, the market has likewise gushed with enthusiasm, sending public trading comparables into orbit.

Surviving Platform Evolution

Last year, The GamePC Consortium considered introducing its own specification standards for the desktop PC, which once again focused the debate about what playback platform dedicated CD-ROM game players will eventually migrate toward as the 16-bit market atrophies, and how long it might take for a clear "winner" to emerge.

The short-term view held by many industry analysts is that incumbent technology companies like Sega and Nintendo (now joined by 3DO, and Sony) have the inside track on gathering the lion's share of the hardware (not to mention software) markets.

The theory supporting set-tops is that 1) There is a high degree of "brand" awareness among consumers already; 2) Software developers are less spooked about making upfront production commitments to support those brands; and 3) Shelf space is already scarce. Retailers (i.e. mass merchants) are sure to stock both the titles and hardware.

At the present time, just about all developers and publishers support

Chapter 1

PC CD-ROM, but most of those products are often classified as "edutainment" or as special interest titles, "which represent less than 20% of the business," according to Lee Isgur of San Francisco-based Jeffries & Co., and developers have yet to crack into the action genre.

Isgur speculates that "the economics of the hardware business appear to support the set-top box through the end of the decade," given that the all-important "cost/benefit" ratio of competing hardware platforms favors consoles. "For $500, game enthusiasts can get a terrific experience from a 20" TV set, and it takes far less of an investment when compared to the computer counterpart," says Isgur.

Nevertheless, with Microsoft and a host of hardware peripheral vendors (witness ATI Technologies) now working closely together to better guarantee the PC's overall performance (spelled PLUG-N-PLAY), it's still a race that's too close to call. The battle cry being heard from the PC group is that Windows '95 is solving many "driver-related" issues (even though some don't ship with the operating system, but only with upcoming software titles), and the introduction of PC 3-D add-on cards in '96 that will bring desktop performance up to the level of set-top boxes.

The goal: Offer game players an "arcade-like" experience on the desktop. ATI Technologies (Toronto, Canada) collaborated with Microsoft on a new software interface called DirectDraw, which effectively reduces demands on the CPU by permitting "block transfers of data" and therefore dramatically accelerates graphics display. DirectDraw technology reportedly yields the mind-breaking action that gamers have come to expect and demand.

In addition, despite the much-publicized problems at Apple Computer, the MAC operating system has always been a favorite in the development community because of its ease of use, its unencumbered "Plug-and-Play" capacity and its extremely loyal base of users.

According to Ken Nicholson of ATI (a member of the GamePC consortium), title developers working with Windows '95 and DirectDraw are quite impressed. Nicholson says that developers are rapidly finishing

The Market

up a cycle of DOS-based product, and will soon turn toward creating a new genre of "PC action" games began "trickling out at the end of '95, but could turn into a flood of product by mid-'96."

Nicholson also said 26 chip makers are competing to supply the 3D chip-sets for PCs, which should boost feature sets, while driving down incremental costs per add-on card. For technology vendors like ATI, codification of a GamePC "standard" could be an important step in the journey to capture a piece of a potentially large, lucrative, but so far uncommitted, consumer game segment, despite the early success of Sony's PlayStation.

Case Study: Mortal Kombat in the Arcade

Releasing a game through the "arcade" window is becoming somewhat analogous to theatrical distribution in the motion picture business because the street buzz that it creates typically goes a long way toward driving title profitability at retail.

But beyond being a bellwether indicator for retail sales, arcades are valuable proving grounds for title developers with the right mix of assets in place to exploit it. It's also business that several major developers (witness Time Warner and Acclaim) are gearing up to enter, despite that fact that it's a tough market to crack because the "value chain" of assets necessary to establish a position (from creative development to stand-up arcade box design) is usually fortressed under one corporate nameplate.

The entrenched competition is fierce. WMS Industries, Capcom, Konami, Sega and Hamco are already major arcade entrants and have a hammer lock on the segment. The dominant player, WMS Industries (best known for its *Mortal Kombat* franchise), has already cornered about 40% of the $500 million (at wholesale) coin-operated video game business, according to Allan S. Roness of J.W. Charles (Boca Raton, Fla.) and other game industry analysts.

According to Roness, *Mortal Kombat I* sold about 10,000 arcade units

33

Chapter 1

worldwide, and *Mortal Kombat II* close to 25,000. Stand-up arcade boxes normally sell for between $3,000 and $4,000, while game "kits" (games sold for existing consoles) cost about $1,000 to $2,200 per unit.

As for *Mortal Kombat III*, WMS Industries CFO Howard Bach, while not disclosing *Mortal Kombat III* arcade sales, says, "Arcade games that sell 5,000 units are considered strong titles." Bach did say, however, arcade games that ship 10,000-20,000 are a bonafide "hit," and *Mortal Kombat III* can be listed in that category. And talk about cross-promotional synergy, the *Mortal Kombat* movie grossed an excess of $80 million at the box office.

The *Mortal Kombat III* title was released at retail on October 13, 1995 for the Super Nintendo and Sega Genesis platforms, and according to the most recent information, WMS has shipped about 1.1 million copies of the game, with 350,000 units already sold through. The key to the whole thing, according to Bach, "is the platform that goes into the arcade, which is getting more sophisticated every year."

The reason is, the typical kid who has a home set-top box goes to the arcades from time to time for the super game play those venues offer. Arcade games have bigger screens, more complex controls and generally offer a more intense experience. WMS releases about 4-6 games per year through the arcade window, and Bach says games that take off at the arcade level establish the following and enthusiasm to drive retail sales.

A typical development cycle for a WMS arcade title includes creating the game, then fitting onto an upright platform. That platform and game are then put out in a beta test. Based on player response, the game is modified, or new characters and action features are added.

Then a sample "run" is distributed to the arcades. Based on that additional "bottom up" input from players on the game, the final version is released anywhere from nine to 18 months after the design document is first started.

Acclaim Entertainment (former distributor for WMS) is in the process of developing its coin-operated business and should release its first

The Market

title (*Batman Forever*) by early 1996.

Its second title is scheduled to utilize the *NBA Jam* property and will incorporate full motion sequence shots using movements of Juwann Howard. Howard spent several sessions in Acclaim's Glen Cove, N.Y. motion capture studio to add authentic movements for the characters in the game.

Acclaim's strategy is to own the title franchise, from arcades to comics, home video, online (multiplayer experiences) and TV network distribution (in partnership with TCI).

Time Warner has a partnership arrangement with Acclaim for both *Batman Forever* and *Demolition Man*, even though its interactive/arcade subsidiary (formally Atari) has a staff of about 280 and releases about 30-40 titles per year.

TWI's *Primal Rage* title reached number one at the arcade level in June of 1994, and the company is now in the process of creating 12 home versions of the title. The first five versions of *Primal Rage* came out about a year after the title's arcade debut (in August) and sold in excess of 1 million units. Another six versions were released in November, 1995.

Similar to the long-established Hollywood studio model, game developers are finding new ways of extending their software franchises into new exploitation windows as the interactive title publishing industry matures, and technology opens up new avenues of distribution.

That ability to capture more of each revenue dollar in the game business is a crucial element to profitability, and that typically begins at the arcade level. That's why the major players have stepped up and made the incremental investments necessary to hedge their distribution bets going into that street level starting gate.

CHAPTER 2
the customer

In theory, anyone who has read a book, played a video game, watched a TV show or gone to the movie theater represents a potential market for interactive titles. The real issue is how to court those users who are faced with thousands of software choices, particularly as distribution avenues proliferate. Those "eyeballs" belong to individuals, game enthusiasts, large and small communities of interest (niche/personal preference segments) representing all demographic categories.

Determining the target audience for a product is probably one, if not the most important, step in the development process. The second most important step is to follow those audiences wherever their leisure entertainment hours are spent: Online, with CD-ROMs, in front of a TV, with a game box, etc.

The questions every developer must ask about a proposed title are:

- Who is the audience?
- Can it be identified, quantified and justified as a community of interest?
- What are the best promotional channels to reach them?
- What are the product "sell-through" assumptions, and can the proof of concept be justified against that forecast level of buy-in?

Chapter 2

- What companies are potential "poker" partners?
- Where does that audience expect to purchase the product?
- What distribution avenues are available to get the product in those channels?

A good concept, well thought-out user interface, compelling visuals and jarring audio are all key pieces of a successful title. But, no matter how good the title, if there is no audience or community of interest that a product resonates with, or if there is insufficient marketing support to promote it, then sales will not meet expectations, and the product will become an expensive lesson in what not to do.

Audience research can be crucial in formulating a quality document design strategy and can be done in a number of ways. There is a voluminous amount of third party research available on the market to guide developers in making a sound decision, but common sense plays an important role as well.

If a developer knows that millions of people like American-rules football, and a large portion of them own computers or console video games, there is a likelihood that the union set of those two segments might result in a definable community of interest that a product can be quantified against and eventually sold into.

Focus groups and testing are also a useful means for determining your audience. In other words, if you test football fans and none of them like your prototype football game, it will likely not sell as a full-blown product at retail.

Creating Motivated Buyers

Once interactive developers have identified a core market group or product constituency, the next job is to create product for or target a known core enthusiast community that will act as word-of-mouth (i.e. hyped) "barkers."

The Customer

That strategy serves two purposes: 1) Development costs can be amortized over an expected sales base of a core constituency; and 2) Those "hyped" user segments form an asset (i.e. revenue) base over which to expand the product's retail reach (see graphic) into adjacent or less attractive segments.

Hyped enthusiasts are not only avid purchasers of product, but can also be counted on to find multiple uses for that same product. For example, a core user segment can also be an attractive way to experiment with new uses of that product (i.e. online and multiplayer environments). What developers should strive for is to make an enthusiastic customer out of each buyer. That can be a function of game play.

Brand Loyalty

One of the basic goals for the developer to consider during the proof of concept stage is how to create a series of products that compel user loyalty to that brand. Brand loyalty is an extremely valuable product differentiation tool and is, by definition, a "hyped" user. Brand loyalty can be further broken up into four discrete flavors:

1. Hard core (hyped) users typically will buy a preferred or favorite brand all the time. For example, many parents are attracted to Disney's kidvid titles because of a long association with that company's product. It's a known, comfortable product zone that has built up a large degree of trust between both supplier and purchaser. Some game enthusiasts will always prefer Sega products to Sony. 3DO has a similar, albeit smaller, core group of enthusiasts that buy the company's products.

2. Softcore users are loyal to two or three brands. Those could include Acclaim, Activision, Interplay or Byron Preiss titles in the game segment. That divided loyalty can be an attractive source of incremental revenue and

Chapter 2

marketshare for developers if they can find one or two product characteristics that appeal to that segment but that were not present in earlier versions of product.

3. Shifting users move from brand to brand, favoring one brand over another based on price, feature sets, word-of-mouth endorsements, availability and key influencer groups (i.e. name endorsements).

4. Switchers are users completely driven by price or deal.

Q & A

Ken Goldstein, Executive Producer
Broderbund Software

Q. Where does the product concept come from? Who evaluates the available market? How do you strike a balance between developing a concept and targeting the end-user?

A. It's slightly different with an edutainment product than it is with an entertainment product. With a Carmen Sandiego product, we clearly ask ourselves: What is it that both the parent is looking for in terms of an educational experience for their child, and what is it that the child is interested in? And what is age-appropriate content?

We have a pretty good understanding of that here, having produced these products for 10 years. So what we're always asking ourselves is: Who is the current customer, as well as who is the current purchaser? In the case of a Carmen product, it's not necessarily the same thing.

If a parent is purchasing it for their child, the parent is looking for one thing, and the child is looking for something else. But most of all, what the parent is looking for is whether the child will stay with the product for a long time, and whether the product will have a great deal of value.

So, one of the things we look for with our concepts is, do they appeal to the user—to the child? How can we make it more appealing and more interesting? How can we make the content more age-appropriate, and then once we have that nailed, how can we frame that information well for the parent who may be buying it?

We work very closely with children in the development of the concept, in the development of the interface, in the development of age-appropriate clues, in the development of age-appropriate database information, make sure that the language is clear, make sure that the content covered is broad and interesting, make sure that the jokes are funny to the right customers.

There's a lot of user testing that goes on in the development of that concept. Those products—the *Carmen Sandiego* products—tend to be developed internally by people who have worked on products before. I serve as the executive producer of all of those products because I have done quite a few of them now, so I have a pretty good feel for what needs to go on there.

But in terms of leading the design process, I usually assign a producer to be in charge of that, based on work they have done in the past and demonstrated sensitivity for the needs of the customer.

With educational and edutainment products, we do a tremendous amount of early testing. The focus testing is more for the entertainment products, where you've got a brand-new concept that you are laying out there to see if people will react to it.

With the educational products, we're pretty clear whether we have something that's marketable or not, going into it. What we need to do is to hone those concepts, so I wouldn't call those so much focus tests as much as *play tests*.

We're constantly (bringing testers into the) development process, letting them bang on it, letting them tell us what they like and what they

Chapter 2

don't like and reacting to that and rolling it into the design. A focus test is usually—with an original piece of work—something we haven't done before, something we haven't tried.

It's something we lay out there and say, "Here are the parameters of the technology we are exploring. Here are the parameters of the game. This is the game play, this is the story, these are the characters, this is the interface." (Then we ask them), "Is this something you would like to spend the next 20 hours of your life with, and if so, would you feel comfortable paying us "x" price for it?" That's the traditional focus test.

And, you know, with entertainment products that are moving into the 7-figure budget, you need to get a sense of that pretty early on. As I was telling one of my producers—who has been developing a treatment with an outside developer—today, our fate is pretty much committed in the first 20-40 pages. If that 20-40 pages is good, it's only going to get better from there. If that 20-40 pages is bad, there really isn't any reason to proceed until it is good, because that is what you are going to produce.

Q & A

Mason Woodbury, VP Marketing Services
Broderbund Software

Q. How do you market to a particular audience once you have a product in-hand—whether it's an educational title or an arcade game?

A. Well, the first step is the name of the product, so that's where the marketing group gets the first contact. Once they have a reasonably tight beta and the concept is pretty nailed down, we will start working on what the name of the product will be and also trying to determine those kinds of issues in terms of the age (appropriateness)—Is this really going to appeal to a 5-year-old, or is this going to be too sophisticated for a teenager?

And all of that sort of gets rolled into the beginning development of the name and what we call the "why to buy"—it's sort of like the tag line. Historically, the product development people have pretty much just walked in and said, "Here's the product. Now put it in a box and sell it for us."

With the shift, over the last year or so, to a more marketing-driven orientation, I have been working with people right from the very concept stage. In terms of, say, what is the demand for chicken raising: Should we do a chicken raising CD-ROM product? How many CD products are out there that talk about raising chickens? What does the market side look like? Who's the market leader? What's the price point for that type of stuff?

The marketing manager and the marketing research manager would get involved with focus groups in terms of we've got three different interfaces—which one seems to work best and appeal to the customer? At this point, I would say that we're reasonably involved almost from the moment that they start thinking about going down a certain road. It still varies a little bit from product to product, particularly (with a product we are publishing for a third-party developer).

With a product that we are publishing, marketing would have far less of that early involvement because, in that case, it's an outside person that usually walks in and has a fairly complete product or concept. But if it is something we are doing internally, marketing would be involved almost from the inception, in terms of does this sound like a good idea, is the market there.

Really, the first time that we start to do real work is pretty much when they say, "Okay, now we need to come up with a name." That is where we start. Product development might say the age range is 4-12, but when we start working on the name and the box design, is when we really start saying, "Is it really 5-9, or 4-12 or 6-7?"

Chapter 2

What Do Consumers Buy?

Customers make purchasing decisions based on a number of factors, but the most compelling reasons are need, product appeal and availability. In order to feel compelled to buy a product, customers must first be made aware of that product's existence. Advertising, promotions and public relations are all appropriate methods for getting the word out about new and existing products, although the marketing mix varies by product genre, scope and target audience.

A well-branded developer, backed up with preexisting content in the marketplace and word-of-mouth buzz, contributes in a positive way to a consumer's purchase decision. According to research, buyers who own dedicated platforms (Sega, Sony, Nintendo, etc.) buy the most software. While computer owners purchase entertainment software to some degree (.8 titles per year, according to Dataquest research), that's far less than the 1.8 titles per installed dedicated game platform.

Home productivity software—ranging from reference to word processing software—is probably the next, most sought after category. Educational, hobby/craft and home improvement categories fall last on the list and have a much smaller potential market than entertainment or productivity.

Kelly Conway, VP Marketing
Multicom Publishing

Q. How do you pick ideas for your products?

A. Multicom's product strategy is one that somewhat mirrors the book business. A couple of underlying pieces of that strategy are that all products should have names—most people call them brands, but names can take many shapes—that consumers are familiar with in the particular category of product that we have decided to do.

Take *Better Homes and Gardens*, Warren Miller in the skiing world or Home Depot in home improvement category. So, number one: All products will work to have a well-known consumer name to *attract* the multimedia buyer.

Number two: The content is sourced either from the name that is the expert in the field or an expert in the field, the two may not come from the same source. How we determine what products to do is a function of looking at the book market and determining what categories of books have been perennial best-sellers, large volume categories, etc.

As an example, cookbooks are one of the highest volume by title and in number of titles in the category...art, history, sports, cookbooks, travel, etc. We do research that helps us to understand that. Then, the second part is just general market research that we can access which helps us focus in on where the interest is in these lifestyle product categories for multimedia products. Really that's third-party research for the most part, that we subscribe to and pay for.

Michael Pole, Executive Producer
Electronic Arts

Q. How are your titles and concepts picked, and how do you know what is going to sell?

A. What I like to do in the children's market is acquire pre-sold content

Chapter 2

(meaning content that is recognizable to the consumer), which makes for an easier sell when you bring a title to the retail channel. That's what we did with *Madeline*. The difficult thing with this is that anyone who controls high-profile content usually has their hand out for a huge advance and sizable royalties. In the children's market in particular, it's very difficult to make your financial model work under these circumstances. It's in those rare instances where people are willing to become your partners—as we did with *Madeline*—that you are able to create a remarkable program in a cost-effective manner.

The advances that we paid for Madeline were very reasonable, and we put every dollar that we could on the screen. There are companies that have made a name for themselves by acquiring great content—in particular SunSoft, Acclaim and some of the others. But they have (generally) paid out a lot of money in the advances, and they didn't put the money or care into the development of the property, so the titles weren't very good and didn't sell very well. The best thing you can do is work very closely with the people that you acquire content from and explain to them the model and make it attractive on the back-end.

Q. When looking at a couple of your affiliate labels and subsidiaries—like Origin and Bullfrog—those developers had original ideas and then built popular titles.

A. Right. But then again, they were small development companies—100-125 people strong—that were acquired by EA. What we've done is given them complete autonomy to continue doing what they do. Peter Molyneux and Robert and Richard Garriot are three of the most talented people in the industry. They make ground-breaking product.

Bullfrog is just now becoming successful in the US. Garriot's group has been successful with *Ultima* and Wing *Commander*, and now they are doing feature-length movies within *Wing Commander IV*. They are working on their franchises—they may be new to EA, but they have been around for many years. Once you create something of value, you try to continue to create franchiseability with that and continue on. This business has changed so much.

Whereas the development of a title on a cartridge could be done for $125,000, the budgets are in excess of $1 million for most of the titles now, and you have to be much more careful about which titles you develop and continue to invest in, in the successful line you create.

Q. Is the platform important?

A. Yes. The platform strategy is very important. EA has been successful in that. We develop everything with multi-platform in mind.

How Do They Buy?

Most customers still purchase software through the traditional retail software store channel. That is beginning to change, however, because software content is expanding greatly in scope, to reflect a wider range of needs and tastes of the growing software consumer market.

Consumers buy multimedia titles based on a number of key behavior sets that are functions of 1) Price; 2) Brand; 3) Availability; 4) Convenience; 5) Perception of value; and 6) Need. These behavior "influencers" to purchase may be scrambled and recast in a variety of permutations. No two consumers are the same, which is why those sets of buying preferences and pricing sensitivities must continually be factored into a product developer's forecasts and sales expectations as projects move to completion.

Consumers can now buy or acquire packaged media in just about every retail channel. The chart on the following page outline the current retail channels.

One successful way to introduce product to the consumer is via hardware and software outlets that allow customers to sample titles before a purchase decision is made. But, one of the main issues that must be solved is making multimedia appealing to women, namely young adults, because this segment of the population is most often doing the shopping—and they frequently look for bargains.

That's why multimedia title sales success will, in large measure, be

Chapter 2

defined by the level of success developers have in grinding down costs, even while getting quality product flowing into commercial channels and on store shelves where the maximum number of shoppers can find it.

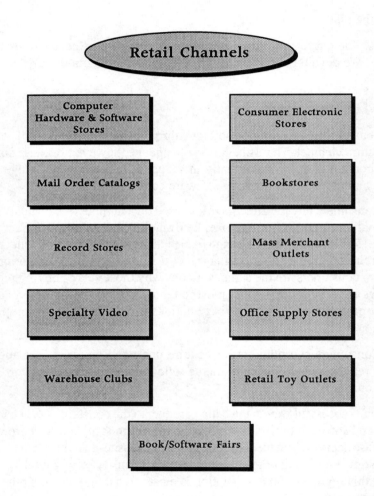

Q & A

Gary Hare, President & CEO
Fathom Pictures

Q. Do you buy market research? How do you know your market?

A. We had a relationship with ABC Sports—a formal one—for a while. Now that's not quite so formal, but we use their research facilities. We also use one of the other broadcasters which needs to be nameless for the moment. And then also, we've found the most interesting thing about the Internet is that almost any question that's on the tip of your tongue you can get the answer to if you know how to look.

We look at things like—let's use the auto category as an example—who is our market? And then we start seeing how many people watch what on TV. We have a regular report that we get telling the bestselling books, magazines, films, music—all of that kind of stuff, country-by-country each month. How many people take what kind of car magazines or boat magazines, etc.?Most of that is fantasy market, however, because only about 10% of the people who take boating magazines own a boat. The other 90% think they'd like to.

And then auto racing—who's interested in auto sims? Could you do an auto sim that's so sophisticated that the new computer technology that's going to come out 3rd Quarter 1996 would buy it just to put on their machines? Those kinds of questions. We try to answer those questions in as much detail as we can before we come up with a concept.

Most of those magazines have done in-house research and can tell you how many of their readers have a PC and when they bought it—within reason. You can call *Car and Driver's* marketing department and probably get that information right now. They're pretty free with that information, and we've never had a problem with it.

Chapter 2

In the past, when I was on the publishing side, I used to try to figure out if 3% of the installed base would find it interesting and then run the installed base figures and see if it was interesting to do. You have to take into consideration (say with a baseball simulation) how many sims are out there—and can you do a better one.

If you use that 3% number and looked at baseball as an example, you'd find that there's seven or eight games out there—four or five of them are really good. Is that something you really want to do? Are you different enough, or is your license important enough? There are some names that guarantee you a certain amount of shelf space.

I think that in the sports arena, EA's name means something because they've spent so much money in *EA Sports*. But beyond that, I don't think there are too many people that know the names.

The "Satisfied" Customer

As technology allows suppliers and customers to form closer "gain-sharing" relationships (via online services, the World Wide Web and better, more finely-tuned direct marketing thrusts), the actual sale of a CD-ROM unit becomes only the first level of contact. Content in that context is simply the carrot that brings both parties together but, nevertheless, provides both sides a powerful vehicle to satisfy wants and needs.

Customer support is a key means of building customer loyalty and is really a matter of living up to promises made in publicity releases and promotional packaging. Developers typically budget from $3 to $5 per CD-ROM for technical support, localization (i.e. voice-overs for foreign markets) and other enhancements.

Those enhancements could include a Web site tie-in that allows a game or enthusiast title purchaser to update the ROM client, add new characters and scenarios in real-time, and find a community of interest based on the genre of entertainment or information.

Q & A

Mason Woodbury, VP Marketing Services
Broderbund Software

Q. Technical support. How important is it and how expensive is it? How do how you view tech support?

A. Well, I run tech support, so I view it as essential. Actually, Broderbund considers it fairly important, and over the past four years I've been given a blank check to get the service up to be what it should be. I've never been constrained by head count or budget issues. When I told them I needed 10 more people and a new phone system, the answer was: "Do whatever it takes." It's crucial. Tech support/customer support—we added it up the other day—I think it's close to 25% of the total head count of the company.

Q. In creating your tech support department, do you look at it on a per title basis. If you release a new title, do you plan on adding a number of customer service reps?

A. No. We try to look ahead and say, "A *Myst* is going to generate more calls than a *Carmen.*" We know that *Print Shop* generates more calls than *James Discovers Math*. We watch it on a day-to-day basis.

Q. Are the calls typically problem calls or calls from people that don't know how to use the software and need some help with it? Can you give me a percentage break down of those two?

A. We don't break it down, but it's all over the map. The reality is that very few of the calls relate to problems directly associated with our product. They don't have the latest video driver or something like that. Say a consumer buys *Myst*. *Myst* is a pretty stable product, but it does require the latest video and sound drivers—so you get someone with a two-year-old machine that goes out and buys *Myst,* and then it won't work.

Chapter 2

There's really nothing wrong with *Myst,* and at the end of the call we tell the consumer to call their computer company's BBS and download the latest video drivers and get it up and running. With *Print Shop,* we get a lot of calls from people who can't find the right printer, or it's printing sideways, or they can't find the graphics. Very few of the calls actually are because of bugs or poorly-designed products. Most of the calls are from people who really aren't familiar with computers and need help.

Q & A

Gary Hare, President & CEO
Fathom Pictures

Q. What about Tech support?

A. Our publishers do it unless it's a bug, then we deal with that issue. As the machines get better it, however, becomes less of an issue. Today, it's a horrendous issue. There are 29 different video cards out there, and half of them probably aren't any good. We released a title 2Q of last year (1995) that we called *The Skins Game*—lot of full motion stuff on it.

We found out, much to our chagrin, that five video cards don't support QuickTime. These people call up, and until you go through the whole decision tree figuring out which video card they've got, you don't even know whether the title was built to support it. As we start getting more and more of a standard, a lot of that kind of stuff will go away, and that's 90% of the calls.

Q. Does Windows95 help or hurt?

A. It helps it a lot. Windows95 and the Apple platforms don't have nearly as many problems. It's been a massive problem. Also, the MPEG standard that they tried to announce for Windows95 doesn't make any sense, and they're trying to correct that now.

CHAPTER 3

Any project has to have money in order to survive, particularly entertainment titles. One way of getting it, is through private funding sources. Venture capital firms (VCs) spend everyday auditioning the future. That future needs to be different and unique because that's where VCs are willing to place their investment bets.

Ann Winblad, partner in Hummer Winblad Partners (investors in such companies as Humongous Entertainment) provided a host of strategies for courting scare investment dollars. Hummer Winblad "auditions" about 1,000 companies per year and has about $95 million under management, which is spread across 31 investments. The average size of each investment is about $2 million, and that fund generates annualized returns of about 47% of net management fees. This formula is exclusively focused on software companies.

Despite the fact that market opportunities are large and there are few winners, Hummer Winblad is very bullish on the future of the market for some key reasons:

- Software-driven entertainment sectors are experiencing 30% annual growth.
- There are 3,250 game titles available, as of December, 1995.
- Ten titles made 25% of all revenue.

Chapter 3

- The top 100 titles generated 90% of segment revenue.

While it's bad news for developers that the top 100 titles capture 90% of the market, the flip side of that is no one supplier has a greater than 7% marketshare. According to Hummer Winblad, that spells opportunities to find and fund a growth company from among the developer ranks. Venture capitalists love to fund companies that have a chance to capture marketshare. By contrast, in the edutainment sector, it's a little different because Disney and Broderbund own a combined 20% of that market.

Venture capitalists are often knocked by game developers because they have a reputation for driving hard bargains. But, Hummer Winblad puts a positive spin on the VC/game developer relationship. Private sources of funding are also valuable for the experience and breadth of contacts they can add to the business, as well as some other strong advantages they bring to the table:

- Experience at building companies.
- Expanded network of customers, influencers, press, bankers and analysts.
- "Rubber ball" consultant for immediate feedback.
- Understanding of strategic issues, operations and industry trends.
- They also formulate business models.

What interactive developers have to realize is venture capitalists are opportunists, and developers must be the visionaries. It's a VC's job to provide an environment for the vision to grow. VCs act as evangelists to move the business toward an IPO (initial public offering) or "sell-out" (private sale to a larger company). VCs know the liquidity process very well. They focus on achieving liquidity (IPO status). That's where they make their money.

Venture capitalists are looking for a unique combination of creativity and breakthrough technical talent. Winblad says Silicon Valley has numerous venture capital attorneys who are often willing to work for reduced fees to get a company financed and build a long-term relationship. Many VCs and VC attorneys are willing to work with companies from across the country. But those attorneys are often looking for companies that already have a "number of dogs in the dish," or users that love the product, or a previous success indicative of what the company can do.

As for striking up a relationship with a VC, Winblad suggests one of the best ways to do it is to stop by a Web site. She advises game developers target only three or four firms, research the right one for them and then get introduced by a key influencer (somebody who knows a decision maker at the VC company). Winblad suggests prior to the meeting developers:

- Prepare a business summary of 2-5 pages.
- Understand the market opportunity.
- Have a unique product and technology.
- Have a solid development team.
- Have a good fix on the competition.
- Have a well prepared demonstration.

Hummer Winblad advises that one of the most important things to remember when pitching a VC for investment capital is they are always looking for a sense of product style and the ability of the developer to show the "signature" of the business.

In addition, game developers can achieve much richer valuations for smaller parts (equity) of the company during a second round of financing. That second round could take place, for example, once a company has already established a relationship with a larger publisher (i.e. affiliate label deal). Initial financing rounds typically require that game developers offer up more of the company to lure VC support because of the increased risk associated with that level of financing.

Chapter 3

The Golden Rule of Interactive Title Development

The golden rule of interactive title finance, nowadays, is: The company with the gold makes the rules. Title developers, like everybody else in the entertainment or edutainment business, need access to a ready source of investment capital to sustain operations. The problem is that developers are artists and engineers, not MBAs, so the thorny issues surrounding product finance expose the classic "geek vs. suit" hurdle that all developers must get beyond in order to keep their product vision alive.

The first step, according to developers who have run the financing gauntlet and survived, is to be prepared for a lot of rejection. Developers should also be prepared to stick it out in order to let both publishers and potential investors know that you are really serious. Beyond that, there are several ways to boot strap a start-up developer, and a good one is to take the product to OEMs and strike a bundling agreement.

Developers need to keep an eye on the marketplace and pitch a product idea to hardware companies that takes advantage of a specific technology (i.e. 3D). That could take the form of a bundling agreement with an upfront advance paid against royalties. OEMs often have a desire to put a game into a box with another product, and that gives small start-ups a chance to make a name for their company and break a product into the channel. Another way to attract venture capital is through investment forums, where private companies are looking to invest in high-risk developers.

High risk investments are often struck for small pieces of equity, which might be sufficient for "bridge financing" to complete a design document. Another angle is to go for funding of $1 million to $2 million to completely finish the title. An important point to remember is developers looking for money must be able to show investors an "exit strategy," a business plan migration eventually leading to an IPO or a sell-out strategy. Many investors don't want to "bail- out," but they want to know the option is available. For companies looking to sell, larger publishers are always looking for key pieces of technology and talent that sits behind the terminal.

Financing

One possible strategy to fund a project is to identify a niche market and submit product proposals to fill that market gap. But developers must be able to justify the market and successfully go through a "proof of concept" phase. The "model" for getting signed to a development deal can take several paths. First of all, developers do not need a complete, finished product. Publishers don't want developers to come in with a finished product because so much is changed (music, art, storyboard) once a publisher jumps in.

Making a Successful Product Pitch

Developers beware: Eight of the most frightening words in the English language are "I have the greatest idea for a game!" And publishers are the first to recognize this fact. Great ideas are a "dime a dozen." There is not that much work in the idea. It's the marriage of the developer's vision and passion with the game idea that is valuable and interesting to publishers and investors. Passion is necessary because that enthusiasm must be maintained through 18 months of development. Passion is also necessary because developers must sell the publisher long before the public ever sees it.

Project proposals are not only a good idea, but the only evidence prospective investors and publishers have to determine the merit of your concept. It's a lot of work and can take several months to put together. But the process forces developers to think about putting functional product together.

At the end of the day, what matters in a proposal is the information conveyed in it. Here are some of the key elements that should be included:

- The **working title** give the publisher and their marketing staff an idea of what the project should convey to the consumer. Marketing may have other ideas after they've seen the final project.
- The **target platform** (i.e. MAC CD-ROM, PC CD-

57

Chapter 3

ROM, SEGA, Nintendo) determines projected primary core audience. This is an important gauge in determining the potential profitability of the proposed project.

- The **target audience** defines the primary core user This should include gender, age, income level and special interests. The target audience further defines the total market for the porject.

- A concise **project description** should convey the essense of the project not only to the potential publisher, but to the potential consumer. Describe the special attributes which will make this product stand out from others. Special attributes include licensed characters potential co-marketing arrangements, sponsors, talent (name actors, name writers, name animators). A special attribute is an element of the project the publisher doesn't have access to or the time to access.

- A **sample interactive sequence (script)** provides the publisher with an inclination of the playablity and overall concept of the project.

- The **scope (characters and levels)** defines the ultimate creation in terms of usage and visual stimulus. In the game market the character can be the most important part of the game and have.

- Describe in detail the **features** (game play or interface), the technology and what makes this project different from others in its genre.

- A reasonable **competitive analysis** describing similar titles, the selling points of those titles and how this marketing data compares with the project under consideration.

- A complete **development plan** (proof of concept) describes how the developer is going to produce the project and what is required of the development studio.

Financing

The importance of honesty as to the strengths and weaknesses is important here.

- The **budget and schedule** determine the milestones and the scope of the project. The publisher sets the milestones and negociates the advance based on these documents. Do not under estimate the time and money to produce the project. This can lead to irreparable damage to your relationship with the publisher.

- **Biographies** are extremely important to any monitary source. The experience of the team working the project is usually the key factor determining whether the project will be financed.

Developers must also have a strategy to make a successful pitch. Making a product pitch is, and will remain, an integral part of the entertainment business and should be considered very carefully prior to actually going before decision makers. Deals are made from personal relationships. Securing money and striking publishing deals will come down to three factors:

- Do they like the developer on a personal level?
- Does the developer have the capacity to produce what they are promising?
- How strong is the concept?

The key will ultimately be, does the publisher personally like the developer. If this is true, publishers have a habit of helping development companies with strong concepts put together teams to bring those concepts to fruition.

If all meets with publisher approval, the publisher will commission a design document, which is typically paid for with an advance of anywhere from $35,000 to $50,000. But a word of caution: Once a developer receives the $50,000 to do a 200-page design document, the publisher owns it, and the developer could wind up with a successful design document experience and a little cash—and nothing more.

Chapter 3

Case Study: Mondo Media and Zipper Interactive

Interactive game publishing is often a "hits" driven business that generates very few legitimate "hits." That creates a strong market for quality content, as well as the talent that produces it. In today's high stakes game market, even the largest media giants (i.e. Time Warner, Viacom and MCA) will fund a title developer which offers the company something it can't do in-house and which appears to have a strong likelihood of finding an audience. For small developers with a well-designed product and business strategy, there is still plenty of opportunity to break into the major leagues of interactive game publishing. The challenge developers face, however, is to keep those projects alive until publishing deals are sealed, and advances are issued to complete the product or fund additional ones.

Zipper Interactive President and CEO Jim Bosler and Mondo Media's CFO Tim McNally provide an example of how different approaches to getting a deal done can still lead to the same successful outcome. Namely, keeping the company solvent while pitching for a deal. Both executives are key players in two firms that have recently signed (or completed) deals with major publishers.

While these two development shops have slightly different corporate personalities and market strategies, they have successfully exploited those unique characteristics to establish themselves as "branded" players in the interactive game business.

Zipper Interactive announced in Spring 1996 a multi-title development deal with Viacom New Media. The first title, *Death Drome*, is slated for a Fall 1996 release. Mondo Media just wrapped up contract work for Activision's *Zork Nemesis* sequel, and is well-known for its development contributions on such projects as *Rebel Assault II* and *The Dig*. Mondo is also the developer of *The Daedalus Encounter*, published by Virgin Interactive Entertainment, which sold about 200,000 units into the channel.

According to both developers, publishers are looking for two basic business attributes: 1) Experience; and 2) Capability (i.e. an assembled creative and management team), which mean the ability to meet project

Financing

milestones. That includes forecasting budgets and milestones and then managing to them. In addition, with the rigors of 3D systems, publishers are looking very critically at a potential partner's technology.

Many games and multimedia titles require if not bleeding edge, cutting edge 3D engines and environments, and those properties are not available as shrink-wrapped assets. Jim Bosler says, "Content can cover up a lot of sins because publishers will work with developers to beef up the creative or technical teams if there is killer content." But he cautions, "Developers must have one or the other."

Staying Alive

Long before a project pitch is made, however, developers have to cover initial development costs. Mondo Media uses a hybrid model that balances original production with contract work (about a 50/50 split). Internal projects compete for resources with external projects. The aim, according to McNally, is "to make internal projects as competitive as possible with the best stuff in the industry." Plus, he says, "It keeps everybody paid."

McNally believes that is very important in the early days of a company because the work flow of a typical title varies depending on what stage it's in. There are peaks for artists and peaks for programmers. And once you come off those peaks, the question is: How do you create a stimulating environment for that talent?

The projects Mondo has done for other clients, as well as its original work, have helped the company get major contract gigs with other companies. The company started with contract work back in 1988 in the corporate CD ROMs and eventually was contracted to supply art for Microsoft's Encarta title. The company kept its Daedalus title alive by using a small core team in the initial stages. That team included an artist, game designer, programmer and producer. Creative bridge financing also helps. Daedalus, for example, was partially funded (about 20% of the $1.5 million budget) by pre-selling some of the foreign rights against royalties.

Chapter 3

Zipper Interactive, by contrast, does not do any contract work. The company initially funded operations by cranking out its first title in two weeks. That "skunk works" approach, says Bosler, was partially the result of a design team that had been together for about 12 years and possessed the know-how to shave about a year off its game engine development time. Revenue from the first game was used to put together the Viacom pitch, according to Bosler. But industry contacts help, too.

Bosler (when head of Boss Studios) had developed a casual relationship with Viacom in the past based on mutual respect. And when Bosler left Boss (a company he helped found), the director of business development at Viacom called the next day and said the company wanted to work with him.

Where is the Cash?

One of the biggest issues confronting a start-up developer is whether to seek an alliance with a publisher, or pitch for VC money. McNally believes publishers are often the best partners for new game developers in the current market environment because they "help guide the project, set milestones and create a risk/reward relationship based on performance." Start-up developers will have to give up a lot to work with a publisher (creative control, a large share of any profits), but the publisher is there to keep the project on track if it (and it usually does) runs into stumbling blocks.

McNally says any developer looking to attract VC money has to be of sufficient scale to crank out a lot of product or to eventually go public. That means developers have to be in "a state of readiness to kick on the turbo engines when a venture capitalist comes on board." That places a lot of pressure on the company and can spell disaster if the management team is not tested.

Bosler says, "VCs are looking for something different than a hits-based business. They want an initial public offering or big exit, and that's not a classic fit between developers and that community." The primary upside from VC support, though, is creative control. Bosler says it's a

Financing

mistake for a start-up developer to come out of the chute and publish games. "With only one game to live or die by, it's too risky," he says. But he continues, "With a publisher covering game costs, a developer can live to fight another day if the first title is less than successful."

A successful product pitch, however, is what stands between a project making the leap from concept demo to gold master. Getting funded this year is tougher than ever because there are reportedly fewer publishers scooping up proposals. In addition, with the collapse of the 16-bit market, and the fact that advanced platforms have yet to take off and drive up software sales, that makes everybody's job harder.

But, the industry is growing at a compounded annual rate of 35%, and that's healthy by any measure. To claim a share of the potential upside, however, developers need to show publishers or VCs what they are buying.

- **Sell the company's strengths**: Make the publisher or investor believe in the team first, and the product second. For example, Zipper Interactive has a very robust 3D development engine developed by a crack engineering team that gives the company an advantage in the military simulation market. Mondo has a very strong proprietary asset integration tool (MechaVision) that company engineers have continually updated as successive titles have come to market.

- **Provide a "high concept"**: "High concepts" in the Hollywood fashion are considered creative breakthroughs in storytelling and composition, and of course every film producer will tell you their project falls into the category of "high concept." The "story" in storytelling has not changed much in over 2,000 years, however story presentation has undergone a major "face-lift" since the Greeks' presentation of their tragedies. A "high concept" is a story which incorporates elements from different stories in a unique way, creating

Chapter 3

a new type of story. It is becoming increasingly difficult to find quality "high concepts" in Hollywood, however the interactive medium presents creative talent with a whole variety of new story paradigms for "high concept" stories. If interactive developers can find a way to provoke an emotional response from their storytelling, interactive is destined to become a powerful medium. Interactive developers in the product presentation should understand how their project is "high concept" and be able to articulate it in the pitch.

- **Hit your target audience**: For any game, one audience that must be nailed to make publishers comfortable is the young, male market. If the product has enough depth, explain how it could capture a wider audience or form the basis for a series of titles.

- **Focus on one or two delivery platforms**: Don't get so tangled up in the "portability" issue to the point that you lose sight of the top one or two primary market segments; today that is PC CD-ROM and Sony PlayStation. With porting costs averaging $100,000 to $200,000 per platform, any incremental revenue has to cover those expenses at a minimum.

- **Deliver a product demo**: Show publishers the actual game level graphics and game play. That can cost upward of about $15,000. Zipper used an action-packed demo (put together inside of two weeks) to sell Viacom, for example, which is very similar to one the company will show at E3 in May. Mondo showed Virgin a working prototype of The Daedalus Encounter that had the look and feel of the game. The tool has also been used and improved throughout numerous contract work cycles.

Financing

- **Know your business**: The goal is to put out a great game, not take on technical risks of evolving technologies. Zipper tries to stay on the "lean" edge, not the "bleeding" edge of technology, according to Bosler. Mondo is known for its high production values (i.e. live action), but it is moving to digitally rendered environments to supply the level of randomness that twitch-enthusiasts demand.

- **Beware of "slick" presentations:** Publishers are looking for reality, not a lot of development dollars thrown at hype. While Zipper had a strong demo, it typically works with fold-out tables with expensive equipment on top; but the company watches its overhead very closely, and that is crucial to selling a deal.

In a publisher-funded model, cash is usually dispensed on a monthly basis against milestones. This "keeps both parties from getting hurt," says Bosler, and he notes, "It's good discipline." In the early days of game publishing, so-called soft project milestones often were not met. Bosler warns, "It doesn't do any good to string out the relationship for a year and then realize that the game is not going to be completed on time if the milestones were too soft."

Know What Your Product is Worth

Interactive profits may be hard to come by in the current marketplace, but those companies making money are growing their margins faster than royalty rates paid out to developers. That's the opinion of Brian Napper, founding shareholder and VP of The Barrington Consulting Group in San Francisco. Part of the reason for that disparity is that, in the past, developers have been happy just to find a licensor for their titles, and have taken a "less than analytical" approach to striking deals.

Chapter 3

Napper says rights holders can take several different approaches to determining royalty rates, which currently range anywhere from 1% to 25% of wholesale revenue. The four basic types of deals:

- A **fixed rate** deal could involve a straight development deal, whereby a publisher pays the developer an upfront development fee, plus a minimum "backend" participation based on product sales. The advantage for game developers is that the product is funded externally and distributed through an established entity.

- **Rate-based** deals are struck for a percentage of sales (wholesale revenue) sold into the channel, minus an allowance for returns and defective product. The main concern for developers in this type of deal is to structure an "audit clause" into the agreement. This type of clause allows the developer to audit sales figures and determine if royalties match with product units sold through. Napper says these types of arrangements typically uncover a trend toward underpayment.

- The **cost-based** royalty model focuses on how much a publisher can save by licensing the product of a smaller developer. In that type of deal, developers and publishers typically sit down and calculate how much the former avoided in R & D investment, carrying costs (production costs) and in some cases, marketing.

- The **income-based** model is calculated as a straight percentage of wholesale revenue. Nowadays, publishers are often willing to structure those types of deals with higher royalty percentages paid at the front end of the product's life cycle. That, in effect, better coincides with more robust sales during a product's launch and early purchase patterns. As the product matures, rates are then calculated on a sliding scale.

Financing

Trends rippling through the industry have placed upward pressure on royalties. Those trends include:

- A hot mergers and acquisitions (M & A) market for quality companies
- The WWW and its potential for ancillary revenues
- Rapid technological change
- An increase in game interactivity, multimedia applications and level of software sophistication. Copying (i.e. software pirating) was also listed as a reason that royalty rates have been moving upward.

Napper believes the best strategy a rights holder has when negotiating royalty rates with a potential licensor is to know what types of deals have been struck in the marketplace before (referred to as "comparables"). He suggests licensees take the time to investigate financial documents for the public companies in order to determine a base royalty rate paid for third-party product.

In addition, rights holders should consider whether the contract calls for a period of exclusivity, the state of product development, licensing alternatives, breakthrough/pioneering technology, licensor promotional support, teaching, size of market, protection costs, administration costs, field of use (in other products, for example) and "grant backs." *Grant back* agreements give the licensee the right to recover profits from certain derivative products created as a result of the original deal.

CHAPTER 4
the product

Interactive title developers are creating new ways of delivering content to core communities of interest (hyped users). These communities of interest are based primarily on user engagement. The industry is in a perpetual state of re-defining its product mandate, however, because technology is constantly providing alternative ways for users to access that information and entertainment, and audiences fragment as a result. At this point, storytelling has taken a back seat to technology, but that is quickly changing.

Motion pictures have survived for almost 100 years because they found two major conceptual justification: the suspension of disbelief, and the repeatability of story-telling. Interactive title developers could learn something from Hollywood, namely, that one of its untold secrets is that people often don't know what they want.

But, once developers discover what users do want, those "wants" turn into habituated cycles of consumption. That's the nature of brand loyalty. It represent the fruits of long years of labor, creating content from scratch with a healthy dose of intuition and "guestimation."

That's why the Internet is going to be so useful to developers, because once they find categories that work, it can be combined with CD-ROM clients to add new characters and play scenarios in real-time, which essentially extends product life. In addition, those products can be fed

Chapter 4

into dedicated game/entertainment networks which will provide a more lucrative aftermarket for developers beyond the retail level.

It's the same path of evolution book technology took during this century. It's far easier to read today than it was 100 years ago, so it can be enjoyed more, and therefore it encourages the reader's willingness to explore. That's the crucial foundation for making a mass market for CD-ROM product and interactive content in general. There has to be a willingness on the part of the user to explore.

There are three macro end-user markets that developers can mine for marketshare:

> **Adult Edutainment/Personal Growth**: Material presented should be useful, logical, entertaining, compelling and familiar. This means scouring the magazine rack as a starting point, and presenting that content in a new way to an old audience.
>
> **Children**: There is considerable opportunity for developers in this segment based on repeatability of content and thematic treatments, which can be leveraged into additional titles and incremental distribution avenues. Children will spend hours with a movie learning dialogue. The key is to provide a compelling reason to do so with a multimedia title as well.
>
> **Games**: Repeatability of storytelling, the level of action, technology and high concepts (a concept presented in a unique fashion) generate the street buzz which keeps gamers flocking to retail shelves or online dungeons to participate in the experience.

Entertainment has been around for thousands of years. The real foundation of the longevity of the art form is the repeatability of story-telling. So-called "high concepts" often can effect paradigm shifts in the entire creative process of what is considered viable and profitable entertainment. Examples are *Star Wars* and *E.T.: The Extraterrestrial*, from the film market. As for multimedia, the two most recognizable titles to have had that kind of impact on the business are *Myst* and *Doom*.

As developers begin to invest more resources in storytelling, the market will see more and more high concept titles emerge that not only have an impact at the retail level, but spawn numerous imitators who will attempt to take advantage of the ground-breaking nature of the content and the manner in which it was presented.

Better Storytelling—Bigger Franchise

Interactive product, like other entertainment product, is based on a four-legged stool: economics, money, technology and creativity. One of the problems with multimedia today is most of the money has been thrown at technology and not the message, namely, better storytelling.

Moreover, interactive product today is experiencing technology shifts that are confusing the end user and limiting greater market adoption (i.e. software sales) because of a fragmented platform universe at the retail level. *But the medium and technology are not the message. The content is the message.*

Developers can't get too caught up in machinations of the hardware market and should go after the safest platform investment in today's market. In other words, developers need to focus on the largest installed hardware base—in this case PC CD-ROM, Sony Playstation and Sega Saturn game consoles—not to mention the networks that already feed both the PC and TV.

The second step is for developers to simply concentrate on making interactive content as compelling as its linear cousin. And a good way to understand that is to co-develop "with the audience." That's why all developers use beta trials and consumer feedback to hone the product. Developers do have the answers but not the questions; Those can come only from a closer relationship with the end user.

Chapter 4

Supporting a Product Development Decision

For established developers, a great deal of the decision making process in determining what type of product to develop is based on past experience. For new developers, identifying potentially exciting product concepts is an important step in getting off the ground.

This can be done in a number of ways. Proven market stand-by's like flight simulators or 3D *Doom* clones are one choice to create potentially popular product. But original ideas and unique implementation often make for the biggest hits. *Myst* and *Wolfenstein 3D* (perhaps the first real *Doom*-style shoot-em-up) persuasively illustrate the benefits of this strategy.

If the developer is repurposing content from an established franchise, he should be able to gauge the potential success of a title based on the content's popularity in its original incarnation. Content based on franchises that have sold well as books, movies, TV shows, etc. will likely do well in the market when integrated into a interactive title—assuming that the new product ties in well with the original, and provided that a sufficient number of the content's prior audience are also computer owners/software buyers. Those are big assumptions, and a lot of gut-wrenching decisions must be made long before those types of projects are greenlighted.

Some of these factors can be gauged through market research, as well as by building a case for production from prior development experience with a particular title or market. With new, unproved products or concepts, developers sometimes use focus groups and user testing to spot-check viability in the marketplace.

These tools can help reveal what could be insurmountable technical hurdles and can work out "kinks" in basic product concept. Testing can also help to determine potential market size by allowing a developer to determine what sectors of the population would find a particular type of title interesting.

There are, however, no magic bullets available to developers to penetrate markets nowadays, given the hyper-competitive nature of the marketplace and the number of large players throwing lots of promotional money at the channel. Development and investment in multimedia title development is a risky business at best.

Platform Decisions

Platform decisions are often problematic. Choosing whether or not to develop for more than one platform can also be an important choice. Some of the industry's most successful and long-lived software companies have survived primarily because of their ability to quickly identify and move onto emerging platforms.

Larger publishers, like Acclaim Entertainment and Electronic Arts, can afford to port a title to four or five discrete playback platforms. That is not the case with other smaller publishers. Porting to additional platforms can cost from $100,000 to $200,000 per iteration. For big sellers, like LucasArt's *Rebel Assault* series and EA's *Madden* sports franchises, it's obviously worth it. Those titles sell hundreds of thousands of units (the first *Rebel Assault* has sold through well over 1.5 million units), and a $100,000 investment in that context is well worth the effort.

Nevertheless, combine platform instability with the fact that development budgets are now pushing seven figures for many multimedia titles destined for the market, and that adds up to a lot of caution. Investment decisions to back the development of a product must be carefully thought out—especially for smaller developers and publishers.

The Doomed Production

Tens of thousands of dollars can easily be spent in title creation without a final product (gold master) emerging. Many development concepts are cut at various stages of production milestones. For the time being, interactive development is a series of milestones designed by the publisher. As the developer meets the milestones without technology problems, thematic problems, art problems or a distinct shift in the marketplace, the

Chapter 4

publisher continues to pay monthly on those milestones.

There are five possible reasons a publisher will abandon a production:

- Developer consistently misses milestones.
- Developer's promised technological advantage never comes to fruition.
- Concept and story disintegrate on implmentation.
- Art does not meet licensed specifications.
- Publisher's sales and marketing can't justify the project (i.e. shifts in the marketplace).

Although it is better to stop development in mid-stream rather than release a title that doesn't have much of a chance to succeed at retail, avoiding the situation altogether through careful and ongoing product planning is preferable.

CASE STUDY

The Only Multimedia Constant is Change
Rocket Science

The volatility of the multimedia business is being exposed on a routine basis, with many companies either going out of business, deeply in the "red" or merging with larger entities to defend and fortress marketshare. No matter how many quality titles a company produces, or the strength of its distribution machinery, those titles still must find an audience willing to pay for them. The market is the absolute arbiter of success and failure in the multimedia business.

the product

Rocket Science President and CEO, Steve Blank, has been quite frank about the company's restructuring efforts. Blank says the company, which he helped cofound, has been through some "interesting shifts in the last three years," when it began corporate life as a game console developer.

Rocket Science was founded in July, 1993 and was positioned as a great technology and graphics company. That was a time when the "hype of multimedia and Hollywood meeting in Silicon Valley was at its zenith," says Blank. The reality was, however, that "the company was not a multimedia company but an entertainment company in a hits-driven business," says Blank.

In addition, while the company was founded on spectacular technology, "That did not default into great games," according to Blank. Compounding the overall problem, "was a poor choice of platforms to develop for."

The result was Rocket Science "produced weak games, with abysmal game play," according to Blank and market analysts. The irony was that Rocket Science had hired a lot of great talent from Hollywood's effects and graphics communities, but their component skill sets did not translate well into a game company environment.

In this market, however, companies have to "reinvent" themselves to take advantage of market preference shifts. Blank says Rocket Science went through a period of reevaluation and put together a 12-step program for reviving the company. Rocket Science was then committed to making major repositioning and structural changes. Blank says the company is "now in the process of sitting and executing, and executing very hard." He quips that employees of Rocket Science all wear buttons around their work spaces that reflect the company's new operating philosophy: "It's the Game Stupid."

Rocket Science also initiated an intense prototype process which occurs before any art is submitted. Blank says funding the repositioning plan was made complicated by the fact that "the game console market has collapsed dramatically over the past two years." The problem for Rocket Science and other game developers is fixing companies takes

Chapter 4

time and money. But, according to Blank, "Multimedia is no longer a play for venture capitalists. Its an entertainment business."

That meant Rocket Science had to "reposition the company where the money is." Blank says the "money in the business is now riding on three waves of platforms: Consoles, PCs and the Internet."

Despite the company's market travails, Blank says this is his sixth start-up, and four of those have gone public, which could be in the cards for Rocket Science. The company's Firewalker 3D tool (developed in conjunction with SGI) is now coming to market, and dynamics of the Internet appear to offer game developers a strong vehicle for maximizing the value of established game titles.

Blank believes Rocket Science finally realized the company had to deliver what the market was asking for. The market always rules, according to Blank, and the companies that can deliver what consumers want at a price they are willing to pay for it will always come out on top.

Ken Goldstein, Exec. Producer
Broderbund Software

Q. Can you talk about the computer or PC side of title development and then about the dedicated game console market—from Sony PlayStation to Sega Saturn? How do you decide which platforms to develop for?

A. We're in the desktop computer business. That's where we've been making our money for the last five years. For at least the foreseeable future that's where we see it continue to happen. It's an open architecture, and it's a free publishing environment (i.e. I don't have to pay a predetermined technology royalty to someone else to put a title out).

the product

We're very excited about the *Windows95* platform and the *Windows95 SDK*. We're very excited about the technology in the *PowerPC* and the *PowerMac*. I think those are both going to be very viable platforms for the foreseeable future. I think you're going to see growth in the online gaming environment—in some way, shape or other exploitation of the Internet in the multiplayer setting.

I'm thinking the Internet right now is more about connectivity—in terms of people sending e-mail, and chatting, and sharing thoughts and information, and doing research at Web sites—than it is about putting people together for multiplayer gaming experiences. I think a lot of that has to do with the technology limitations. I think that in the next several years some of those will go away and some of those won't.

As those limitations go away you'll start to see more online gaming. I think that the issue with online gaming has more to do with how the people putting the products out continue to enjoy enough of a revenue stream to make it a worthwhile business venture. No one has yet to articulate a business model that makes a lot of sense.

Q. Does Broderbund have any multiplayer or network games?

A. We are working on a couple of things right now that support multiplayer involvement, although they—like most of the things we do here—exist primarily in stand-alone mode where somebody can drop the CD into their machine and start playing. We are trying to add a connectivity element to some of those products.

Q. Are those entertainment titles? Or are you doing multiplayer educational titles for school networks, etc.?

A. Well, we've been on school networks. Local area networks are easy for us. *Carmen* has been on local area networks in schools for—I don't know—six, seven years or something like that. But we're starting to explore it more from a point-to-point environment where kids can play cooperatively as well as competitively. I still think that the real opportunity there is in bringing the kinds of games that people have enjoyed over local area networks to server environments where people can play in two

77

Chapter 4

remote places—where they would previously have played in the same location.

Q. What about dedicated platforms? Is Broderbund interested in that market?

A. We're certainly interested in it. The economics of it are pretty terrifying. If you look at some of the best-selling games on the PlayStation, a frightening number of them are Sony-published titles. The odds are still with the hardware manufacturer on those types of business models.

The licensing agreements tend to favor the licensor of the hardware and software. There are economies of scale there as well, where, if you're going to market those aggressively (which you seem to have to do in those kinds of games), if you don't have a dozen games out there, it's pretty hard to really spend your marketing dollar well.

I think that the technology on the PlayStation is real exciting. I don't think that the machines have been positioned as edutainment type machines. I don't see us getting real aggressive there. We have had some projects go over and be licensed. *Myst* has done real well on the Sega CD. *Prince of Persia* did terrific on the Nintendo. I can do sub-licensing, but I don't foresee us in the immediate future getting into the publishing business on those platforms, although we're clearly keeping an eye on it.

Brian Farrell, President
T*HQ

Q. What platforms do you develop your titles for?

A. We are primarily in the console business—the dedicated game system business—as opposed to the PC multimedia platform. The reason for

the product

that is two-fold. Number one, although people keep talking about convergence of console games and PC games, it hasn't happened yet.

We can see the argument that PCs are getting more powerful and therefore more game-oriented and that with *Windows95* you may have something closer to the plug-and-play environment found in a game console.

But, we also see the argument—we vote for this with our own capital—the game consoles are generally found in the entertainment section of the house—either the den, family room or kid's room—whereas the PC is currently used more as a home productivity device. In the PC market, bundling is also an issue.

When I bought my own multimedia PC, I must have gotten 30 different forms of entertainment software, so there wasn't a big need for me to go out and buy four or five new entertainment concepts for me to do. So while I won't say there's not an entertainment market on the PC, even the 16-bit market—which everyone is singing the death knell of—is bigger than the entertainment side of the PC market right now.

Q. Especially the arcade side of the PC market?

A. Absolutely. When I look at PCs, I look at straight entertainment—different from what I'll call edutainment, different from productivity software. So if you take all those three things, then the PC market is pretty broad. But when you are comparing apples to apples with just straight entertainment software, the 16-bit market is a bigger market on the entertainment side than PC entertainment.

Q. Are you doing the multimedia-type titles that are big on the PC—*Myst, 7th Guest* for example?

A. Not at this time. That's not the kind of thing we would do. We are actually working on two concepts for the PC market, but they are more console games that we are going to port to PC, rather than the other way round. The other point I wanted to make is in the PC market there really are no barriers to entry—the cost of goods is very low. You don't have to pay these high "path charges" to the Nintendo, Sony and Sega franchises

Chapter 4

of the world. You don't have to get your product approved and licensed. You just ship it.

If you have an IBM-compatible product, there's really no barrier to entry. That has resulted in a really crowded marketplace and a real bitter battle for shelf space. While in the console market, you still have to battle for shelf space and have some darn good product; Maybe I'm competing with 100 other Sony PlayStation games, not 2,000 PC wanna-be's.

Everybody said, "Wow! Here's this open platform, worlds of opportunity, huge installed base." But the flip side of that is it's really crowded for shelf space.

When somebody buys a Sony PlayStation they buy it for one reason and one reason only: to play video games. A PC can be bought for home finance, so you can work at home, have your kids learn to do math. Currently they are different experiences.

Q. Are you primarily developing for hand-held and 16-bit consoles? To what extent are you going after the market for advanced platforms?

A. Obviously, the future of the company lies with the more advanced platforms. But being a public company, our shareholders pay us to earn money. Right now—particularly the GameBoy, Sega has virtually abandoned the GameGear—there is a market there (hand-helds). Everyone else moved into 32-bit, and we're making a living on the older platforms. Like anything else, when a market matures, there's still business to be had there. The only difference between us and other publishers is that we're not turning our back on those markets.

We know our future is in 32, and maybe 64-bit, and we are investing in R&D. We're signing licenses. We're developing games. It's funny—we've kind of gotten this moniker as the hand-held company only because we are making good money at it. It's a nice business because we didn't have a lot of competition to get the kind of licenses like LucasArts' *Return of the Jedi*, the EA stuff—*Madden, Fifa, NHL, Pocahontas* and *Toy Story* with Disney. It's a nice little business. It's not great, and I wouldn't recommend people to go into that business now because it's on a downward slope.

the product

But for somebody in that market who has the contacts, has the game design, has everything to do—they can still make money in that business.

Building the Assets

The steps involved in creating a interactive title are fairly uniform, although the process, sequence of tasks, technology employed and production terminology vary from publisher to publisher and title to title. According to developers polled for this book, the typical production process includes 13 steps.

Interactive development typically consists of three major phases: pre-production, production and post-production. The pre-production phase begins with the concept treatment and includes goal definition, user/audience analysis and the intricacies of authoring design and specification, and target platform (s) of the title.

The script and the storyboard provide the developer with a creative "blueprint" for the design of the project. They provide the developer and the publisher with the entire creative scope and scale of the project. They are critical for determining the use of technology, new technology needed and the schedule and budget of the project. They are the precurser to the design document, which adds the technological specifications to the project.

Technical design document specifications explain how the title's goals will be accomplished. It will typically include what kind of interactions and media elements (graphics, animations, video, etc.) the title will contain and whether media assets are available for re-purposing, or if they have to be acquired or created. The design document includes a brief description of each section of the title.

Typically, all of these elements go through a revision process, as the scope and scale of the project are defined and redefined. These redefinitions are usually directly attributed to the budget. As the budget is built from the design document, the project goes through a kind of "argument,"

Chapter 4

> ## The Interactive Decision Tree and Production Process
>
> ### Preproduction
> 1. Title concept pitched, and decision process initiated
> 2. Informal analysis and group brainstorming
> 3. Discussion of broad treatment commences
> 4. Development or purchase of script
> 5. Storyboard layout
> 6. Prototyping
>
> ### Production
> 7. Make/acquire media assets (initial production phase)
> 8. Alpha testing
> 9. Beta testing
> 10. Final testing
>
> ### Post-Production
> 11. Porting media assets to target platforms
> 12. End user validation
> 13. Ship gold master
>
> **Source: The Carronade Group**

the question being: How do we develop this concept for the budget without denigrating the original vision of the project? Here lies the dark pit for every development team. With careful consideration, the team redefines the project to meet the scope and scale of the budget. This is not necessarily a bad thing.

One question for all production managers, directors and producers alike: Does this cut hurt the playability, user engagement and reusability

the product

of the project, and how will this cut ultimately detract from the consumer's experience? If the answer to those questions is, "Yes," then ask, "How do we make it simple with the same effect?" Often the simplest solutions are

---

Broderbund's Interactive Title Product Development Cycle

Pre-Production—The collaborative team made up of lead interactive designer, writer, sound engineer, programmer, art director and product manager, begins piecing together a general outline. Sketching, brainstorming cycle, preliminary script development, assembling images, rough story board are completed. The discussion of licensing/purchase of technology needed. Target platform (s) delivered on.

Graphics and Animation—Development begins. Character designs based on gestures and body language are produced; professional actors are contracted for voice overlay.

Sound and Video—Analog video shoot. Taped results are digitized, then adjusted for balance image and quality with intended screen size. Sound team is assembled which comprises musicians and composers. Sequences are selected for incorporating classic cartoon sounds.

Computer Programming—Technical requirements (disk space, colors, screen size, what code modules must be original or used from in-house programming library) are created. Technology is possibly sourced from 3rd party (work-for-hire) development shops.

Post-Production—Quality assurance testing, third party validation (parents/teachers), consumer and beta release testing is conducted.

Source: Broderbund's annual report.

83

Chapter 4

the most elegant.

During pre-production, prototyping (typically a 40-60 day job) starts, once the creative and design statements are done, and while the script is being written. Sound and video production begin about two weeks to 10 days into prototyping. At the same time, the interface guidelines are developed.

The production phase involves the creation or acquisition of media assets and then, the preparation, capture and editing of those assets. Still photographs, graphics and other flat artwork can be captured using scanners. Image processing software is then used to edit captured images.

Original graphic images are created using drawing and painting tools. Video can be captured using video frame grabbers or scanners. Once still and motion images are created, they must be converted to the resolutions and formats used by the target platform. Audio is recorded and modified using digital audio processing.

Once the authoring or programming is complete, simulation testing begins, followed by pre-mastering. During pre-mastering, images and audio are converted into the formats used by the target delivery platform.

Michael Pole, Exec. Producer
Electronic Arts

Q. How do you develop project milestones with your developers?

A. A lot of people figure out what they want their release date to be and work backwards. I'd rather work with the knowledge of how long each of the elements and tasks are going to take to build the game. We build a really good design and then require a technical design document. That

the product

technical design document and the game design will basically dictate what our milestones are going to be and how long it's really going to take to do a project, based on the amount of people working on it. Then I figure out when we are going to ship. You can promise the company anything you want, but being able to deliver product on time is what you are judged by.

No milestones are broken down until we have our technical design document. At that time, we build in preliminary deadlines. We want to get to the prototype stage very early on in the process—spending as little money as possible in the process. We like to jump over the most important technical hurdles as early as we can. Then basically, it's delivery of levels and game tuning as you move forward.

Q. Do you find that method of scheduling works best for meeting deadlines?

A. Set a realistic schedule and you can be successful. Once you have a design and technical design, you can give a realistic release date.

Q. What does creating a technical design document entail—what goes into it?

A. It basically outlines the steps involved and the technical aspects of it—the game engine or engines. Some games have one, some have more. There is a lot of "proof of concept" stuff going on at the early stages. If you want characters that can roam in eight different directions, then you need to prove that you can do it technically. Those are some of the technical hurdles we want to get over.

Q. So you need to know how to take care of all of the technical aspects—creating graphics, etc.—before you back a product development decision?

A. Exactly. Show me one room of an enviroment that includes art and animation up and running, some collision detection and some game play. And if you can move all of those assets around in a limited space, then you can expand. If you can't, then there's no reason to move forward. Honestly, you can spend half of a million dollars and have nothing to show for it. That is scary.

Chapter 4

Q. How quickly into the development process do you want to have a prototype or working prototype pieces up and running?

A. I like to see preliminary artwork and a preliminary prototype in four months. Once you have this, you can intelligently schedule the remaining game development.

Q. What is your worst nightmare in dealing with a developer?

A. Being late is problematic. Not being able to get over a technical hurdle is also one of the most difficult situations to be in. My biggest fear with a developer is that they will fall on their face technically and not be able to deliver on milestones having, already created the technical design document.

Q. Where in the design process do you start working with your marketing assets? From the very beginning or later?

A. Producers have to wear two hat hats. We are responsible for product creation, but we must also be salesmen, and that begins from the very start of the project. We work with the marketing department to make sure they believe content and design are demographically correct. So that starts very early.

We go in as partners. We sit down, and we talk about the genre. We decide if the content and genre work together, and then we decide what game to build. You have to marry the right concept to the right genre. Madeline doesn't belong on the Sony PlayStation—*Gen13* does.

Q & A

Gary Hare, President & CEO
Fathom Pictures

Q. Can you give me some information about how you work with publishers?

the product

A. We've done it two ways. One is advance against royalties. We go in and say, "We'd like to do such-and-such a title, and it's going to cost so much money." And they advance us that money against future royalties.

Q. Do you have a prototype in-hand?

A. We have a title treatment or even a more fleshed out design. Literally, we've done titles on the back of a napkin when we're talking to somebody and say, "We'd like to do this." Somebody will say, "What will that cost?" And I'll throw a number off of my tongue, and we sit there and write down about five deal points on the back of a napkin and fax it to our respective attorneys. One of our most successful relationships began with a situation like that. About 50% of the time, publishers come to us and sit down and say, "Here's what we'd like to do, and here's our agenda. Would you like to do that, too?" So we've done it both ways. We've seldom done any blind mail stuff out to people.

Usually, I'll call somebody and say, "I'm thinking about doing thus—is that the kind of thing that you might be interested in?" They'll say, "Yes, we might be interested, so let's take a look at it." Then they do, and sometimes they are interested and sometimes not. Either one is fine. The only kind of relationship I hate with publishers is when you don't here from them for 90 days or not at all. If somebody can call you up and say, "Nah, that's crazy," that's fine.

Sometimes publishers have a specific agenda and that's nice, too, because they can sit down and say, "This is our strategy and the stuff we like to do." Some of the very best publishing relationships are probably the hardest to find. That's when you sit down and figure out what you want to do together as a two-way deal. We don't have that yet in the long term. I'm envious of the few companies that do because they can sit down and try to figure out the publishing strategy together.

Q. Do you do any of your own publishing?

A. We've done a little bit—where we've funded our own titles and had them distributed and marketed by others. Interplay is distributing one of our products—actually two. We did a title not long ago that has been picked up internationally by Adler Communications out of Washington

Chapter 4

D.C. They are doing all of the international licensing, and I think it's going extraordinarily well.

Q. Can you detail the budget structure for an average title?

A. For PC or Mac, about $700,000. We are probably somewhere between $500,000 and $900,000, so let's say $700,000 on average. On an average conversion—let's say you do a PC title, and you want to convert it to PlayStation, that's a couple of hundred thousand dollars. Depends on the title, how much JPEG you have to do and that sort of stuff. We're not doing $3 million titles or anything like that.

Q. The PC is your primary authoring environment?

A. Generally speaking, yes. We develop on the PC or the SGI, and generally we'll port it over. It's usually a rewrite, code-wise. Using golf as an example, we have a ball flight engine that can be transported across platforms pretty easily.

Q. What is an average wholesale price for one of your products?

A. It varies a lot based on the publisher. I guess the average these days is $20 to $25 for most folks, but it's changing so quickly these days. We're seeing an erosion in the wholesale and retail price, which theoretically will raise volume anyway, so it's a wash. I could not give you an intelligent answer about what the wholesale price might be six months from now. It's going down.

Q. What about retail prices?

A. Those are coming down, too. I think that most people are talking about $39.95 as an average, where they were $49.95 a year ago. On the platform side it's higher.

the product

Q & A

Kip Konwiser, VP of Entertainment
Graphix Zone

Q. How do you pick a title or a concept, and how do you know when it will sell?

A. We're in the business of selling emotions. We're not in the hardware business, not in the technical business. We don't care if the delivery system is on a potato chip—if that's the delivery system the audience has... and there is an opportunity to get an expanded emotional availability between themselves and the artists...then it works for us.

We pick our titles based on whether or not they strike us as emotionally veritable, useful, worthy and applicable to this format. Do they belong on an interactive format, and do they ring emotionally true and fat enough to make enough juice out of the real estate that we are starting to occupy on a CD-ROM.

Q. Do you look to the music and movie industry to know what sells and what audiences prefer when you are choosing a title?

A. Sure. I mean you can pay attention to the world, too. Look around and see where are people going—what's their stream of consciousness, and what's the music that defines that stream most accurately, and does it apply to this medium. If the answer is "Yes," then that's the deal.

Q. Is it a formula or is it intuition?

A. I don't think it's a formula. I think it's life. If you recognize life, and you know what it is that your company does and what you do within that company, then things can line up.

Q. What about your titles?

Chapter 4

A. We produced Bob Dylan Interactive, perhaps the leading seller in interactive music, and it's peaking just below 100,000 units in its first nine or 10 months. We've done "Prince" Interactive, which is about 93,000 units in its first 12 months. We did the Nixon soundtrack with a John Williams score.

The Nixon soundtrack, by the way, was nominated for an Academy Award, which is the first time that the Academy has recognized an interactive property. And it's the first time ever that a film score was released solely on an enhanced CD platform— i.e. the only way you can get the soundtrack is as an enhanced CD that you can play in your standard audio CD player, as well as in your computer at home.

Q. Is that deal still exclusive or is it available in other formats now?

A. That's it. Exclusive. One SKU. That's the way it's going to be forever, except in countries where they don't release CDs— Zimbabwe or some place like that. We are doing the Nixon CD-ROM, which comes out at the end of March, 1996 and is based on an Oliver Stone film as well.

Q. Is that a cinematic decision or a documentary style decision?

A. It is everything. It's the world's largest term paper based on the movie, with Oliver all through it. It is a complete annotated screen play. It has interviews with actors, cast, real people from the Nixon era— 75,000 pages of never before seen text and documents that have been dug up by John Dean, who we went into business with Cinergi Pictures in order to make all of this stuff come true.

It's hyper-linked all throughout the disk, as well as onto the Web with an Internet browser site that goes through more documents and insight. A 3D White House that the user can navigate through to uncover all of the stuff. Tons and tons of robustness. It is a thick disk, and it's entertaining. It's not just documentary.

We are doing a jazz music CD with Herbie Hancock that basically traces the history of jazz from its landing in America. It does not go back into the African diaspora and the beginnings of rhythm and sound that actually gave birth to jazz. To a large extent, though, it does touch on

the product

those elements. But what it does really get into is Congo Square in New Orleans in the 1900s, Chicago in the '20s , New York in the '40s and New York in the '60s, Los Angeles in the '50s.

It has environments to transport you, such as river boats and trains and things like that. It's a fully-navigable 3D environment for each of those periods, where you can uncover more material on music, and jazz specifically, than you would ever uncover in any other disk. It blows Dylan away in the opportunity that a user has to get close to the artist because in this case— unlike Dylan and Prince— the artists themselves are all over it. It is robust and deep, as far as all of the resources and material that are available on the disk. So it is pretty thick. We are doing three titles with Herbie—that's the first.

We are also developing new technologies and producing record albums on CD+. We are doing three blues releases on unheard-of blues artists that will be dueting with Clapton as CD+s. We're doing a bunch of movie scores as enhanced CD or CD+ from all kinds of top features, from Oscar-winning directors almost exclusively.

We are doing Bob Marley as three CD+s with 49 tracks of never-before released or heard Bob Marley— tracks that just came available legally. The first of three titles is already out. The next title will be released on February 6, 1997 to coincide with Bob Marley's birthday. We will be doing a Bob Marley CD-ROM as well— that's to be done with the Marley family, as well as with Danny Sims and Chris Blackwell and the whole group. We are striking deals with major labels like Philips, Capital Records and others, depending on the material available.

We are dalso creating a Southern California music scene CD-ROM, which traces the music history of Southern California from the Mamas and the Papas all the way up to Pearl Jam and also includes The Doors, Joni Mitchell, Crosby, Stills, Nash and Young, Jackson Browne, James Taylor, America and many, many more.

Chapter 4

IInteractive Title Budgets

Increasing amounts of interactive content is driving production budgets up, and that is a long-term phenomenon that is not going to change. Development costs for some titles are now averaging more than $1 million—with super high-end titles such as Origin's *Wing Commander IV* exceeding $10 million. Titles for 16-bit console machines can range from $250,000 to $500,000 or more, depending on complexity (Nintendo's *Donkey Kong Country* probably ran as much as $1 million). Titles for 32-bit consoles can run as much as those for the PC CD-ROM— $1 million or more.

One of the most expensive aspects of creating a software title is the time spent by the development team. Graphics, sound effects, music and video are all very expensive to create—especially at the volumes required to fill one or more 650+ megabyte CD ROMs. As compression and storage technologies improve those costs will continue to skyrocket. The average 16-bit title can take between six and 12 months for development. Titles for 32-bit and PC CD ROM platforms can take anywhere from one to two years or more to develop.

Fewer resources and smaller development personnel can extend those development times considerably. IT can be quite expensive to license existing content for repurposing as an interactive title , both in terms of up-front fees and factoring in back-end royalties. Licensed content can lend considerable appeal to a retail product. Paying a large up-front fee for a content license can be devastating for smaller companies with smaller development budgets, as it limits the amount of money that can be directly spent on creating the project. Partnering and reduced fee/higher back-end participation are two means of coping with those difficulties.

Budgeting and scheduling is an art which would take another book to cover, so here are the basics:

> **Design Document Breakdown—** a composite breakdown of all of the elements in the project. This is the master shopping list containing all of the artwork (characters, landscapes, 3-D design, animation, mecha-

the product

nized gadgets), live- action video, 3-D animation, and programming code.

Schedule— How long will each element of the breakdown take to acquire or create, and in what order does it need to be done in to complete the project. The schedule should have achievable miletones. This is imperative.

Budget— Each element will have a cost involved either in salary or acquisition costs. On top of the basic production costs there is usually a 10% administration cost, finge, contingency padding and special costs related to the project (i.e. special hardware and software).

Q & A

Gary Hare, President & CEO
Fathom Pictures

Q. What kind of titles do you do?

A. We do two—primarily sports and sports-derivative products. A couple of examples:

We're doing a title called *Nick Price Golf*. It's Nick Price at the Prince course in Hawaii. It was all shot on 35mm film and is completely controllable. It's basically a golf game that is completely real. There are three new pieces of technology in it that have never been used before—something like that.

We're also doing an auto racing simulation called *Bob Bahnderan's High-Performance Driving*. The Bahnderan School is the number one

Chapter 4

school for race car drivers to learn and train at. We're basically putting the Bahnderan course into digital format and then letting you race. And then they'll pull you off of the race and tell you you're off-line, or you're this or you're that. It will be the first title where you can race cars and actually learn how to drive them. Your performance can get better. So it's a true racing simulation. It's probably aimed at an older, more sophisticated audience than *Need For Speed* or something like that.

Q. Does the golf product have a tutorial aspect as well?

A. No. Well, there's a help section where you can ask Price how he plays short irons or how he plays out of the sandtrap or something like that. But its intention is really to be a pretty high-profile golf game, as opposed to a sim. Now we've got the data that would allow us to make that into a sim. In the course of making the Bahnderan title, we've written the physics of the race car.

So we now have physics that are sensitive enough that we can race any vehicle on any surface. In fact, let's say we did a title where you could race a Porsche at Laguna Seca. You could take the car into the garage, change the air pressure in its tires and ratchet down the anti-sway bar a little bit, and the car would actually behave differently out on the track.

Q. You're planning on doing something interactive that allows a user to actually customize a car?

A. Yes. And we hope to announce that on the 12th of this month in Europe. We are heavily involved in all of this car stuff. And then our third sports area is what we'll call "left/right control sports," and we are doing a title that is controllable full motion. When I say "left/right control sports," I'll just give you some examples because I can't talk about this title yet.

That would be skiing, snow boarding, surfing and all of that kind of stuff. We're doing one that will actually give you control in a photo-real environment. We've written tools for that. So primarily we do sports. We do three sports titles, currently, and then we do one non-sports title.

We are doing a science-fantasy game called *Dregs*. This is a different

the product

kind of thing. It's an action-adventure— original story, original character development. We have mixed live-action characters with 3D characters but not probably like one has seen before. They're literally mixed, where a 3D character can actually go up and grab one of the live-action characters and drag him down the hallway for one reason or another.

The logical question is: Why would you do mostly sports events and some sci-fi? And the answer is we use the sci-fi title to test and sometimes create technology which we apply back to our sports titles. It becomes sort of an R&D production for us. The stuff in our latest science-fantasy title—two of the things we're doing in it we are applying to two new sports titles.

Q. What about production techniques?

A. What interested me from the very beginning was how you could use traditional film and television methodologies in the body of interactive product. So we've used miniatures and motion control, live-action shoots, controllable still and motion 35mm. We've used a lot of pretty traditional stuff. But we were the first company to ever use blue screen. We were the first company to ever use interactive sound maps in the body of a title, so that what you hear relates to what you just did.

We used a lot of this kind of stuff. We looked around and in those days (this was around 1989)— so our first CD-ROM title was for CD-I like a lot of people's were. We had the number one and number two titles in the world.

Q. What were those?

A. *The Palm Springs Open*, which is a golf title, and *Escape From Cyber City*, which is a sci-fi title. If you've ever seen CD-I— our golf title is the one most often demoed. That's been the number one best-selling title since the system came out— over four years.

What we didn't want to do was cartridge stuff. But really, in those days, cartridge stuff was what was most successful. I just wasn't interested in figuring out how to move pixels around a screen— that didn't interest me. Interactive entertainment interested me.

Chapter 4

Average Action Title Production Values Rise

Game developers like Activision, LucasArts, Origin, Interplay, Virgin, Blizzard, GTE, Mindscape, Rocket Science, Electronic Arts, Cyan and Philips are routinely creating titles with multi-million dollar budgets. Payback for an investment of that type can take a couple of years and in many respects depends on the number of aftermarket windows producers can push the product through.

For example, WMS Industries' *Mortal Kombat* franchise was not only a hit at consumer retail, but the movie of the same name earned well over $70 million at the box office. A video rental/sell-through window will add even more payback punch to the company's coffers. Activision is set to license its *Zork* property to one of the major studios for a feature film project as well.

MULTIMEDIA TITLE PRODUCTION COSTS
Per Unit Breakdown

PC CD ROM
Category Per Unit Costs
Home improvement — $2.75 - $4.00
Education — " "
Aesthetic Environment. — " "
Entertainment — $4.00 - $6.00
32-Bit CDs — $9.00 - $10.00
Carts — $15.00 - $30.00

Packaging Components
Box — $0.60 - $4.00+
Jewel Case — $0.10 - $0.20
Documentation — $0.50 - $3.00
CD Duplication — $1.00 - $1.25
Carts — $10.00 - $25.00

Source: Carronade Group

the product

That franchise leveraging paradigm can also go the other way. For instance, George Lucas leveraged his *Star Wars* franchise into a lucrative multimedia window with such titles as the *Rebel Assault* and *Dark Forces* series. Even though the characters, scenes and storyline are not duplicated, the Lucas brand is a well-known commodity to both consumers and retailers.

LucasArts released the second installment of it's much-anticipated *Rebel Assault* franchise in November 1995, amid industry expectations of yet another million unit sell-through success, and the title has performed very well at retail. Given the $3 million dollar budget, it had to. At this point in time, *Rebel* is designed to run on PC CD-ROM and MAC CD, with Windows 95 integrating into the mix sometime early in 1996.

Rebel Assault II (suggested retail price $54.95) has already shipped well over 250,000 units, and sell-through sales have reportedly been brisk. With some re-orders already booked, LucasArts says, "Rebel II is on a pace to equal or surpass the original retail success of *Rebel Assault*, when it was released back in the fall of 1993." LucasArts preliminary forecasts for the first *Rebel* had been somewhat modest, but the title opened up with over 200,000 units selling through by Christmas, surprising everybody.

The original *Rebel Assault* continues to be the company's best-selling title to date, with about 1.5 million copies sold through (not counting OEM bundling). Hot on the heels of that franchise, however, are LucasArts' *X-Wing* and *Dark Forces* titles, each with about 1 million units in retail sales and budgets to match.

And despite the glut of multimedia titles on the market, LucasArts titles have managed to stay on store shelves for as long as a year and a half with the strength of the Lucas name behind them, enabling the properties to perform more like annuities rather than two-month wonders.

Part of the reason for shelf life longevity is the company, at the ripe old age of 14, literally grew up with the multimedia business and has cultivated a number of direct accounts with the retail sector. Another reason is retailers are comfortable with the quality of LucasArts products and are willing to allocate shelf space to those titles on an ongoing basis.

CASE STUDY

LucasArts

LucasArts cranks out about one dozen titles per year and has 220 total employees in development, production and administration. Even so, development time for *Rebel II* was about 1.5 years. And while the average game title nowadays costs anywhere from $2.5 million to $7.5 million to produce, LucasArts was able to grind down costs because of the level of pre-production planning that is built into the process.

Looking at the economics of a typical million unit seller, LucasArts appears to be publishing families of cash cows. While the break-even point on a $3 million title is around 250,000 units (see chart, next page), a number which was unheard of several years ago, once it does break into the 750,000 to 1,000,000 unit range, the ROI can run anywhere from 50% to 60%. That's assuming LucasArts sells directly into the retail channel and by-passes two-step or national distributors.

Assuming *Rebel II* reaches the million unit plateau, it will have generated close to $46 million in gross retail revenue and contributed more than $9 million to the bottom line. That's more than many theatrical motion picture releases nowadays.

One reason the economics for *Rebel II* are so favorable is the basic game engine already existed, even though it was overhauled to improve its compression and playback capabilities. This allowed developers the use of full-screen, full-motion video.

The authoring engine, called INSANE (Interactive Streaming Animation Engine), has also progressed to the point where LucasArts can present a number of intricate set images and integrate them seamlessly with computer-generated designs, adding to both the game and entertainment experience.

In addition, Hal Barwood directed the production, and *Rebel* benefited from his work on *Indiana Jones and the Fate of Atlantis*. He also knows George Lucas well and was tapped because of his long years of film expertise.

REBEL ASSAULT II: ECONOMICS OF A MILLION UNIT TITLE

Sell-Through Units	(000)	250	500	1,000
SRP	($)	54.95	54.95	54.95
Street Price	($)	45.95	45.95	45.95
Gross Retail Revenue	($000)	11,488	22,975	45,950
Wholesale Price#	($)	19.23	19.23	19.23
Wholesale Revenue	($000)	4,808	9,616	19,233
COGS	($000)	769	1,539	3,077
Gross Margin	($Mil.)	4,039	8,078	16,155
Marketing/Sales	($000)	481	962	1,923
Development Costs	($000)	3,000	3,000	3,000
G&A/Tech Support	($000)	385	769	1,539
Contribution	($000)	173	3,347	9,693
Margin		4.3%	41.4%	60.0%

\# = Net of Promotions/rebates and distributor incentives

Source: Paul A. Palumbo

Chapter 4

Development Deal Financial Models

DEVELOPER PAYBACK SCENARIOS—PER TITLE
Straight Upfront Payment Model With Percentage Backend

Units Shipped	(000)	25	50	100
SRP	($)	49.95	49.95	49.95
Street Price	($)	39.95	39.95	39.95
Retail Revenue	($000)	624	1,249	2,498
WholeSale Price	($)	24.94	24.94	24.94
Wholesale Revenue	($000)	624	1,247	2,494
Developer Royalty @20%	($000)	125	249	499
COGS	($)	0	0	0
Marketing/Sales	($)	0	0	0
Development Costs#	($000)	450	450	450
Development Fee	($000)	450	450	450
G&A	($000)	65	65	65
Contribution	($000)	60	184	434
Developer Margin		47.9%	73.9%	87.0%

Source: Paul A. Palumbo

DEVELOPER PAYBACK SCENARIOS-PER TITLE
Affiliate Label Deal Model

Units Shipped	(000)	35	75	125
SRP	($)	49.95	49.95	49.95
Street Price	($)	39.95	39.95	39.95
Wholesale Price	($)	24.95	24.95	24.95
Wholesale Rev.	($000)	873	1,871	3,119
Affiliate Label Markup	($)	10.00	10.00	10.00
Affiliate Label Revenue	($000)	350	750	1,250
Pressing/Packaging	($000)	105	225	375
Coop Funds	($)	0.65	0.65	0.65
Returns Reserve	($000)	53	113	188
Gross Margin	($Mil.)	193	413	688
Marketing/Sales	($000)	0	0	0
Development Costs	($000)	500	500	500
G&A	($000)	65	65	65
Developer Royalty	($000)	123	263	438
Contribution	($000)	-250	110	560
Developer Margin		-129.9%	26.7%	81.5%

Source: Paul A. Palumbo

PUBLISHER PAYBACK SCENARIOS—PER TITLE
Self-Publishing Model

Units Shipped	(000)	50	75	150
SRP	($)	49.95	49.95	49.95
Street Price	($)	39.95	39.95	39.95
Retail Revenue	($000)	774	1,161	2,323
Wholesale Price	($)	24.95	24.95	24.95
Wholesale Revenue	($000)	1,248	1,871	3,743
Marketing/Sales	($000)	116	244	581
Development/R&D Costs	($000)	650	650	650
Returns Reserve	($000)	100	150	300
Developer Royalty	($000)	0	0	0
Packaging/Pressing	($000)	150	225	450
G&A	($000)	70	105	209
Total COGS	($000)	1,086	1,373	2,190
Contribution	($000)	162	498	1,553
Publisher Margin		13.0%	26.6%	41.5%

Source: Paul A. Palumbo

Kip Konwiser, VP of Entertainment
Graphix Zone

Q. What type of budget range do your projects fall into?

A. It depends on the format. A CD+ has a significantly different budget than a CD-ROM. A CD+ is music first and interactivity second, and a CD-ROM is the other way around. Interactivity is a lot more expensive. CD+, if the music comes delivered— if we don't have to produce the music, which has its own cost, can be anywhere from $15,000 to $50,000 or $60,000— certainly no more than that.

Chapter 4

A CD-ROM can be anywhere from $100,000 to $650,000, depending on the size of the artist and the advances and how the deal is structures and all of that sort of thing—depending on how many 3D environments we want to create and how much content we need to fill up those environments.

Q. What is the typical retail price of each of those formats?

A. CD+ prices are all over the place right now because it's such a new bird on the market. Nixon was released at $16 which is the exact same SRP it would have had as a standard CD. Marley will be released at $17.98. We can do that because it is more competitive music material and a buck more is not that much to ask. They can range anywhere from $12.99 to $24.98.

On the CD-ROM, Dylan and Prince came out at $59.95 and still sell lots of units at that price because there are very few artists who can demand $60 from the consumer for a CD-ROM— unless that CD-ROM shreds, and unless that artist shreds in that person's opinion. So if we have competitive artists and competitive titles, then they release at $59.95 or $49.95, somewhere in that range. But generally, they are $29.95 to $39.95. You can say anywhere from $30 to $60, depending on the artist.

Q. What price do you sell into the channel at?

A. You can generally take about 40% to 50% off of that for wholesale prices.

Q. Do you work with third-party developers at all?

A. To date we have done it all ourselves because it's the only way we can really guarantee the look and feel we really need out of the product. But that should be changing. We can't do all of this stuff by ourselves. As it is, we are totally tapped. If we are going to continue to grow and expand our roster and get that many products out onto the market, then we need to start finding some kinds of partnerships that make sense for us. We are making those kinds of partnerships happen right now.

Q. How will you structure those deals?

the product

A. It will vary. It's a publicly-held company, so we can do stock swaps and outright purchases and mergers and strategic alliances. It all depends.

Q & A

Michael Pole, Exec. Producer
Electronic Arts

Q. What are the average budgets for different types of titles?

A. Development budgets can range from $500,000 to well over $8 million dollars.

Q. Can you compare the costs involved in producing a CD title vs. a cart title?

A. It's hard to compare, but let's say that the cost of development for a CD is 8x that of developing a cartridge.

Q. What about developer partners? Can you discuss how you work with some of your partners and the relationships you have with them?

A. The risks are so much greater now because the development costs are so much higher. We base our choice of partners on past experiences with those developers. It's those loyalties that make us go back again and again.

We've gotten burned because the cart companies aren't always the ones who are going to do well in the 32-bit market—it's different because the dynamic of the business has changed. There are now so many new elements needed to create a top selling game. We're looking for new partners each and every day.

Personally, I like to marry really talented art and animation resources

Chapter 4

with really talented programming resources. Interactive development is more like movie producing now—not everyone can do it all, it's not one-stop shopping anymore. So you need to have great art, animation, great music, sound effects and great programming—as well as a terrific design—in order to be successful.

Fact is, if it's not a great game, none of the other elements matter. It is a combination of all these elements that make a great game. To protect our interests, we like to see prototypes. I want to see early stages of development. I don't want to see the developer jumping over the most difficult technological hurdles at stage alpha. I want to see it early on. So that's how we choose our resources. Great planning, design, art, animation, programming and sound are needed to build a great game.

Q. How do you develop project milestones with your developers?

A. A lot of people figure out what they want their release date to be and work backwards. I'd rather work with the knowledge of how long each of the elements and tasks are going to take to build the game. We build a really good design and then require a technical design document. That technical design document and the game design will basically dictate what our milestones are going to be and how long it's really going to take to do a project based on the amount of people working on it. Then I figure out when we are going to ship.

You can promise the company anything you want, but being able to deliver product on time is what you are judged by. No milestones are broken down until we have our technical design document. At that time, we build in preliminary deadlines. We want to get to the prototype stage very early on in the process—spending as little money as possible in the process.

We like to jump over the most important technical hurdles as early as we can. Then basically, it's delivery of levels and game tuning as you move forward.

the product

Q & A

Kelly Conway, VP of Marketing
Multicom Publishing

Q. Within your genre, how many units do you need to sell a particular title to break even?

A. A lot of our time and energy goes into database work, those kinds of things. Depending on the title, break-evens are probably in the 30,000 to 60,000 unit range, based solely on retail sales. OEM is an incremental opportunity. International is incremental as well.

Q. What is the budget range for one of your titles?

A. Well, they probably range in the neighborhood of $400,000 to $750,000 per title.

Q. What analysis models do you use to come up with budgets and break even numbers for a title?

A. It really is based on experience, and it's also driven by content—what are the appropriate multimedia elements for a particular category of products. On one hand, if you look at our home improvement products, they are very illustration intensive because that's the way consumers said they liked to be able to understand how to change light switches, build shelves, etc.—even in a multimedia environment. The *Warren Miller* product has lots of video and music. It has a different feel to it to appeal to that particular consumer.

Q. What is your price range?

A. Generally, retail software is in the $35 to $40 range, and with a complimentary book—we do bundling with books as well, it's about $10 higher.

Chapter 4

Q. What about wholesale into the channel?

A. About $65% of the shelf price.

Q. Do you think that's high or low for the industry as a whole?

A. That is about average.

Q & A

Ken Goldstein, Exec. Producer
Broderbund SOftware

Q. Are budgets developed by formulas? Is there a model that Broderbund can plug numbers into and think about how many units you can sell, or is it intuition?

A. No. Clearly, once we have the concept framed, it becomes the question of a business opportunity. That's the context under which I run the studio. I own the P&L for the studio, so what I have to do is—based on the concept we are looking at, based on the projected budget we are looking at, based on the projected schedule and time to market that we are looking at, based on the first year projected sales and lifetime projected sales at a certain wholesale price,(determine) what the business model for that product is.

I have to set the business model and make a case for whether it does or doesn't make sense. Yes, once we're excited about the creative concept, we do a fairly formal business analysis of it to see if it makes sense.

Q. How do you come up with break-even numbers for different titles? How do we need to sell this many titles to pay for development? How do you judge the budget?

the product

A. I have certain tools that I have developed and that we have developed internally here—certain financial models that we can plug some numbers into and push and pull. I have different returns on investment that I need to deliver and different budget thresholds. So there are different, if you will, proprietary formulas that we apply to it. So I go...can I can get this much marketshare based on this investment, this amount of time in development and this time to market (i.e. we're developing early or late in a platform's cycle, that means a lot).

If we're right at the beginning of developing for Pentium technology, we're going to get to market in the middle of that curve, as opposed to at the end of that curve. There are different expectations that I apply and play with the numbers on the spreadsheet and pretty much know whether something is a good business proposition—if my assumptions are correct. There's virtually nothing that I do here that we don't break even on. I won't do it if I can't break even in a worst case scenario, and there aren't a lot of people who can say that.

If I can't show a reasonable model—where over eighteen months of sales I break even—I will not do it. My assumptions have to show me that the worst case scenario is that I will break even. The interesting thing about the business model that I apply to things is I say that in the worst case scenario I will break even, and in the best case scenario I won't even be able to predict my return on investment. That's the way I like to look at things, and that's the reason Broderbund has been successful. We don't say that you can spend "x" amount of dollars and reasonably expect to make "y" amount of dollars.

Instead, we say we can spend "x" amount of dollars, and we can reasonable assume that in an average case scenario we will make "y" amount of dollars. But the ceiling on that is unlimited. That is why you see hits here like *Carmen Sandiego*, like *Print Shop*, like *Myst*, like *Living Books*. While the business model is entirely conservative—which is how we approach the business, the upside is unlimited, and that's what our stock holders like to see.

Q. What is a general or rough estimate for what Broderbund sees as a

107

Chapter 4

budget for an educational title such as *Carmen Sandiego* or for an entertainment title such as *Myst*?

A. We generally don't quote budget figures because it's not a real comfortable place to be, but let's just say that they've all been creeping into the seven-figure range pretty consistently in the last year.

Q. Is that because of the need to create more content to fill a CD-ROM?

A. The word content is really obscure to me. It doesn't mean anything anymore. People say to me, "Well my budget is 'x' dollars because I have got to go out and acquire 'x' video assets and 'y' music and blah, blah." That stuff is all cheap. That stuff doesn't cost very much when you think about it.

What costs me a lot of money is people's time. The thing that goes into stuff here is people's time. If I'm going to have a team of eight to 10 animators work for me for six months—and they're top notch animators, that's going to cost me a few bucks, especially if they're staff people—fully-loaded and receiving benefits and all of that. But all of the money is going into people's time. The hard costs are a fraction of the product.

Q. But in terms of people's time, doing a *Myst*-type title takes a lot of investment in modeling, rendering and that sort of thing?.

A. That's correct. But when people say "content," it's not about acquiring content.

Q. What about third-party developers at Broderbund— for example, a relationship like Cyan or Living Books?

A. *Living Books* actually is a very unique relationship in that it's a joint venture between Random House and Broderbund. Each of us owns 50% of the company. One of the things that Broderbund still does in that relationship—aside from distribution—we treat them as an affiliate label. We actually developed their software engine for them.

All of their engineering is done on proprietary tools developed here. So it's sort of a unique relationship. From a business model—we bill them back for that, the same way we would bill back anyone else for

the product

doing engineering services. But with Cyan, that is simply a publishing deal where they do all of the work in exchange for a financial circumstance, and we handle the marketing, public relations, distribution, sales, etc. The one thing we are doing with Cyan—that we did on *Myst* and will also be doing on *Myst II*— is the *Windows* engineering. That's another unique service that we have been able to offer people over time. They're very comfortable developing on the Macintosh, and we have a very strong set of Windows development tools. So we are simultaneously developing the Windows version as they are developing the Mac version.

That's one of the things that we're very good at. Rather than forming a lot of hard, fast traditional models—saying we only work this way or only work that way, one of the reasons Broderbund has been so successful over the years is we'll do whatever it takes to do good work. So in that particular instance, what they want to do is develop the creative assets on their side, and they want us to do the Windows programming. That works for us. We can always find a business model for whatever a developer needs.

Q. So would you be open to someone coming to you with concept sketches and a few computer models and graphics—how would you proceed from there?

A. Again, somebody like Cyan is a lot different than somebody just coming in cold. Cyan is on their fifth software product—somebody with a track record who had developed a couple of products, who has had some early success in the industry, who knows what they are doing, who comes to me with a Macromedia prototype and a design specification, and one of my producers gets excited about it.

There is virtually any number of ways that we can proceed. Somebody that's just coming in with an idea? It's not very often that we buy ideas. They have to generally bring something to the table in terms of development capability or history. Otherwise, they're better served working on my staff—in which case, if one of my staff come forward with an idea, that's a much easier way for me to proceed. We don't pay royalties to staff people.

Chapter 4

that profitability. It's just a different kind of relationship. I would hardly call their deal typical.

Q. What about with another developer—a typical one?

A. I wouldn't want to be quoted in print as saying what the parameters for our deals are. There are traditional publishing models—very much based on the book industry. We fund advance against royalties. If we pick up some hard costs, those are our hard costs. The amount of dollars that I advance is inversely related to what royalties you can receive—so at a certain point it declines beyond being reasonable. We want to be able to put a reasonable number of dollars into a product to bring quality work to market, and if the developer does a good job, we want them to make money too.

Q. Can you give me an idea of the percentage of royalties you can expect to make as a third-party developer who brings you a title you fund?

A. Overall, it is extremely difficult to fund development advance against royalties in this market. Generally, people need to come in with some kind of backing, some kind of finance structure. A lot of times, what we see is people who have done very well in other parts of the industry who can carry themselves for a while— the money that I put in all goes on screen.

Generally speaking, if you are developing a title as a start-up business, you need to have some seed capital. The people that I see get into trouble the most in the multimedia world are the people who go out and make a deal for $500,000 advance against royalties and suddenly realize that isn't going to be enough money to make the title.

In this market, that's not enough money to make a quality title that is going to have any kind of life at retail. On the other hand, I'm not comfortable widely spreading seven-figure advances around. I'd rather do a shared risk with somebody. Those are the kind of deals that are most appealing to me because it shows faith on the developer's part and doesn't put all of the risk on me.

CHAPTER 5
marketing and public relations

Stimulating product demand begins when the customer is made aware of the product and picks up speed when a purchase decision is made. It's an expensive process that is made more complicated in the multimedia business because the channel is saturated with product, and shelf space is at a premium.

At the same time, the channel is still relatively immature, and there is a growing list of entertainment giants that can throw a lot of promotional firepower behind their title launches and command shelf space, even if they don't actually "buy" it.

The battle for shelf space is going to intensify as the number of multimedia titles expands, despite the fact that new retail opportunities and sources of distribution will emerge as the industry matures.

A lot of marketing muscle formerly placed in the hands of advertising messages, is becoming more and more a hands-on part of every developer's product creation cycle. The goal of this chapter is to explore and examine marketing and public relations within the interactive community— how it works and the strategy of niche product positioning. Niche products can include "how-to" series, educational and courseware entrants, as well as entertainment sub-segments such as reference titles about the business.

Chapter 5

CONSUMER RESPONSE MODEL

AWARENESS: The comsumer must be aware of the product.

KNOWLEDGE: To make any decision the consumer must of knowledge of the product.

ACCEPTANCE: The consumer must accept the product of what it claims to be.

PREFERENCE: The consumer coms of a prefer of one product over another.

CONVICTION: The consumer is convinced there is a personal need for the product.

PURCHASE: In response to the consumer's personal need, the consumer buys the product.

Marketing and Public Relations

Most entertainment titles are designed with a broad-based consumer audience in mind, which is typical of a "hits" driven Hollywood model. That model often requires titles sell through well over 100,000 unit sales to reach payback. The demographic characteristics of that audience are male, 12-34 years of age. Developers and publishers have to nail that demographic at a minimum, and if the product has broader appeal, then attempt to capture incremental audiences as well.

In the past, the process of awareness building was built on gross advertising and promotional impressions, whether in print, TV, radio or point of purchase (POP) merchandising thrusts in retail environments, such as Blockbuster Video. But as new technolodies bring suppliers and consumers closer together, the industry is looking at developing marketing strategies based on "net" impressions—namely, marketing to audiences that have a specific interest in the products or services a company is promoting. The best examples of that philosophy, today, are specialty magazines, such as various computer magazines or sports magazines (Running, Walking, Bicycling, etc.). On a much broader consumer scale but still part of that more tailored advertising strategy, is the World Wide Web.

Hollywood studios, for example, are throwing up sites to promote awarenes of every movie hitting the theatrical window. Game company developers aggregating content on such sites as Happy Puppy or Splash Studios (www.happypuppy.com and www.splash.com) are courting niche audiences that play games and surf the Web. The union of those two demographic segments is attracting a lot of advertiser interest (i.e. game companies eager to promote retail sales of packaged media, comic book publishers, merchandisers and retailers).

Developing marketing strategies for specific potential customer groups will be essential for interactive titles being developed. A good example of this trend is advertising a skiing title in a magazine or venue which attracts targeted communities of interest around skiing. Advertising dollars are targeted investments driving sales. Matching the correct message with the medium and the target audience creates a powerful advertising investment.

Chapter 5

Creating Customer Relationships

The whole concept of corporate America's merchandising and marketing thrust is based on getting closer to core market–essentially bringing the manufacturer and the consumer together without intermediary interference. That philosophy (product on demand–when, where and how the consumer wants it) is becoming a more closely watched awareness building strategy as the interactive title development industry matures.

And that can take many different flavors. So far, we have been talking extensively about entertainment industry models, which are based on large audiences. This model is focused primarily on producing multiple titles and amortizing the profits of successful ones against those that are less successful. Even though unit sales of a particular product may not achieve success, it is all part of a library building strategy or the ability to establish corporate "brand" in the consumer marketplace. A library building strategy makes sence for an up and coming developer even though one particular title may not perform well in the market place:

- It gives publishers confidence that a developer can deliver a steady stream of product.
- It better establishes "brand" in the marketplace.
- It amortizes development costs against a more properties lowering the cost of development for any particular one property.
- It creates more opportunities to extend the value of that francise into other mediums and ancillary markets.

Another way to leverage and establish "brand" is to cater to a very specialized audience. For example, Stanley Kaplan's course preparation for SAT, LSAT, MBA, GRE examinations are developed for consumers interested in self-study. Kaplan, as a seminar and print company, has developed a strategic consumer relationship with a renewable audience of potential graduate school college applicants.

Another example is Davidson & Associates, an educational publisher that has developed a close relationship with key influencers, such as

Marketing and Public Relations

teacher and parents, and is dedicated to a K-12 type of product.

Bottom-up relationships between title developers and end-users are being enhanced daily by the existence of the World Wide Web. While consumers often flock to retail outlets or peruse catalogs to find a title of preference, that's long after the developer's investment in the title has been made.

An even closer relationship with consumers would yield *data* about preferences that could be profiled into needs or desires, which developers could then utilize when they consider new title concepts. This goes a long way toward ending the "hit or miss" character of the development business. For example, abridged or beta versions of titles could be tested on Web sites, with consumer feedback used to improve performance and gameplay.

Jay Williams, VP of Research and Development for Webcaster Serve.Net (www.serve.net) says, "There is going to be a reversal of the paradigm, to one where producers are listening to their audiences and providing them with entertainment they want to see."

He goes on to say the business will have to acknowledge the fact that "the Web will allow multimedia producers to distribute entertainment product every bit as good as what comes over network TV or the big screen." This will further fuel the competitive move to get closer to audiences that pay the bills.

Defining a Core Audience

What are characteristics of your audience? Are they college graduates? What specific interests do they have? Do they ski? Surf? And if so, what are the cross-promotional opportunities that exist to a publisher in the case? Where do they shop? How much do they earn? What do they read? What brands in other market categories cater to the same segment? What are other co-promotional opportunities in that segment?

For example, consider a "how-to" title focused on deck or patio building. It would most likely have a male audience between 30-50 years of

Chapter 5

Consumer Communication Model

EXPOSURE: Expose the audience to a new behavior.

RECEPTION: The audience receives the behavior.

RESPONSE: A direct reaction to the new behavior.

ATTITUDE: A conversion or aversion to the behavior.

INTENTION: A created need or repulsion for the behavior.

BEHAVIOR: The behavior is modified.

Marketing and Public Relations

age. That buyer would typically own a home with a backyard, shop at Home Depot or Orchard Supply, purchase hand tools, subscribe to various "fix-it yourself" types of publications and make between $50,000 and $100,000 per year.

Audience Information Consumption

What seminars does your target audience participate in? What magazines, books and publications do they read? What type of TV programming do they prefer? Do they subscribe to cable TV? Do they have a computer? What sites on the Web do they visit?

Our deck builder probably has purchased a "fix-it" series of books, and most likely he attends Home Depot seminars on various topics, watches Bob Villa on TV, watches the Home & Garden Channel, and visits various similar Web sites.

Creating Audience Awareness

Advertising, promotion, street buzz, co-marketing thrusts and public relations (PR) are all elements that drive increased consumer awareness of products. The goal of any marketing program is to maximize the budget across a media mix that has the best chance to reach the defined target audience. That investment should lead to product sales and can then be quantified as a return on marketing investment.

The marketing thrust depends on the marketing budget—the higher the budget, the more advertising "buys" available through various media. A more limited budget will depend more upon an ability to create market buzz through PR. The most effective marketing tool, perhaps, is the so-called "word of mouth" advertising because it is a result of users that are hyped about the product or service.

PR is all about creating a "hyped" user. A hyped user is a product's best salesperson. One hyped user can potentially influence a wide circle of friends.

Chapter 5

Q & A

Andrew Maltin, President
Insights Software

Q. What is your philosophy for marketing a title?

A. First of all, it's expensive. How do we go about it? Well, first of all, we participate. We really are choosy in the different marketing programs that come across our desk. There are a lot of programs out there in working with the different retailers—from advertising to in-store merchandising and stuff. Our basic philosophy? I guess for us it really is dependent on the program and where it fits with what we're doing and in what retailer or distribution channel it is in. There are certain distribution channels that just don't work for us.

Q. Which ones?

A. Like entertainment. There are certain retailers that are strictly entertainment or Nintendo-oriented retailers, that our types of market just won't shop at that store.

Q. What are the stores you are thinking about? A Software Etc.?

A. Right. Not that we would not go into Software Etc., but we would limit the marketing dollars that we would spend with a company like that. We are always looking for as much shelf space as we can get—maximum shelf space is what we are all looking for. What I like is to really find the programs that work with our market. Then, that's where we spend our marketing dollars.

Q. What about PR? Can you compare PR and advertising as marketing tools?

A. First of all, PR is really where we are focused. We are very focused with our PR campaign. We took a turn about a year and a half back when

Marketing and Public Relations

we launched our product *Pure Motivation*. We went directly into national advertising without having distribution. I think we learned our lesson there with the print media, and I think we turned at that point and made a decision to really work with PR. We're finding that people read reviews.

People read stories and respond better than direct response advertising. Now, we are definitely willing to support our retail distribution efforts with advertising, with print media. At this time we are only looking into doing trade publication advertising to make the buyers more aware.

Q. What kinds of publications do you take out ads in?

A. Magazines like *Success* and *Home Office Computing*. We worked with *Windows*. We did the airline catalogs and the in-flight magazines—*American Way*. Like I said, our advertising is now more focused and will appear in *Computer Retail Week* and other industry trade publications. *Success*, *Entrepreneur*, *Home Office Computing*, *Inc.*—those are the types of magazines our customers are reading.

Q. How do you work with your PR firm?

A. It is more about positioning than just getting the articles written. The process that we do is we sit down with the PR company and work out our angle—where's our market, what's our position, how do we want to be known in the marketplace. And then we devise a campaign around that position.

Q. How much input do you have in that process? Do you direct them a great deal, or do they bring you plans?

A. It's a very directed approach. I think it needs to be very closely monitored to make sure that the positioning is continuing at the right angle. There's definitely a part that we play in that. I'm not sure if all companies play a similar role, but we play the role because we feel that we have the creative side as well.

Q. Do you think your PR could be better handled in-house or out-of-house?

A. I think it's better handled out. I enjoy out-sourcing as much as pos-

Chapter 5

sible. Everything that we do, we out-source. I think that's kind of the model of the '90s. I think it's better handled outside, and the reason we picked the people we're with is because of the relationships. They have great relationships within their field, their industry. That's really what you're buying.

Q. What about distribution channels? What channels are available, and what types of marketing are necessary to get the product into those channels?

A. All of them. We work with all of the channels—there are so many channels available to plug your product. You see so many opportunities come at you once you get into the distribution. We were kind of a one-product company for a while, and we really learned our lesson with distribution and so forth. We weren't touched. Everybody was afraid to touch a one-product company. No one wanted to work with a company that had money but only one product. That's where we realized that we needed a line of products.

Q. Do you think that might be a given in the industry? You need more than one product before anybody will take you seriously?

A. No question about it. That's the one rule that I would tell anybody getting into the business. You'll see that any of the successful companies in the industry right now are definitely more than one product.

Q. How do you create a buzz on the street about your products within your demographic? Is it the PR?

A. It's actually our other channels. We've become really well known within the personal development channel—via catalogs. We work with the speakers and the authors. We work with the cream of the industry. So in the personal development industry—which I see as a totally separate channel than the software business—we have established ourselves as the leaders of the electronic part of that business.

We have actually been contacted by speakers to put their books on the software, and we do custom products for them that they take and sell in the back of the room. They don't have enough retail pull. We'll actu-

Marketing and Public Relations

ally create a product for them and package it in the SuccessWare product line. But we won't put it onto the retail shelves or even introduce it into the retail channel. They sell it in the back of the room or through their own channels.

Q. So you might consider doing something for Amway?

A. We actually do that. There's an Amway product that we do. We develop the product and put a sticker on the box that says, "Developed exclusively for this market."

Q. Can you give me an idea of what percentage of your business comes from off-the-retail-shelf products?

A. I'm not sure. We've just begun shipping a few months back, so for us, it's a major part of our revenue, of our market. A year down the road, I'd like it to all be electronic distribution—no more retail. That's the future I'm hoping is on it's way. We are really betting on electronic distribution in the future.

Q. Is that your key focus? Is that where you'd like to be?

A. It's not our key focus. Mainly, what we want to do is establish ourselves as the engine for this type of product. We start at the top by acquiring the best books in the business and move from there. The goal is 60 titles before year-end, 1996.

Q. Can you reach that?

A. Yes. We know most of the titles. It's just the issue of retail space. That's why we're hoping electronic distribution will be a big avenue for us. The retail specialists will pick up our top 10 titles—but not our other 45 or 50.

Q. Are you seeing a lot of product sales from the Internet already?

A. Like I said, that's new for us. What we're doing is just giving away free software instead of charging for it. We agree that we are looking at a couple of years before we begin to see any substantial income from it. I'd like it to be 100% of our business at some point, but we need to deal with

Chapter 5

this retail channel until then.

Q. In terms of Internet distribution, how will you market to that audience?

A. We'll use all of the search engines. We'll use all of the marketing everywhere else—we've got another marketing company to do that. We will put the word out in our PR campaign and in our ads. We'll have incentives for the distributor, the end user and the retailer.

Q. You mentioned catalogs. Do you do your own, or are you in with someone else on that?

A. Our catalog is really just a four-color sheet right now, until we grow the number of titles. When we do, we'll put together a little catalog, and we'll out-source that. Right now since there's only 14 titles, we just send out our four-color brochure.

Q. What is your largest retail channel?

A. It's bookstores.

Q. Do you buy shelf space with them? How do you work with them to promote your product?

A. It depends on the retailer. We haven't been in the situation where we've had to buy shelf space or been forced to. We have been asked to participate in many of the different coop programs. Some of them we have accepted, and others we have not. There are many different avenues for participation. For us, an end cap isn't necessarily viable because it's expensive. Our products are a lower margin, and we need to move a whole lot more product. We do ads and catalogs with them.

Q. What is the retail price of your SuccessWare products?

A. $17.95.

Q. And you put them out for $9?

A. Yes.

Public Relations and Market Effects

Public relations represents the cheapest, but most unpredictable, marketing method for developers. Software reviews can be an important part of marketing as well, and good reviews for a product can mean increased shelf space or better shelf location and increased customer awareness. Conversely, bad reviews, whether deserved or not, can be the downfall of a title—especially for lesser-known developers. Competitors often use poor reviews as ammunition for convincing buyers to choose their products over others.

Moreover, a good review can really boost consumer awareness and product sales. Title reviews in magazines, TV, radio, newsletters, etc. introduce and in many ways validate a product in the consumer's mind.

Interviews conducted with development talent also contribute to strong product awareness and street buzz. Hollywood has been very successful at playing these models to the fullest degree. Hollywood loves to book its key theatrical talent on David Letterman, Jay Leno, and Saturday Night Live, as well as doing the morning AM-network program talk show circuit.

Interactive publishers might find a receptive audience on high tech shows such as *Next Step* (shown on The Discovery Channel), *Beyond 2000*, *PC Magazine*, *Interactive Gaming News*, and *Home PC Magazine* and on Web sites. There are also a number of AM radio talk shows discussing technology and computers, which are open to guests whose content takes advantage of that technology and level of computer sophistication.

Public Relations in the Product Channel

National buyers (distributors, product reps, retail buyers and affiliate label reps from major publishers), faced with a looming wall of new software choices, will often make purchasing decisions based solely on reviews, or go with publishers they know. Often bad reviews are given to a good product when the reviewer's preferences do not coincide with the

Chapter 5

product's qualities. This can be particularly true for entertainment software that crosses over the PC/console boundary.

PC games tend to be more complex but less action-oriented than console games. The difference can cause reviewers who typically stick to one of the two platforms to dislike products created for or ported from the other. PC reviewers often say arcade-style games have no depth and console reviewers usually feel that PC games are too complicated. The difficulty is compounded by the fact that reviewers usually only spend a few minutes with the products they are reviewing.

PR relates directly to national buyers as well. However, due to the immaturity of the interactive channel, it is increasingly difficult to pitch for that shelf space because a buyer isn't necessarily the buyer responsible for a particular piece of retail real estate. For example, in the case of a home improvement title, it would probably end up in the interactive title section of a bookstore and not in the home improvement area. This is typical of many of the retail channels nowadays. Even if our home improvement title is written up in *Homes & Gardens*, which national buyers would be aware of, those buyers aren't necessarily charged with acquiring interactive product.

Q & A

Gary Hare, President & CEO
Fathom Pictures

Q. What about PR in terms of sneak peeks and reviews?

A. PR is really important. Probably press releases and all of that kind of stuff work reasonably well to get the word out about a title. It gets you some reviews and that sort of thing. You have to be careful about the

Marketing and Public Relations

reviews. We've been on both sides of this. We've gotten far worse reviews than we deserve and we've gotten far better reviews than we deserve. The difference between the two is technical philosophy of the reviewer as much as anything.

We got a reviewer once that just absolutely hated one of our titles—said it was one of the worst things he had ever seen. Then at the very end of the review, he said that he had to admit that he just really doesn't like photo-real stuff. Some of the other reviewers were far more subjective about it, and they basically gave us sort of "B+" reviews. He gave us a flat-out "F"—said it just didn't work for him.

You also have, because of the growth in the industry and the tremendous number of magazines reviewing titles and the tremendous number of titles being made, the average time that a reviewer spends with a product is probably a few minutes.

If you do anything that is very difficult to get into, then they just don't get into it. They give you bad reviews. If you do *Doom,* and you get to shoot the first guy in eight seconds and the second guy a few seconds later, you go, "Bingo! This is an action game to play." Then if you do something where there is a whole bunch of setup involved and it's really a true interactive thing, you'll find that the reviews will be strongly slanted one way or the other. The reason is that reviewers don't spend that much time with them.

Q. Does an extremely good review for a mediocre title hurt you, too?

A. There are some titles that fall into the "Mercedes Benz" category. If you buy a Mercedes, you don't tell your neighbor that you hate it because you look bad. There are some titles that fall into that category—and then you don't tell people that you didn't care for it very much because everyone else bought it, and it got great reviews. You feel like maybe you are the problem. There are a couple of titles that have gotten extraordinary press and that everybody bought, and I can't find anyone that spent more than 15 minutes with it. There will always be stuff that falls into that category. I don't know if it hurts anybody all that much, to be honest with you.

Chapter 5

I think what hurts you is if you get a really bad review on a title that you release in 1st quarter or 2nd quarter. Then you are in big trouble because it affects the Christmas buyer. What really happens with bad reviews is that your competitor's sales-force Xeroxes them and takes them to the buyers. And the buyers don't have a chance to review everything, so they don't want to pick up something that someone else said was bad. That's the real impact. 3rd quarter and 4th quarter, depending on your publisher, these things get onto the shelves anyway.

Q. Is it harder being a small company trying to get good reviews?

A. There are a lot of people that think there is a correlation between ad space and quality of reviews in some of the magazines. I would not argue with that case with a number of certain magazines. So a company is not buying as much space and may find it difficult to get much attention. We have big publishers, and they get a lot of attention.

Q. Can you talk about promotions?

A. There are a lot of titles that can benefit from sponsorship and/or specialty distribution. Let's say that we can do a really cool truck racing sim using a specific truck. We would go to the manufacturer of that truck and say, "Let's use your truck, and when people come in and do a test drive they get a free sample product." The numbers are large enough for something like that, and it benefits the manufacturer because they need that kind of promotion anyway. It benefits us as well.

We get a lot of stuff we would not normally have access to. The installed base of PC is getting high enough that some of the major consumer product companies are seeing it as a premium item that can help them with what they're trying to do marketing-wise. Let's say we did something that's really great that sells for $40, and you can get it for $5 if you also buy a case of oil. We're pretty active right now in that area. A large enough percentage of the customer base of some of these companies have PCs.

Marketing and Public Relations

Trade Shows

Industry trade shows can be an important part of a product's launch cycle. Many publishers schedule launches and announcements around shows like COMDEX, E3 and CES in order to obtain the maximum bang for their marketing dollars and capitalize on the press coverage associated with those shows. Meetings with the press provide the PR platform to initiate an industry buzz around a new product. These meetings offer an excellent public relations vehicle for upcoming product by putting the press and the publisher in the same room.

Resellers comb conventions to find the latest products (i.e. "hits") to enhance market position. Many resellers make inventory purchasing decisions at these conventions because it's convenient to meet suppliers at one location, and also it gives them the opportunity to comparison shop with hundreds of software vendors attending the same trade show.

The drawback to launching titles and making announcements at major industry events is smaller players tend to get lost in the shuffle. Major developers often gain the most media attention, and they spend a lot of marketing and PR dollars to do just that. The largest benefit of trade shows such as COMDEX and E3 is the gathering of resellers in one location.

David Crane, President of FlagTower Multimedia, Inc. says, "Aggressive press coverage, exciting channel marketing strategies, a focus on quality products, and listening to what your customers, distributors and retailers have to say" are necessary facets of a well thought-out distribution strategy. Crane believes that the classic approach to distribution and marketing includes a sales force, direct to customers (via the Web and catalogs) programs, not to mention working with resellers and partnerships with national distributors.

The problem, says Crane, is as simple and complicated as "getting distributors to notice the product." FlagTower's approach was twofold: 1) The company first took its products to **E3**; and 2) It created a promo-

Chapter 5

tional buzz when it drove a fully-functional tank into exhibition spaces to get people talking about its WWII-based product line. The fact is that the strategy worked, and the company's products have locked up key distribution accounts nationally.

It's a similar strategy used by id Software in an electronic environment, when the company released part of the *Doom* development code over the Web. It allowed users to create their own dungeons and situations. The key message here is getting attention of the target market by creating a word-of-mouth buzz.

Q & A

Kelly Conway, VP of Marketing
Multicom Publishing

Q. Can you compare marketing and PR as tools for making the public aware of and attracted to your products?

A. I think one thing that we're trying to understand and that we're testing is the value of advertising software products in the mass market publication that the multimedia content has been taken from. The specific example is running an ad for *Better Homes & Gardens* product in the magazine of the same name. We feel like it is the time to do that. We are testing it to see which types of ads are most effective. What we are trying to figure out is if it is time to advertise in mass market publications, as opposed to computer-oriented publications. We think it is probably the right thing to do to tell the *Better Homes & Gardens* reader that *Better Homes & Gardens* recipes are now available in software form in the magazine that they are so comfortable with.

Q. What about PR in those same magazines?

Marketing and Public Relations

A. Reviews are very important. Still though, I think we're realistic about what reviews mean in terms of overall marketing mix, and we don't count on reviews alone to drive awareness and acceptance of the product. It takes coop and retail marketing, and it takes some consumer marketing. We put reviews, in terms of the launch of the product and timing of that, about third on the list because we are kind of honest about being able to get finished, reviewable copies to publications happens about the time that product ships to retail.

We do consumer and retail advertising right at the launch of a product and then assume that reviews will start to hit in the second, third or forth month after release. That is kind of the tail-end of the launch plan in terms of timing.

Q. What is your base philosophy for marketing a title?

A. We use trade shows to announce products. We use whatever "sneak-peek" opportunities we can create. Then, at release, we like to have retail promotion and retail advertising in place, as well as some selected consumer advertising. We then follow that up with the next piece of PR which is to get reviews out of the dailys and the syndicated writers for the dailys. Last comes reviews in the monthly's.

Q. What are your best channels for marketing product right now?

A. Still the core software channel.

Q. Then the book channel after that?

A. Yes. But still the majority of business comes from the software and computer superstores.

Q. What arrangements do you have with your distributors and retailers?

A. We have our own direct sales staff that work directly with the retailers, sets up the products with the retailers. Then we sell the products to the retailers through the traditional wholesale distributors. Depending on the product, we'll put a focus on it in terms of coop support or put a special buy-in incentive on the product. Those are two of the variables that we look at in terms of creating some additional interest in the title.

Chapter 5

Promotions

Promotions can be an important means of getting the word out about a new or existing product and often give customers the feeling of maximizing value from their purchase. Promotions can encompass simple purchase rebates or complex bundling agreements with related goods ranging from mouse pads to golf balls, depending on the target audience of the title.

For preexisting content, cross-promotion with other products from that franchise can prove quite successful and thereby attract fans who might otherwise not have bought a related software product. Unfortunately, promotions are generally quite expensive, leaving smaller developers with little opportunity to employ this valuable marketing tool.

Sometimes, less well-known companies can successfully team with other well-known partners for cross-promotion opportunities. Promotions have always been important and will become even more important as distribution routes expand even further beyond the software channel.

Q & A

Brian Farrell, President
T*HQ

Q. How much of your own marketing do you do?

A. Part of the EA deal that makes it so wonderful is that when we launch our *Madden* GameBoy or GameGear— they are launching their 16-and 32-bit titles— we just piggyback. We are not bashful or ashamed about that. That's just part of the deal and part of the great thing about working with EA, that we don't have to spend our own marketing dollars. We pay

Marketing and Public Relations

them a royalty. In our mind that's not part of the deal— it's to be able to piggyback on their project.

But for our own projects like *Mask* and *BassMasters* and some others, we try to figure out who the target market is and then hit that market as cheaply as possible. We will do a fair amount in the game publications because gamers are reading those. A great example of the kinds of things we do is a promotion with Nabisco this last year that included two of our products (*Mask* was one of them).

Nabisco put it on something like 30 million snack cracker and cookie boxes and then put the promotion on TV. We had the equivalent of 10-12 seconds of exposure for our game in their promotion.

It cost us only the $5 rebate on some minuscule amount of games. Some people call it guerrilla marketing, but I think it is an excellent example of effective cross-promotion with another type of company. It didn't cost us a lot, and we got a tremendous amount of impressions. We have a terrific marketing department that has a small budget.

Q. Is advertising, or PR, more important for T*HQ as a marketing tool?

A. We are very heavily weighted towards publicity and PR. Let's get coverage in the form of publicity, and let's do promotions like the Nabisco deal. We did one with Howard Johnson and Sega. We have a lot of things coming up with our Olympic slices coming up this year—the Summer Olympics. *BassMasters*—we did something with them. Promotions and publicity can buy you a lot more impressions than sometimes even the best advertising.

Q. Some PC developers have said reviews are less and less important to them. How do you look at reviews?

A. Video game magazines do help. That brings up what I consider a global issue, and that is game magazines are more geared to the hard-core or more active gamer. And people in this industry seem to forget that what really made this industry re-happen in Nintendo 8-bit was *Mario*—because anyone could play it, and it appealed to everybody. It appealed to a

Chapter 5

gamer, a 5-year-old kid or a 40-year-old adult.

My point is that if you just concentrate on the video game magazines, you can miss a lot of your market. Like when we had *BassMasters*, we hit the game publications, but we also did the bass fishing things, and we did the bass pro shops. There's just other things you have to do, particularly on things like *Pocahontas* for GameBoy. We're not going to put that in game magazines.

Hard-core gamers are not *Pocahontas* people. We are probably going to tag with Disney a lot, but we'll try to get some coverage in women's magazines. It's a gift purchase. It's not a traditional video game buyer, we don't think.

I'd like to add that the importance of publicity for us now is that buyers and retailers don't play the games themselves, so they're dependent on previews and reviews. One problem we're facing is getting product to these reviewers before the title hits the retail shelves. The lead time for PC and CD-ROM games is a month, whereas for carts it's three months. We are having to reassess how we do publicity, how we get previews and reviews out to our editors. Retailers really seem to depend on these reviews more and more. As the games become more complex, they do rely on reviews. We have a game that got terrific reviews across the board, but one reviewer just slammed it. It was more of an arcade-style game, and a more PC type of publication picked it up and just didn't like it. It can really hurt you. You can't get hung up on that.

Q. What is the average wholesale price?

A. Roughly, our cost on GameBoy carts (it depends on the price of the cart we purchase from Nintendo) is somewhere between $10 and $11.50, and we sell it at between $19 and $22, and it ends up retailing at $29 to $35.

Q. So the cost of the cart is a major thing for you guys? What about 3DO and others?

A. Huge. When 3DO first came out, their deal was as follows: You pay for your own cost of goods. The cost of a CD, including jewel case, is

Marketing and Public Relations

around $3. Initially, 3DO wanted a royalty of $3. Then they upped it to another $3 to $4 marketing contribution about sixteen months ago. You can call it whatever you want, but it ends up at around an $8 to $9 cost, even for a 3DO item.

The real killer is 16-bit. Our cost on a 16 megabit 16-bit cart is around $23 to $25 dollars, which is ridiculous. That means we have to sell it at $40 something, and it ends up retailing at $64 to $69. We are hoping that Nintendo and Sega will realize that 16-bit has a life as a mature product at a lower price point and lower their prices on it—but I'm not holding my breath on that.

Q. What about promotions with retailers?

A. That's something that's very difficult and expensive to do. In a perfect world, I would like to do more. And we keep looking at it, but it is very difficult to execute, unless you have a mega-hit property. I've seen it done successfully with *Nintendo's Donkey Kong Country* and EA's *Madden Football*. I would like to do more of that, and if we ever have what we think is a mega-hit, we will try like hell to do it.

Q. Can you ride along on a partner's promotion?

A. Absolutely. We are doing that with Madden. We are on a display with EA's other versions of the product. To do that on even a successful product like our BassMaster—you just can't do it at a cost that makes sense.

Advertising

Advertising messages are all about creating a corporate identification in the mind of potential consumers. It can be very expensive, particularly if a TV campaign is designed. Advertising budgets are running anywhere from 3-5x development budgets in today's market. It requires deep pockets, or publishing partners with ready access to cash, an understanding of the channel and a large product base over which to amortize that investment.

Chapter 5

In developing an advertising program, developers and publishers must always start by identifying the target market and buyer motives. Then, they can proceed to make the five major decisions in developing an advertising program:

- What are the advertising objectives?
- How much can be spent?
- What message should be sent?
- What media should be used?
- How should results be evaluated?

For any company, however, collateral (brochures, product spec sheets) print is a good place to start. Product packaging is one of the best forms of advertising, assuming a developer can get it on store shelves, and it is a good reason for the industry to standardize the size and shape of boxed media assets.

The media planner has to know the capacity of the major types of media to deliver reach, frequency and impact. The major media categories, in order of their advertising volume: 1) Newspapers; 2) Television; 3) Direct mail; 4) Radio; 5) Magazines; and 6) outdoor billboards. Given the media characteristics, the planner must decide how to allocate the budget to the major media types. For example, launching a new interactive title, a publisher may decide to allocate $2 million to Saturday network television, $1 million to game enthusiast magazines and $500,000 to coop advertising with retailers.

If a Web site is thrown up, it makes sense to pull in existing work (key messages, themes, visuals and copy) from other advertising media. Web sites are an attractive advertising medium because they are not a time-based expense. They can archive comprehensive content, and users can control the experience.

On the other hand, Web sites are a lot of work and expense. And if customers aren't out there, they make little sense. That requires developers to be sure their potential customers have modems.

Marketing and Public Relations

CASE STUDY

Advertising and Promotional Mix

The Acclaim Entertainment Model

The proliferation of multimedia PCs in the marketplace may be beginning to change the way software is advertised because a larger, more eclectic crowd of users is begining to purchase titles. For some companies, particularly those with larger audiences, advertising in non-computer magazines and other forms of media is becoming a viable marketing option.

The console game market was perhaps the first to pick up on this possibility a few years ago. They began to advertise computer games during peak child viewing hours. Today, for example, a developer of a how-to series of software titles would likely find a measurable audience for its product in a mainstream magazine such as *Popular Mechanics,* or during a television show such as WGBH's *This Old House*, or even at office supply stores that parents frequent. This trend will grow, as powerful computers become more prevalent in homes across the country.

Developing an advertising budget, however, is part science and part instinct. Acclaim Entertainment is well-known in the business for launching titles across multiple game platforms, including day and date with motion pictures (witness *Batman Forever*), and spending as much as $10 million per title to get the street buzz going.

Acclaim has never been bashful about glittery marketing extravaganzas, and 1996 will be no exception. The company is unleashing a $2 million marketing campaign to support its *D* title, which will be released for the PlayStation, Saturn and PC CD-ROM in March, 1996.

"Your marketing options change a lot when you can release the same game title on more than one format," says Acclaim's VP of Marketing,

Sam Goldberg. Goldberg says the majority of those marketing dollars will target at least five computer gaming magazines and a host of video game and horror genre publications.

Acclaim is planning to polybag more than 750,000 demo versions of the CD-ROM with the computer magazine thrust. The company will also direct about 150,000 demo discs to selected consumers, and thousands more will be made available to video game retailers to sell at a nominal cost.

But that's not all. Acclaim funded a national, in-store sweepstakes, which was promoted via the company's web site (http://www.acclaimnation.com). POP materials will round out the marketing blitz. Acclaim also bought more than 10,000 theatrical size posters, 8,000 banners and 4,000 sweepstakes displays.

Acclaim's marketing thrust is built on building awareness with a key demographic: young adults of college age. Acclaim is also mounting a "grass roots" national radio promotion that will run in 50 to 60 college markets. Television is not part of the advertising mix, according to Goldberg, because it's not the most economical vehicle to deliver a good ad impression.

Product Pricing Decisions

Today's pricing structure for multimedia software seems to fall into three distinct categories: *Premium*, *Standard* and *"BudgetWare."* Premium titles include multimedia extravaganzas like Cyan's *Myst* and Origin Systems' *Wing Commander IV*. Software within this range is typically priced from $45 to $65 per unit at retail. Some "new release" titles within this category, especially those which include a number of CDs, can go as high as $75 per unit.

The BudgetWare category includes packages from bundles of lower-quality titles, combined on one CD for one low price point to a single, smaller, no-frills productivity or game title. The acknowledged leader in this category is SoftKey International. BudgetWare is typically priced from $5 to $25 per unit.

The Standard category houses anything in between—from last year's title, to a title that didn't quite make *Billboard's* top ten list. Products within this category range from $25 to $45 per unit on the retail shelf.

Pricing over the next couple of years, provided there is an expansion of the market, will probably begin to find equilibrium between $20 to $35 per title. One model to consider is the video cassette business. Ten years ago, video sell-through tapes were priced at $99 per tape. Today, that figure is between $14 to $25 per tape. Many categories of tapes (box office duds) can be purchased out of specialty video isle bins for about $4 per tape.

Eventually, there will probably be three levels of pricing: 1) Rental; 2) Sell-through; and 3) Remainder/OEM bundling. Rental outlets will pay a premium to rent the title for multiple "turns." This price will likely resemble current premium sell-through pricing. Sell-through pricing will likely follow the evolution of video cassettes and books, as tonnage shipped escalates. OEM/remaindering will basically be inventory clearance for unsuccessful titles.

Developers can generally expect to sell their products into the channel at 50% to 65% of the suggested retail price. That margin depends considerably on the type of product, the distribution agreement, royalties and overall brand strength.

PRO-FORMA MULTIMEDIA COMPONENT COSTS—PER TITLE

$39.95 Retail Price
$12.00 Retailer Mark-up
$7.00 Distribution Costs
$5.50 Development Costs (talent, etc.)
$3.50 Manufacturing/Packaging
   ° $1.00 Disc/Jewel Case
   ° $1.50 Product Box
   ° $0.75 Manuel
   ° $0.25 Other
$0.50 Package Design
$4.00 Marketing
$6.00 Distribution
$3.50 Technical Support

Source: Compiled from public information

Chapter 5

Q & A

Gary Hare, President & CEO
Fathom Pictures

Q. Can you give me an idea of OEM prices?

A. This year, in the last couple of quarters, we were approached by a company that wanted to distribute 500,000 units of one of our products for free. I asked him why I would do that—what's in it for me? He said, "Exposure." I said, "Well, if you distributed 20 million of them for free, then I'd have the entire market." There are a lot of people now that have said that—"We'll put your title or a piece of your title in a bundle, but we're not going to pay you anything for it."

Then I have seen deals ranging from 50 cents per unit to a high of $4.00. We have done deals in the past as high as $12 per unit and as low as $7.00. This year, I think, will be far less attractive on the OEM side. A couple of dollars is more common. There is a new computer coming out, and they are trying to do 30 titles in their bundle. And if they pay $1 per unit, they have $30 for their costs. A lot of the software is garbage, but the problem is the new computer buyer has 30 new titles to wade through before they have any interest in buying another one. That's one of the reasons why the rate is so bad.

Q. Do you see OEM as a positive force at all in building new customer loyalty or brand-name recognition for your products?

A. Well, it's exposure. We were approached by a company for our new *Nick Price* golf title saying we want to put nine holes on it and the incentive would be that people will go out and buy the other nine. I don't know whether that's true or not. I just think that it's so overwhelming when you buy a new PC and you get a stack of software.

You don't know much about who they are, how many kids they have, how old they are—you just give them a bunch of stuff. At one time, Apple was looking at it and wanted to kill bundling because people were so dissatisfied with the stuff in the bundle that it made them dissatisfied with the technology as a whole. If you went and bought a CD audio player and they gave you 35 CDs, we wouldn't see people buying eight CDs that year—that's a pretty high tie rate. We wouldn't see that anymore if you got all of that stuff for free. I wish bundling would go away.

Q. Do you see it as something you have to do?

A. Depends on the deal. It also depends on your publisher.

Q. What about older titles that you are not selling many of through retail? Would you throw those into a bundle—would they make people more or less likely to buy your current titles?

A. It depends on how good the old title is. Some of them are very, very good. If you have a good older title, it doesn't hurt you in the slightest to bundle it. But most of the bundles now, they want stuff that people haven't heard of. They even want an exclusive or six month windows or that kind of thing.

Packaging

Packaging is an important part of presenting an interactive software product to consumers. Software packaging ranges from shrink-wrapped CDs at almost no cost to the manufacturer, to oddly-shaped die-cut boxes covered with splashy artwork. Costs for packaging can range from a low of around 25 cents for the simplest, no-frills boxes, to $4 and up for fancy or specialty packaging.

Some software retailers, however, have found it difficult to integrate nonstandard shaped boxes into their shelf displays. So, although an uneven package will likely capture the consumer's eye, good shelf placement might be sacrificed to accommodate the convenience of the retailer.

The industry has not come up with a standardized product packaging format. This has limited the opportunity for interactive titles to be re-

Chapter 5

leased through nontraditional channels (i.e. video specialists, book stores, mass merchants, etc.). A standardized interactive package will help to provide more shelf space availability in the future.

"A lot of companies are getting a shrink-wrapped product—not including the box—for under $1," claims Gary Hare, President & CEO of Fathom Pictures. "That's why it's so interesting to the music industry and the movie industry and everyone else. The actual cost for a disc these days, in any volume, is under 60 cents, pressed."

Manuals are also important for ensuring consumer satisfaction with a product after they get it home—especially for complex products. This documentation can be an extremely expensive component of the manufacturing process, ranging from 50 cents for a simple booklet to as much as $2 or $3 for more expensive literature. To alleviate some of that expense, many developers are putting much of the documentation on disk, either as Windows help files or in another format, like Adobe's *PDF* document format.

"Most people are putting the manuals on disc now," adds Gary Hare. "That's true, the manual can be expensive. The box can be anywhere. You see die-cut boxes and weird shapes. The box can cost anywhere from 25 cents to $3 to $4 dollars, depending on how razzle-dazzle you want to get. "

Direct Mail or Simply Direct?

Keeping current and past customers informed of product updates and new titles is the major use of direct mail. The medium is quite expensive on an ROI basis, and usually only larger developers can afford to actually mail product literature outside of their own customer base as a marketing tool. Direct mail items can range in size and cost from a simple postcard flyer to full-color product catalogs.

Direct mail campaigns have been relatively successful in general, however, and for MAC-based titles in particular. According to Apple Computer, as many as 50% of MAC owners buy software and hardware

Marketing and Public Relations

through the mail. Similar to video and audio, mail order is a popular way for multimedia PC owners to order packaged media. The trick is to have access to (and be able to afford) a huge mailing list with qualified end users that match the addresses.

Developers can purchase mailing lists from CD-ROM manufacturers who collect names from registration cards, as well as registrants for high-end video cards, peripherals and other computer hardware.

Selling directly via various media, however, is not limited to mail—or print, for that matter. There are book fairs at schools, the online services and the WWW, not to mention the product update circulars that follow existing users of products.

Q & A

Mason Woodbury, VP of Marketing
Broderbund Software

Q. When you advertise, what channels do you use—direct mailing to current customers and that sort of thing?

A. Most of the direct mailing is for upgrades only. We don't really do a direct mailing for a general announcement. The little bit of advertising we do has been a wide variety—a lot in the home computer magazines. But we've also done a lot in the parenting magazines. We're on American Airlines right now with *Print Shop* on the in-flight movie trailer. We sort of dabble around. The gaming products are advertised in the gaming magazines.

Q. Do you get more exposure from taking out ads or from the PR side of things?

Chapter 5

A. We take out ads, but there is far more exposure from the PR side of things. If you add it all up, it's probably a factor of 100 to 1.

Q. What about schools? How do you market to schools?

A. We have a whole division that's devoted to the school market. We have what we call "certified partners in education"—about 100 dealers that we sort of certify as significant players, and they have to go through an authorization process. We have school editions where the content is done with a teacher guide and material to help the teacher use it as part of the course. It's really a different packaged product, and we have site licenses and network versions. If your school district has five schools with 2,000 computers, you can come in and get a district site license for *KidPix*.

Q. In terms of marketing to schools, how do you get it out to the teachers that, "Hey, there's this product ...?"

A. They go to a lot of specialty trade shows. That's the purpose of these dealers—they all have special relationships with the school districts. We're really depending on these dealers to be sort of the beat on the street.

Q. Does it work anything at all like the textbook industry?

A. No. These are true dealers. They either buy the product from us outright, or, in the case of when they sell a site license, we pay them a commission. But they're not reps, as such. The net result is probably about the same, but these are literally 100 different businesses, and they range from fairly large businesses, like Educational Resources, down to a couple of people working out of their basement.

Q. And they all have a stake in actually selling the product because they get a commission or something else?

A. Inventory.

Q. What about electronic marketing—through the World Wide Web or AOL? Do you do very much of that?

A. Yes. We're on AOL, CompuServe. We have a Web site. We're on Microsoft Network.

Marketing and Public Relations

Q. Can you buy product through the Web site?

A. Not on the Web site yet, but you can on AOL and CompuServe.

Q. On MSN?

A. No. Not yet.

Q. What about catalogs? Do you produce your own catalogs, or do you go in with others?

A. Both. We have our own little catalog, but it's really been little more than a customer service tool. If somebody calls up and says, "Send me a catalog," we can't very well say we don't have one. But it's not anything we actively mail.

Q. Do you get one in a box if you buy a Broderbund product?

A. We don't even put it in the box. It's really just to have for when a customer calls up and says send me a catalog. We are looking into an electronic version of the catalog that we can put on the disk. Like I said, it hasn't been viewed as an active marketing tool—more of a customer service tool.

Q. What about selling-cycles—for both the K-12 market and the consumer market? Can you talk about that a little bit?

A. The school market is obviously pretty dead for the summer and in November and December. There is a huge blip when you get around April and May because, in a lot of cases, they've had funding allocated to them, and if they don't spend, it goes away. So what happens is when you get to April and May, all of a sudden these school districts go, "Oh my God. I've got $5,000 left in my technology budget, and if I don't spend it by June 1st, it goes back to the district." We get a huge number of customers saying, "You've got to ship it by the end of the week. If it's not here by then, I can't pay for it."

There are other periods when you would expect the school market to be slow because they aren't there. It's pretty even. You get a blip in the fall when they come back, but the big rush is that April/May time frame.

Chapter 5

The consumer market is basically that December and January are the peaks, but even the slow months, when we've done the overlays, it's not a huge difference. It's not as if we do 50% of our business in December. It spikes up, but it's not to the point where you look at it and say, "Wow! The business is driven by Christmas."

Q. Does 40% of your revenues come from educational titles, including *Carmen Sandiego*?

A. That sounds a little high. It's probably closer to 30%.

Q. What percentage of that comes out of the school market?

A. We've never figured that out. I can tell you that the school market is probably around 13% of our total volume. But we've never figured that number out. Let me qualify that. When we say that's our school business, those are products that we know have been sold into the schools. But there's nothing that prevents a teacher from walking into Egghead and buying *Carmen* and using it in the classroom. We don't know what percentage of the products ultimately end up in schools. All we know is the percent that we sell into the schools. It's probably higher. I sense that in a lot of these schools, the teachers either pay for it out of their own pocket, or it's petty cash or car wash fund—it's not going through the purchase order process.

Q. How do you work with retailers to distribute? Do you buy shelf space? How does the arrangement work?

A. It's kind of complicated. They are all a little different. I don't know that we buy shelf space in the sense that you would associate with a grocery store or something like that. We buy "end caps" for key promotions, but we don't pay a shelf stocking fee on a regular basis. For the most part, we depend on the strength of our product line to drive those relationships.

Q. How are your relationships with the various retailers developed, and how do you pursue additional ones?

A. Again, it varies. There are some retailers like an Egghead or a Soft-

Marketing and Public Relations

ware Etc. where the relationship literally goes back to the beginning of time. It's just one of those things that's always been there. Though both companies have changed and modified their plans a little bit, there's always that base line of a relationship. Then you have someone else like a WalMart that sort of shows up on the scene in the last two years and says, "I want to carry software." We've probably spent two years just understanding who they are, how they do business and how you work with them.

Q. Do retailers come to you now, more than you go to them?

A. I want to be careful not to sound arrogant. What happens generally is when a new channel decides they want to carry software, they come to us. Because someone in their business says, "Hey! This software industry looks hot. Maybe we should put software in our music stores," they go to someone that knows something about the industry and say, "Who should we talk to?" And they go on up the list and say, "Broderbund is in the top three consumer software developers, and you can't really have any credibility unless you carry their products."

In that kind of case, we'll get a call from someone who says, "Let's have a meeting and talk about how you do business." In other cases, we might identify a channel or a partner that we want to see how they do business, and we might contact them. Mostly they call us.

Q. What do you see as the largest untapped channels for software distribution?

A. Right now most people buy software from retailers who carry a large selection. As computers get to be more of a mass market item, what you're going to have is a store might carry two or three software titles relating to whatever their specialty is. You might have a stationary store carrying a *Print Shop,* or Gymboree carrying *Living Books* products. You might have a Nature Company type chain carrying *Carmen.* Historically, that hasn't been the case. They have wanted to carry a big selection of software. I think as the titles get more niche-oriented, you are going to see the channels—you'll walk into a hardware store and see the 3D Home Architect on a shelf next to the cash register.

Chapter 5

Q. Do you expect to see reference titles being sold alongside books in a Waldenbooks?

A. I think the book store will probably carry a wider selection because it's more entertainment. A video or record store market is probably the largest untapped new distribution outlet.'

Customer Support

Customer support is becoming increasingly important for developers as computers begin to fall more widely into the hands of less techno-savvy consumers. Just a few years ago, real customer support services were the stuff of legend and confined to business-only consumers. Now, most established software publishers maintain well staffed and knowledgeable customer relations departments. Even smaller publishers are allocating resources to provide reliable customer service through out-sourcing to specialty service companies—a trend which could lead to better service and lower overhead.

Even a "bug-free" product needs good support because of the wide range of target hardware and software configurations present in the marketplace. There is no guarantee that even the most robust software will function on every PC, and prompt and accurate support is one sure way of building customer loyalty. This is obviously less important for the console market, where customer support often comes down to offering a "900" line for hints and tips.

Michael Pole, Exec. Producer
Broderbund Software

Q. At what point in the development process does marketing really start getting involved?

A. Usually, we are involved at the pre-alpha stage. Actually, when you acquire a piece of really high-profile content, marketing would really start talking to people after the signing of that content. This was a big thing for EA when we acquired Gen13 because we have never been really successful in the action category. Nailing this one was a big win for us because other publishers really wanted it.

Q. How do you approach marketing a title—in stages?

A. Marketing has their own ideas, but I really like to get a taste from the market at the earliest possible stage. When there is other categories of product based on the concept you are building interactively, it makes it easier. We like to start some pre-hype with initial builds getting out to the trades. Then we like to start creating some really cool press events that will expose the characters in their other forms at trade shows, etc.

Q. What about the "coming soon" box?

A. It really ticks me off as a consumer. If the box is going to be out there for a week or two weeks, I'm not uncomfortable with it. If the empty box is going to be there for a month, it really pisses me off because I'm always picking it up to see if it's there yet. I think the displays are going to change drastically over the next year, and I don t think there's going to be as much of that. Hype is one thing, but too much hype is aggravating.

Q. Do you see PR as less or more important as marketing?

A. It's every bit as important. It is a collaborative effort—everybody has to do their part. You can have a great game that doesn't get the marketing and sales support. It doesn't get the PR. It will go away because the market is so flooded. It is when everything clicks—you've got a great game, great marketing and great PR—that's when magic happens.

That's what happened with *Myst*. It's a very user-friendly game with the right PR, marketing and hype. It was the first real CD ROM that was user-friendly. That's what's called catching lightening in a bottle.

Q. What distribution channels are your best channels—next to retail?

A. Online is going to be a much more significant part of our business

Chapter 5

very soon. We are taking great strides in that area. The retail channel is our best channel because we do it so well. We don't ship to distribution companies. We ship direct to the stores. We have intricate selling devices that let us know when they are out of inventory, and we can ship automatically, based on that information.

We have these systems that we've spent millions on that allow us to make sure that when software is not on the shelf, we can address it immediately, so there's never any long-term emptiness on the shelf.

Q. What about OEM?

A. It is great for some titles and not for others. It should substantiate or help retail sales.

Q. Can you talk a little more about electronic distribution?

A. I think there is going to be a huge opportunity to buy things over the net. We'll be doing demos and releases over the net, so that people can demo the product and buy it automatically. I think it is going to be increasingly important for us to really establish ourselves on our web pages and make buying software over the net easy.

CHAPTER 6
distribution

Product distribution is all about developing channels of product sales through publishers, distributors, two-step distributors, OEM bundling and numerous other retail channels. Publishers and/or developers have to first and foremost determine:

- Which distribution strategy makes sense (self-distribution, affiliate label, OEM bundling, direct-to-consumer, catalog, online, free downloads, etc.) for their particular business model
- Which retail channels end users frequent to buy those types of products associated with a particular category or genre
- Which company resources are required and available to get product SKUs into those channels
- A strategy for keeping product on store shelves and a plan of action in case of returns

Distribution deals are being struck in the marketplace everyday, and there is often a great degree of latitude in the structure of those deals. The question to be answered, however, is: How much (or little) will be left for future development, manufacturing and marketing after slicing out a distributor's or affiliate label's share?

The alternative is to determine if sufficient in-house resources can

Chapter 6

be allocated to mount a direct sales force campaign, without endangering development and creative asset building. It's at this stage many developers are at the greatest risk of failure because they often do not want to "turn loose" the project in any way. They can become intent on going it alone, which is dangerous and expensive.

Few developers and publishers, however, have the in-house resources to completely go it alone. In fact, one of the easiest and fastest ways to fail in the multimedia business today is to NOT take on any strategic partners or form beneficial alliances that maximize established relationships.

The multimedia business has matured to the point where venture capitalists are less interested in funding developer start-ups that attempt to go it alone for one very key reason: Interactive publishing is now—and will continue to be—an *entertainment business* and therefore, takes on the business models of that industry. The competition is big, well financed and very well-known in the marketplace. If newcomers don't have access to retail shelf space through partners and alliances, they will have to buy it.

That requires any developer to spend a lot of capital to create product categories that resonate with end users—and even more to crack distribution channels dominated by major players, like Disney and Microsoft, that can afford to buy up shelf space.

In the Hollywood model, producers develop a project to the point of production and then sell the project to one of the studios to raise sufficient financing to produce the film. In the last year, the relationship between interactive developers and publishers has evolved into a similar model.

Even so, both generic (national distributors) and proprietary distribution channels used for multimedia titles reflect the fact that the business model is still immature. Channels are developing quickly, however, as entertainment giants enter the market. It's anticipated that more store shelves will open up to publishers, but the flip side of that maturation process is the cost of informing those channels and getting the product message out above the multimedia promotional clutter.

Maturation of the interactive business is raising marketing and distribution expenses for everybody. More assets are now required to inform potential distributors and buyers about product. Increasing layers of product clutter and the powerful merchandising machines of established media combines, from Hollywood studios to arcade specialists like WMS Industries and Konami, are making retail real estate scarce.

The current distribution model borrows liberally from software, audio, video and book publishing businesses. In fact, many of the key distributors that handled packaged media prior to CD-ROM discs, now also carry a large library of those title, too. Joanna Tamer, a highly regarded multimedia distribution consultant, describes the multimedia distribution contract as a "software model, built on a record industry contract, with a bunch of book publishing terms and conditions."

Tamer believes, however, the business is consolidating around the Hollywood model. "Like independent filmmakers, small multimedia publishers will always have a hard time securing distribution," she says. But the good news is that with large studios and publishers still focused on developing in-house talent, small publishers have an excellent shot at signing affiliate label deals or co-development (work-for-hire) pacts that will guarantee at least a minimum level of distribution.

It can be a tricky balancing act for a new multimedia publisher. Borrowing elements from the contracts of each industry yields confusion, additional consulting expenses and slimmer margins. While a video distribution deal is standard, consisting of four or five points and can be done via fax, multimedia distribution contracts are lengthy documents of 20 pages or more.

Compared to the film and video businesses that have had years to develop and mature around production and distribution relationships, the multimedia market remains highly fragmented by suppliers, categories and retail outlets.

But interactive content developers can learn a thing or two from the

Chapter 6

Hollywood model, which is built on the value chain concept (see graphic). That model implies that the more a franchise is maximized through various exploitation windows, the better chance a property has to reach payback and generate positive cash flow.

The good news for developers is there are now more windows through which to exploit a franchise, including online and web applications, as well as character licensing via the toy and apparel segments, for example.

Educating the Channel

The battle doesn't begin and end with consumers. Interactive title publishers have to educate, inform and persuade the retail channel to take a chance on new products where those products are sold, namely, retail counters. That requires a point-of-sale marketing program, some sort of retailer (not to mention distributor) incentive and a well-staffed in-house sales force. Those are all excellent reasons why developers should seriously consider a distribution deal with an established publisher that already has a concentrated point-of-sale marketing program; it's an expensive and time-intensive channel evolution that will soak up scare development funds.

Tracking is another element in distribution. That can be as simple as making sure once products are shipped, they do, in fact, end up on retail shelves. Publishers' marketing programs need to make titles a familiar and comfortable name with retailers as well as the general public. Salespeople at retail outlets should be taught and informed about the company's products and told how best to pitch them to customers.

Book Channels

Multimedia titles are distributed principally along the software model at the present time, but publishers and developers are looking for ways to expand the book channel. Distributors are playing a role as well. Book publishers are being encouraged by distributors to take a different ap-

Distribution

proach to marketing and merchandising their multimedia titles than they do for their books. The distribution of software is much more diffuse than book distribution. Unlike book publishers, software publishers cannot depend on a single distribution channel to sell their products through to end users.

For book retailers wary of stocking interactive titles, support among the distributor ranks is taking shape. While there is a lot of confusion in the book sector about CD-ROM product, the role of a distributor in today's market is to design opening inventories at various levels of buy-in that enable retailers to simply "get started." The strategy is to not load the channel up with product that is never sold through, but to match the requirements of the store with its customer base. Rental or demo stations may play a more central role in the business as well.

Many industry experts believe the multimedia title publishing distribution model will parallel prior forms of packaged media, and book publishers should study the distribution models in the software, record and video industries.

Consumers will increasingly spend their media dollars through one of several "gateways," whether made of brick and mortar, shipped in catalogs by "snail mail," parked on servers and delivered as digitized bits over a network, or inspired by direct sales pitches.

Book publishers need to build on their experience in marketing and merchandising products in an environment where books are not the only type of medium. Bookstores, in turn, will have to learn not only how to sell books better but also, inevitably, how to sell electronic media.

Packaging seems to be an overall concern for the peripheral retail channels which include book, music and video. If the publisher is interested in these channels, the publisher must accomodate these channels self space concerns. Most interactive product is not package "friendly" in these retail environments.

There are a number of self-help/education titles which would do well in the book channel, however the current display space devoted to

Chapter 6

the book retailer's primary product, books, does not accomodate current interactive product packaging. Bundling interactive product with a book or packaging the title to look like a book might make the book retailer more amenable to stock these titles.

CASE STUDY

Baker & Taylor

Success at retail typically involves the channel support of a distributor as well. Baker & Taylor's (B&T) Director of Market Development Mike Albanese says while there is a lot of confusion in the retail about CD-ROM product, the role of a distributor in today's market is to design opening inventories at various levels of buy-in to simply "get the retailer started." He notes the "issue is not loading the channel up with product that is never sold through, but matching the requirements of the store with its customer base." Rental is also expected to play an ever-increasing role in the business.

In 1993, for example, B&T expanded its efforts to distribute multimedia titles into bookstores, record stores, video stores and mass market channels, including grocery stores. Albanese believes entertainment software has the best chance in the short-term to find distribution through the video channel, while educational and reference titles are a natural fit to flow into the book channel. Baker & Taylor Software carries one of the largest selections of CD-ROM/New Media titles available on the market, with over 1,000 CD listings in its catalogs.

In 1994, B&T announced that B&T Books joined with B&T Software to develop a joint CD-ROM/New Media merchandising program for bookstores, and it instituted a revised return procedure to better manage slow moving inventory that had been clogging the channel. Baker &

Taylor is offering book retailers a choice of three types of merchandising units that come pre-stocked with CD-ROM and new media titles. The merchandising units include a 12-title end cap, a 25-title spinner rack and a 30-title wall unit.

The displays have different software categories, such as literature, reference, children's education, games and best sellers, that can be customized by the retailer. The program attempts to eliminate some of the merchandising guesswork that plagued book retailers in the early 1980s, when they tried unsuccessfully to stock and sell computer software applications. Participating CD-ROM and new media software publishers include Compton's New Media (now a unit of Softkey International), Knowledge Adventure, Sony, Time Warner Interactive and Virgin.

Baker & Taylor reps maintain that the biggest net positive going forward is that "the channel is starting to get its arms around the returns issue." Everybody throughout all levels of distribution is looking at returns with an eye to putting the right level of inventory into the channel, says Albanese.

The emphasis is not on "returns" per-say but on distributors buying the right amount of inventory from suppliers and moving that product into the channel. Baker & Taylor Software representatives provide retailers with ongoing support, expertise and information about the new media products most in demand, including electronic versions of bestsellers, mystery/games, reference and children's titles. The company's program is designed to put opening inventories into the hands of consumers at various levels of buy-in. As part of the program, B&T Software is producing a catalog devoted to CD-ROM/multimedia products.

Distributor Categories and Distribution Channels

Multimedia titles are currently distributed via the classic software channel (Babbages, Software Etc. and other specialty computer software stores), OEM bundling arrangements, catalog mailings, direct consumer sales/mailings, national distributors, two-step distributors, online merchandising or Web marketing. They are also cross-merchandised with books and other pulp-based material. The strength of the computer software channel cannot be overstated.

Computer and software-only stores are the two most popular venues for multimedia title sales to date. Retail chains such as Babbages and Software Etc. (which merged in 1994 in a marketshare grab), Electronics Boutique and Egghead Software are among the leaders in multimedia title sales and generate some of the highest revenue per square foot figures ($540 per sq. ft.) in all of retail packaged media.

By comparison, Hollywood studio stores (Disney, Warner Bros., etc.) generate about $400 in revenue per sq. ft., video stores close to $150 per sq. ft. and music-only stores about $278 per sq. ft. This means product moves off of these stores shelves quickly, or nervous retailers remove and return it themselves.

At present, it is estimated 80% of all CD-ROM software sales take place in computer specialist and software-only retail environments. Research also shows the majority of CD-ROM sales are made to so-called "information households" that have had a computer or other game gear for five or more years. Thus, this would appear to be a mature audience, in a relative sense, because the user who is buying product has been doing so for years. For a publisher to reach these typical product users, deals must be struck which guarantee a certain level of retail presence in the software channel.

These software specialists and other retail chains in the computer distribution channel are supplied by a handful of national computer hardware and software distributors and by distribution subsidiaries of some of the larger entertainment software publishers through direct and affiliated label programs. This means developers can take a "rifle shot" approach to getting a distribution deal done. This strategy is to target a national distributor or a publisher with a national sales force.

A new type of storefront that we haven't yet seen could emerge over the next few years, that would more closely resemble a video superstore that also stocks games, books and music but would be positioned as an information superstore.

Distribution

This type of store would fall into the class of video super store today. It would have well over 10,000 sq. ft. of floor space and around 12,000 titles, but it would specialize exclusively in all forms of digital content.

Distributors and distribution consultants often must advise publishers that they, and not the distributor, are responsible for marketing (i.e. creating "pull" demand) for their titles.

The distributor's responsibility is to broaden channel distribution by building retailer awareness. To accomplish this, distributors will create reseller education and training programs, promotions and buying incentives backed by Market Development Fund (MDF) capital. It is the publisher's role to create market (end user) demand for the products. This is what is referred to as push and pull marketing. Distributors "push" product into the channels. The Publishers' responsibility is to "pull" end users into stores.

Publisher as Distributor

Interactive publishers are a tried and true distribution outlet for start-up and single title developers. Companies like Acclaim Entertainment, Electronic Arts, Broderbund and Mindscape have the revenue base to support national sales organizations. Additionally, some of these companies (i.e. EA and Broderbund) grew up with the interactive publishing business and have long-established relationships with key retailers like Babbages and Software Etc.

For a new developer, it makes sense to use an established publisher because of the costs associated with self-publishing. The large capital expenditures in duplication and building channel awareness are simply out of the reach of a young company. National distributors will not pick up products one at a time but prefer a line of products, and many new companies are not geared up for that level of production. That is not a complete solution, however, because most executives think it's a good idea to keep some distribution capability in-house beyond any partnerships and alliances with classic channels.

Chapter 6

The Market Development Fund (MDF) Question

Informing, measuring and developing successful marketing programs aimed at distribution, retail and end users are issues that all multimedia publishers, large and small, deal with on a daily basis. Max Wurz, of new media consulating firm Levy & Wurz, says, "As the business matures, publishers have to get smarter in every aspect of the business and measure and justify marketing investment."

According to publishers and analysts, multimedia companies are averaging about 25% of total sales on marketing and promotion nowadays, with a small (but significant—about 2% to 5% of wholesale price) portion of that going into so-called Market Development Funds (MDF). Many publishers maintain that MDF moneys are hard to track and account for and wind up benefiting only the retail segment.

Some developers go so far as to call it highway robbery. Publishers and developers are quick to complain that often MDF (also known as coop advertising) is not an option in many cases and often subtracted from product invoices as a matter of course. Their big fear is that MDF is just a black hole which, if it benefits anybody, it's only the retailer.

A sensible way to integrate MDF into overall promotional investment is to look for ways in which retailer goals dovetail with yours. In addition, it's absolutely imperative to insist on compliance with the MDF program. This involves clearly specifying the deliverables associated with the MDF commitment, with a form for "proof of performance." Publishers need to develop a relationship with retailers and conduct these types of negotiations in a clear fashion. If this is done, retailers will respect it. If those negotiations don't occur, then it is the "default" relationship that the retailer will come to expect.

For example, Ed Sturr, President of Fry's Electronics Superstores (a retailer catering directly to the high tech professional) says Fry's does, in fact, require MDF, end caps, or some other POP material guarantees before product will be displayed in the store.

Sturr says "There is absolutely no way around it." Beyond that, the company requires about $12,000 per month in MDF support, which goes toward new product awareness in Fry's ongoing product assortment advertising.

Two-Step Distribution

Two-step distributors are actually marketing firms that "rep" a company's products to other distributors. For example, Hawthorne Marketing "reps" Activision, Sony and Psygnosis multimedia product to national distributors like Baker & Taylor. Those types of deals are typically struck for about 3% to 5% of the wholesale dollar. While it adds another line in the product enrichment chain, it does save publishers from positioning expensive sales personnel in every key area.

Publishers rely on a two-step distributor to get their products to retail but can also strike deals directly with a national (i.e. "stocking") distributor. Hardware manufacturer (bundling arrangements) also offer guaranteed shipments and sales.

Distributors place orders directly with the marketing rep firms (like Performance Marketing, HiTech and Hawthorne Marketing) and not with the publisher. Two-step distribution has proven to be very popular with established publishers because paying commissions are often cheaper and faster than maintaining or creating a full-blown sales force.

National Full-Service Distribution

National distributors have large transport, tracking, warehousing, field rep and channel promotional resources. National packaged media distributors have broad relationships with suppliers and retailers, and they handle stocking, billing, shipping, warehousing and customer service. They also are responsible for product returns, and typically require a portion of wholesale revenue be set aside to cover those costs. There are four major, national software and computer products distributors that a lot of multimedia product is channeled through, and those include: Baker & Taylor Software, Ingram Micro, Handleman Company and Merisel. These national distributors generally pay publishers 40% to 50% of sug-

Chapter 6

gested retail and sell it to retailers at 45% to 55% of suggested retail.

Distributors operate on razor thin margins and typically earn 5% to 10% of the retail dollar, but in 1996 that figure is skewing toward the higher end because of returns and the fact that multimedia titles simply don't sell into the channel at the tonnage rate (and generate the commensurate revenue) that audio tapes, videos and books currently do.

Publishers and consultants agree there is no ironclad distribution deal given the volatile nature of the business. But services typically offered by and contracted for national distributors include: warehousing, banking, carrying risk of collection, insurance, shipping, handling returns and administration. Distribution of multimedia titles also requires an effort to educate the retail channel (i.e. market development funds—MDF), to assist in inventory management analysis and to ensure payments to suppliers.

In addition, publishers must give 100% return privileges to the distributor because the distributor gives it to the retailer. Retailers send product back that sits on store shelves anywhere from 60-150 days. The average return rate for multimedia titles is 12% to 15% but can run as high as 30% or more.

Affiliate Label Distribution

Affiliate label distribution is a deal struck between a small developer and a full-service publisher to introduce product into the packaged media channel. The difference between this agreement and a publishing deal is the title developer pays for duplication, marketing and tech support of the title.

Affiliate label programs are an attractive, but double-edged sword for small publishers who don't have the resources and marketing muscle to sell products directly into the channel. Affiliate label relationships are a long-standing fixture in the entertainment software publishing business, but those deals add another link in the product enrichment chain, and therefore, can siphon off a significant portion of profits (up to 30%

of the wholesale sell-in price). Nevertheless, many multimedia titles are distributed through affiliate label programs, and both sides report the relationship can be profitable.

The main affiliate label publishers are Electronic Arts, Acclaim Entertainment, Broderbund Software, Softkey International, Davidson & Associates and Activision, among others. The Hollywood studios are now significant players in the business as well, and they have aggressively signed affiliate label distribution deals over the past several years as a means to supplement in-house development talent, while keeping fixed costs (overhead) low.

Affiliate label publishing programs are set up to sell to the national distributors or directly into the retail channel, in the case of EA and Broderbund. Publishers that started affiliate label distribution programs back in the 1980s, such as Broderbund and Electronic Arts, have long-established relationships with retailers, offering a natural distribution advantage.

Direct relationships cut out the middleman distributor and add a few more precious profit points to the affiliate publisher's bottom line because it implies a corresponding increase in wholesale revenue flowing back to the publisher. Affiliate label publishers pay their affiliates 45% to 55% of retail and sell to national distributors at 48% to 57% of retail or to resellers at 50% to 52% of the retail price.

OEM Bundling

OEM distribution is selling product *en masse* to a packager who bundles the title with other titles, a book, hardware, etc. The title is usually sold into the channel at severely discounted rates, but it is a proven way to establish brand equity in the marketplace for an unknown developer. It's also a good way to unload slow-moving product and to sell bestselling aged product (i.e. *Tetris*).

Bundling agreements are likely to remain part of the marketing and distribution mix. Hardware manufacturers are getting very selective about what product they align with because they have been burned in the past by titles that either didn't play, or lacked any real technical support. In addition, Publishers are beginning to see the emergence of new aftermarket windows that may eventually benefit the bottom line far more than bundling, such as the Web and via arrangements with online content aggregators like AOL.

Additionally, OEM bundling has lost some of its luster in the developer community. Ken Goldstein, Executive Publisher for Broderbund Software, says there are simply too many "junky" titles out there taking up valuable distribution space, and there are "lots of failures associated with those titles, and that hurts everybody."

OEM should still be considered as a key part of the overall marketing, promotion and distribution mix. But it is an incremental feature of branding that is meant to augment, not supplement, a solid business plan.

Q & A

Gary Hare, President & CEO
Fathom Pictures

Q. What are your primary distribution channels?

A. Retail, by and large. We've done some OEM—particularly when we have done new technology stuff. We have done some MPEG versions of some of our golf stuff that have been OEM'd into the new MPEG machines.

Q. For an advanced racing game for the PC, you might try to get it OEM'd with a next generation PC platform?

A. You said that, I didn't. I don't want to be telling you stuff I shouldn't. We say, "What can we do with this title that makes it compatible with a new piece of technology—an Intel or Apple product— that people are going to be interested in?" If we can do something easily, then we do it. And if we can't, we don't.

Q. What about OEM prices?

A. This year—in the last couple of quarters—we were approached by a company that wanted to distribute 500,000 units of one of our products for free. I asked him why I would do that—what's in it for me? He said exposure. I said, well, if you distributed 20 million of them for free then I'd have the entire market. There are a lot of people now that have said that we'll put your title or a piece of your title in a bundle but we're not going to pay you anything for it.

Then I have seen deals ranging from $.50/unit to a high of $4.00. We have done deals in the past as high as $12/unit and as low as $7.00. This year I think will be far less attractive on the OEM side. A couple of dollars is more common. There is a new computer coming out and they are trying to do 30 titles in their bundle.

And if they pay $1/unit, they have $30 for their costs—a lot of the software is garbage—but the problem is the new computer buyer has 30 new titles to wade through before they have any interest in buying another one. That's one of the reasons why the return rate is so bad.

Q. Do you see OEM as a positive force at all in building new customer loyalty or brand-name recognition for your products?

A. Well. It's exposure. We were approached by a company for our new *Nick Price* golf title saying we want to put nine holes on it and the incentive would be that people will go out and buy the other nine. I don't know whether that's true or not. I just think that it's so overwhelming when you buy a new PC and you get a stack of software. You don't know much about who they are, how many kids they have, how old they are—you just give them a bunch of stuff.

At one time Apple was looking at it and wanted to kill bundling because people were so dissatisfied with the stuff in the bundle that it made them dissatisfied with the technology as a whole. If you went and bought a CD audio player and they gave you 35 CDs we wouldn't see people buying 8 CDs that year—that's a pretty high tie rate. We wouldn't see that any more if you got all of that stuff for free. I wish bundling would go away.

Developing a Distribution Strategy

For a multimedia title producer, developer or publisher, the process of generating positive cash flow begins by getting product into the wholesale channel, and eventually into the hands of end-users. That means moving product from factory pallets to store shelves. And in today's crowded marketplace, once they get there, titles have about 90-150 days to make it (games have even less time than that) before retailers start to pull it, and "returns" begin to not only clog the channel, but also gnaw away at the bottom line. With product returns still averaging about 15% to 17% for all titles, the front end component of any development strategy has to acknowledge a distribution strategy that assures everybody in the product's food chain there is a viable plan to get it into the channel quickly to warrant the risk associated with potential failure. Innovative and creative strategies play a role.

The marketing and promotional strategies directly relate to the channel(s) in which the product will be distributed. For example, for a "do it yourself" title, the channel may include bookstores, warehouse home improvement chains, office supply stores, catalog companies, mass merchants, some specialty video retailers and the Web.

Many analysts speculate that the Web is transforming the way publishers and developers communicate with end users, particularly business to business selling relationships. The Web *can* be useful for developers by providing coop marketing (i.e. hyperlinking) with the national retailer through the publisher or developer's site. That can be particularly useful to developers angling for a national distribution deal or a direct account with a national retailer.

Another example of how the Web has been integrated into the publisher/retailer relationship is that all major players have Web sites, and in some cases (witness Fry's Electronics), they post their "open days" where developers can contact product buyers electronically and pitch their wares via the net. "Open days" mean buyers don't require an appointment or a traditional project pitch, but they are willing give new developers and publishers an opportunity to showcase their product "one-on-one" with the buyer.

The issue, however, for developers is that real success or failure of any title in the marketplace still rests on the strength of packaged media distribution and retail relationships. Packaged media at the retail level is here to stay, despite all the hype about electronic distribution cutting out the middleman.

There may be one or two exceptions, like Netscape Communications which came into industry prominence by virtue of free downloads of its navigator software. But for most publishers, somebody at the distributor level has to notice and become interested in your product to find an audience. It is, however, useful to consider alternative ways of getting product into the channel.

CASE STUDY

Alternative Distribution

The Voyager Company

The Voyager Company is a New York based company which started publishing films on laser discs and in 1988 began publishing consumer CD-ROM titles. Bill Heye, Director of Marketing for The Voyager Company, strongly believes in direct mail.

Chapter 6

The Voyager Company mails out several hundred thousand catalogs each year, but it's somewhat ironic—and quite illustrative of where the market is headed—that about one-third of the direct responses are coming back over the Internet, according to Voyager. Heye says the company will continue mailing catalogs, but more and more attention will "focus on the Internet as a direct marketing and distribution medium."

He suggests, "There is no idealized way to distribute products." He helped to craft a company philosophy that will always be "product-driven." That philosophy is based on channel diversity, with about 40% of revenue generated from schools, 15% made via sales to the U.S. education market through value added resellers (VARs), 15% from rackers (i.e. Handleman), 20% from foreign sales and 20% direct to consumer.

As for international sales, Heye says international markets are "usually done on an exclusive basis, the advantage being that the company's entire line is supported," as opposed to negotiating with individual distributors on selected titles across different linguistic territories.

The company's Web strategy is to support retail as well as to build traffic to the site. That includes actually closing a sale online. The company has a daily title special which is often cheaper than what a store can buy it for. The site is also hyperlinked with all the retailers' sites that carry the company's product line. Discounts are about 30%.

Voyager typifies a new breed of company using innovative promotions to attract attention and even make some sales via alternative distribution avenues. The company has developed an interesting twist on product distribution, for example, by linking audio CDs with online text that describes and discusses the work. The "active" Web text connects with sections or tracks on the CD.

Heye says now anyone "can become a publisher about music, art literature, etc. without necessarily obtaining the rights to distribute the work," the theory being that the user has already purchased the disc, and Voyager is simply uniting what were formerly two separate media—print and audio.

Distribution

While Voyager does the most typical distribution strategy, it is, however, probably one of the most creative. While none of these distribution strategies are rocket science, the real success formula is to have a plan and follow it through in exquisite detail, while allowing for modifications and market shifts. In the interactive publishing business, 18 months is a generation and can completely alter the market dynamic.

Retail Channel Strategy: Breadth and Depth

The retail channel supporting multimedia titles is still relatively small, when compared to the book channel, video channel and music channel. Thus, the margins are often skimpy for the majority of publishers, and it's a market fact that the big "hits" soak up the lion's share of consumer spending nowadays. Therefore, the size and scope of a distribution deal can make or break a title's launch.

Moreover, distribution affects a publisher's future production capacity. The best strategy for publishers is to go for "breadth and depth." Breadth implies multiple titles, and depth means numerous distribution channels supporting those products. The more locations that carry your product, and the more SKUs your company can offer distribution and retail channels, the better your particular deal will be.

Online Merchandising & Distribution Strategies

The Internet is everywhere. At least that's the perception, and it's very important for developers and publishers to embrace the concept that distribution is going to change. This implies there could be a merger of traditional packaged media and new online merchandising and distribution segments.

Bob Vogel, President of Softmail Direct, says the aim in taking messages and products to the Web is to "make sales and generate leads." The Web is at once a distribution medium and an environment to seal the

Chapter 6

deal. He says the action goals of promotion on the Web are no different than print: namely, to build image, create awareness, further the sales process and even close the sale.

The good news for small developers is the Web offers them an opportunity to give potential customers much more content and information than through any other medium. It's also interactive, personal and fast. The Web is a great way to educate the channel because Web sites and content cab begin where traditional promotion and awareness building leave off. Vogel lists several strategic Web promotional concepts:

- Create a unique URL (home page address) for every single product.
- Link direct response Web content to ads promoting that specific product (don't send users to a generic home page with many other products).
- Provide product incentives to capture name/address.
- Test everything: price points, sources of inquires, content, etc.
- Always ask for the order.

A good starting point is to populate the Web site with a corporate ID, collateral material (brochures, product spec sheets), product packaging information, celebrity endorsements and catchy inducements to explore the product further.

The real benefit to smaller developers is Web sites can be as good, or as bad, as the expertise and concept behind them. Even the largest media companies are learning this game, and there is an opening to create awareness in the cyberchannel. In addition, traditional methods of awareness building are not two-way, and opening a dialogue with distributors or retailers is the first step in getting that product on store shelves.

Q & A

Kelly Conway, VP of Marketing
Multicom Publishing

Q. What distribution channels are you going through?

A. We are in the bookstore channel—that is in the early stages of development. There are probably fewer than 2,000 storefronts that have viable software selections, so that's going to be a slow growth channel. We have some good success in the Home Depot stores, specifically selling the home improvement products which has their brand on it. That legitimizes the product in those stores. Interestingly enough, when we did the research, there was a high correlation between computer ownership and home repair/improvement product buyers. It seemed like a natural fit, and that has proven to be true particularly within those stores.

Q. Were you able to break into that channel because of the Home Depot logo—because they were working on the product with you, or would you have been able to get product into those stores anyway?

A. Yes. And then we have had some success on a smaller scale with parks, gift shops and bookstores with our parks products—also in the sporting goods stores with our skiing products. Those alternative channels will be driven by the appropriateness of the content to that environment.

Q. Has the proliferation of multimedia PCs driven the ability to sell through to alternative channels?

A. Of course.

Chapter 6

Q & A

Kip Konwiser, VP of Entertainment
Graphix Zone

Q. What is your channel marketing mix?

A. I think that it depends on the product and which channels we need to access and what the genre of the product. Before we do a deal, we know who it is we are selling to. Before we do a deal and start talking to the artist seriously, we already know who we are going to sell it to, how we are going to sell it, how many we are going to sell and how much we're going to sell it for. That's the way I run projections and find out whether it's a viable business.

Q. Which channels work best for you?

A. Standard brick and mortar music channels are still the places where the consumer turns for music. We also are trying to let consumers look to Computer City and CompUSA and the various software channels, too. Right now, however, the standard channels remain the strongest channels of distribution.

Graphix Zone has also "inked" a deal with GT Interactive which gives the company distribution into all of the mass merchant channels, including Kmart, Wal-Mart, Sam's, Price Club, Target and others.

Q. What about online distribution?

A. Yes. A whole part of the online strategy is too be able to distribute not only our own stuff but also the stuff of our artists on our Web site. I think that will grow and that music is one of the strongest presence's on the Net—next to porn.

Q. What about advertising?

A. We do a lot of advertising, and we do a lot of marketing. We also go to a lot of shows, etc.

Q. How do you handle publicity for launches?

A. We pick and choose projects we think are going to make a profit for us, and we launch them at appropriate times during our fiscal year when we know we can free up the resources to do a serious marketing push—when we know that it complements other releases we have coming out. It really depends on the particulars of the title, but we try to give each title its due.

Q. What kind of PR do you do?

A. All of it. We want people to know we exist. The point is to get the message out.

Q. Do you do a lot of in-store promotion?

A. Yes. Especially at launch. Some huge number of your sales occur in the first couple of months. Some products last forever, and sales just keep coming in. I think music is not like that. I think music is about buying something hot right away.

Elements of an Effective Distribution Strategy

Multimedia title publishers must determine a distribution strategy when their product is still at the concept stage and identify distribution channels before product development and design begin. Product design should be influenced by the chosen distribution strategy because different channels have different expectations for multimedia titles.

Key aspects of forming a distribution strategy include developing a product plan that includes the four "P's" of multimedia merchandising: Product, Price, Positioning and Performance. Following those determinations, then selecting appropriate channels for selling that particular title is appropriate.

Chapter 6

Product plans submitted to distributors should exhibit the publishers vision and strategy over a two to three year period and should clearly establish a "family of products" approach. A product plan should discuss products currently under development, as well as future products, and should include product positioning, target market, list price and packaging concept.

Publishers have to continually evaluate how and where to position their titles to maximize both the end user and the channel that will distribute it. The interactive market is undergoing a rapid transformation because user tastes and new market opportunities (and threats) occur about every 24 months.

Thus, any product started today may, in fact, have to deal with a completely new set of distribution realities when it finally makes its market debut 18 months from now. The distributor needs to be reassured that the product enhances—or will enhance—its current offerings to stimulate additional sales to resellers, how many marketing dollars will be made available for advertising, and how much margin the title offers.

To position a title to both the end user and distributor, publishers must differentiate their product from competitors. Publishers will need to examine competitors' product positioning, pricing and distribution strategies as well as the titles' features and functionality.

Channel selection should be made in terms of product positioning, pricing and the resources available to pursue the channel. Publishers must have adequate finances to penetrate the chosen channel and sustain the program over a period of time. It is not an overnight process, and *commitment* is the key operative word.

Once product is in the channel, publishers have to market in order to get the product to sell- through. Publishers have to push their product into the channel by marketing to distributors and then pull the end user into the channel through advertising, direct mail and promotions.

Publishers must have aggressive marketing programs to get their product on the shelf before somebody else does. The marketing plan should leverage multiple titles in a series or product line. This allows publishers to sell additional titles to the same market. Important marketing activities include public relations, direct marketing to your installed base, merchandising and advertising.

Buying into the Software Distribution Channel

Distribution costs are rising, and this requires publishers to pick the right title categories and go head-to-head with comparable competitors in order to have a reasonable chance at reaching ROI success. Publishers need the tools to play the game, and that includes infrastructure, product marketing and distribution assets or alliances to maintain and grow a strong position in the marketplace.

Jan Gullett, Senior VP of Sales and Marketing for Broderbund Software, says publishers continually ask: "Who are your competitors? Do you have the financial staying power to play hand after hand-after-hand in the same business segment with those competitors?" Moreover, he says profit comes from leading titles; "Unless you win a few hands at the poker table, you will never generate the ROI." He says "ROIs really come back to the company over time, and publishers must be long-term players to generate profit."

Robin Harper, VP of Marketing for Maxis Software, emphasizes the most important aspect is to use enough elements (variables) in your marketing analysis and distribution strategy. She says to wet the appetite of the channel by "coming up with promotions that have a theme that offers a consumer rebate as well as a rebate for bringing product into the store." Furthermore, she says "selling-in" the promotion means targeting specific retailers, and it really makes sense to try to fit the promotion into their marketing programs which creates a win-win approach.

Harper emphasizes that, "Selling-in a promotion requires that the retailer believes it will improve their key measures: sales per square foot, inventory turns and gross margins." She empathizes that, "Publishers aren't the only ones looking for ROIs." According to Harper, ways to

Chapter 6

determine an ROI for a marketing thrust include: 1) Increased product trials; 2) Redemption rates (number of people that return coupons, etc.); and 3) Changes in product awareness, image and increased product usage. For confirmation purposes, PC Data is one of the most reliable tracking firms for quantifying sell-through unit sales.

Kerry Huffman, Director of Channel Marketing for Intuit, provides a very simple and illuminating definition of ROI: "ROI is incremental dollars spent and incremental dollars received back from that investment." He believes any investment in channel promotion must take into account the margin and base line (what you would have received anyway without the promotion) to quantify that investment.

For example, if publishers invest in a retail end cap, and that expenditure is $100, and it generates incremental sales of $1,000, then the ROI is 10:1.

Assuming a publisher was forecasting base line sales of $100,000 on a particular title and was further willing to invest $30,000 in an incremental promotional thrust, the break-even point for that investment is an additional $60,000 in sales (see table below).

If the POP element was an end cap, for example, and the investment was that same $30,000, then an incremental multiple of "2" would justify the strategy.

The Distribution Channel Loves "Hits"

Interactive title publishing is at an important and critical juncture. The industry is—and will continue to be—volatile and subject to the same market forces as any other "hits" driven business. Everybody agrees the "hits" nature of the business is a clear driver behind the strong consolidation trend working through the market.

The problem, however, is an estimated 4% to 10% of CD-ROM products are actually making a profit in any one year. Given that reality, creating a hit is important because, simply put, that's where the money is.

Not only is it where the money is, but a successful title will go a long way toward guaranteeing a developer or publisher a crack at locking up shelf space for the next title. But it's also a catch 22 because the industry is not mature enough to predict with any degree of certainty which titles are going to be "hits."

Ken Goldstein, Executive Publisher for Broderbund Software, says the market is unforgiving, and publishers have to "understand the difference between a great idea and a good market opportunity." Goldstein says, "Lot's of great ideas do not sell all that well, and the best strategy to take is to look at evergreen-type products that have channel staying power."

For example, *Print Shop* has been Broderbund's number one seller over the years, and right behind that title is the Carmen Sandiego series. Beyond the evergreen titles that Broderbund budgets for on a year-by-year basis, the company does try to develop a few hits, which is risky, according to Goldstein. "With budgets that are well into seven figures, we all have to answer to stockholders for our jobs," he says.

Goldstein says another problem with the business is that there are too many "junky" titles soaking up shelf space or still bundled with hardware. He maintains that there are "lots of failures associated with those titles which hurts everybody." For new publishers looking for success, Goldstein strongly emphasizes "category building."

He believes the "industry has always grown by category defining software." He advises developers to "define a category and then attempt to own and defend it." This makes the product much easier to garner channel attention.

Even so, he says innovation is tough because publishers are running out of new categories to exploit. "You have to be very brave to create category defining software because no amount of marketing or distribution studies are going to replace instinct when it comes to picking the winners and bypassing the losers."

Goldstein also has words of caution about Web distribution. He does believe the Internet is a huge opportunity, but he says, "It is also a com-

Chapter 6

petitor because there are just so many viewing hours in the day and entertainment options consumers are willing and able to consider."

Greg Roach, a multimedia producer and graphics artist, says the main issues that define a successful title are: 1) Where is the source of funding and the publishing opportunity? 2) How strong is the distribution machinery? and 3) How could the expectations of the VC (or funding source) developer, publisher and audience best be aligned? The most crucial element, says Roach, is that a producer must maintain the product vision through the 18 months of development time.

Andy Higgy, President of Production of the San Francisco-based First Linear Studios, says there are three ingredients to make a successful title: A strong talent base, design phase and product measurement criteria. Higgy says whenever his company looks at acquiring content, the first thing they do is develop an extensive property plan for that content and figure out which windows and distribution opportunities legitimately exist for the proposed title.

Q & A

Mason Woodbury, VP of Marketing
Broderbund Software

Q. How do new forms of distribution complicate the copyright process?

A. I don't know that it has affected us at all except when we've tried to move characters into movies or TV shows. Then we've had problems because we may have only gotten the rights for the software. *The Carmen Sandiego* TV show has had some complications in that area. We have the TV show on WGBH, and they created some characters. And we have a cartoon show on Fox, and they created some characters. Some of them are in the software, and some of them aren't. So we're constantly talking to these people in terms of who has the copyright for *Zack and Ivy*.

Q. So you might have problems moving a character from the TV shows into a game?

A. We generally take care of that. The problem comes when someone comes, and now I want to make a movie or want to make a line of T-shirts based on *Carmen*. We're doing a comic book with DC Comics. They are looking at a wide variety of sources of characters. We'll get the comic book, and they're using some of the characters off of the WGBH TV show. Then (comes) the question of who owns the rights to those characters to put them in a comic book.

If we do a movie deal, the movie people want to own all of the rights to the characters, but meanwhile we've already assigned some of the rights to other people. We don't really have any problems with the software as such. It's when we're taking a character like *Carmen* and moving her from software to TV to movies to books to comic books to T-Shirts. All of a sudden it gets confusing as to who does *Stretch the Wonder Dog* belong to.

Q. What about warehousing and storage?

A. Other than the fact that we don't have enough of it?

Q. Packaging costs. What are the costs per title?

A. The box is 60 cents. The jewel case is like 10 cents. The books are usually another 50 cents or 60 cents. The actual duplication of the discs is somewhere around $1.00 to $1.25. By the time you end up with everything, I think it's between $4.00 and $6.00, depending on the level of documentation.

Q. Is documentation one of the most expensive components?

A. Yes. We took the book out of *Print Shop* for that reason.

Q. Do you own your own pressing facilities?

A. No. Not for CDs. We did when we were on floppies, but we're in the process of selling off most of that equipment.

CHAPTER 7
online network franchise

For game developers, the cable network distribution strategy has the advantage of offering players the same performance that carts are famous for, but with inventory that is close to 50 titles per month.

The Sega Channel says with existing cable TV technology (premium network distribution), players can have virtually the same game experience as if they rented the cart. Sega is not planning a web site for games, however, and the company's Internet presence is strictly for information and referral, according to spokesperson Jennifer Moffie.

Sega only makes abridged versions of new games available via its network, and the company reports that its service currently passes approximately 10 million homes and is carried on 200 cable systems. But in many cases, electronic distribution at this juncture is still a judgment call because PC household penetration is so low, and the number of homes connected to online services or the Web are relatively small.

Case Study: Sega Channel

Sega Channel has been adding subscribers at the rate of about 3,000 to 4,000 per week, which would put the venture at close to 225,000 subs since service launch back in December, 1994. Looking at it from a penetration standpoint, however, and assuming a 2% take rate for passed homes, Sega Channel is probably looking at a year-end 1996 subscriber figure in the range of 400,000.

Chapter 7

CONSUMER ON-LINE SERVICE SUBSCRIBER GROWTH 1988-2000		
Year	Subs (Mil.)	% Change
1988	0.7	—
1989	1.2	71.4%
1990	3.0	150.0%
1991	3.3	10.0%
1992	4.0	21.2%
1993	5.2	30.0%
1994	7.5	44.2%
1995	10.1	34.7%
1996	16.0	58.4%
1997	20.0	25.0%
1998	24.0	20.0%
1999	28.5	18.8%
2000	33.5	17.5%
Montgomery Securities data.		

At that rate, and further assuming subscriber acquisition costs of about $25 per sub, the channel is grossing $59 million from its electronic delivery service (not including activation fees), with approximately 45% (or $26.6 million) going to MSOs, and the remainder to Sega Channel.

It's not a huge business when compared to retail revenues, but electronic distribution is still in its deployment infancy. And, as broadband network pipes get fatter, the possibility to spin off other niche game ap-

U.S. HOUSEHOLD COMPUTER ON-LINE CONNECTIVITY							
Category	All U.S. (%)	Ameritech (%)	Bell Atl. (%)	BellSouth (%)	NYNEX (%)	PacTel (%)	SBC (%)	US West (%)
PC Homes	39.8%	27.8%	44.8%	36.4%	42.9%	47.1%	39.9%	44.7%
PC w/modem	24.3%	17.1%	21.7%	24.4%	28.1%	30.0%	23.2%	27.4%
Online Homes	7.8%	10.2%	7.2%	7.2%	7.7%	11.2%	5.4%	5.5%
Net Homes	8.1%	8.3%	7.1%	6.9%	10.2%	11.1%	7.2%	5.8%
Source: Regional Bell Operating Companies research.							

plications is more likely. That could mean dramatic aggregate electronic distribution revenue growth going forward.

Because Sega Channel takes up only half the MHz of a typical cable channel (about 3 MHz), the venture is already experimenting with spin-off services. Sega Channel recently rolled out a new sister service, Express Games, which launched in November, 1995 and is the *Pay Per Play* arm of the Sega Channel.

SEGA CHANNEL PRO-FORMA BUSINESS MODEL

Premium Subscription Service Analysis

Year-End		1996	1997	1998
Cable TVHH Availability	(Mil.)	20	35	45
Average System Take-up	(%)	2.0%	2.5%	3.0%
Avg. Sega Ch. Subscribers	(Mil.)	0.40	0.88	1.35
Subscription Fee/Mo.	($)	12.95	12.95	12.95
Total Yearly Revenue	($Mil.)	62.2	136.0	209.8
New Sub Acquisition Costs	($)	25.00	25.00	25.00
Net new sub costs	($Mil.)	3.1	12.0	11.8
Net Sega Channel Revenue#	($Mil.)	59.0	124.0	198.0
Cable Affiliate Compensation	($Mil.)	26.6	55.8	89.1
Sega Channel Net Revenue	($Mil.)	32.5	68.2	108.9

\# = Service revenue only, and does not include activation fees.

Source: Paul A. Palumbo

Here's how it works. First, a game player must already subscribe to Sega Channel to get the service. Subscribers then have access to "day and date" release of electronic versions of video games right along with retail outlets. The game is available (in its entirety) for two calendar days for $2.95 per game, or the same cost as a rental title. The splits are three ways: $1 for the game publisher, $1 for the Sega Channel, and $1 goes to the MSO. Express Game's first full month in operation was December, 1995, when *Mortal Kombat III* was available.

In early 1996, *Mortal Kombat III*, *College Football* and *VR Troopers* will be available. The service is a more extensive version of Sega Channel's Test Drive section on the main service, which allows players to preview abridged versions of games in advance of retail release.

According to Moffie, the company's research indicates that where the channel is available, retail traffic goes up incrementally because players get to sample the product for a relatively cheap price before they lay down the $70 at retail.

Moreover, title availability windows have remained fairly constant since launch. Games are still available pre-retail launch for testing, followed by a 30-90 post-street-date window before the game is once again on the network. Sega says an average player currently plays 39 of the 50 games inventoried on a monthly basis.

Sega has found that add-on features and promotion are the driving forces behind adding new subscribers. Sega Channel learned some unexpected characteristics about consumer adoption since rolling out its service on a business as usual basis in 1994.

First, Sega Channel is considered a value-added convenience. The kids who play the games are not the ones paying the cable TV bill. What's interesting is, those parents typically identified as "early adopters" don't necessarily want their kids playing 50 video games per month on a TV screen. Some would rather see them spend more time studying, while others would rather spend the $300 on a new 32-bit game console and a few of the top games to keep up with the march of technology.

Second, middle income families have really become the market because both parents are working, and they don't have the time to go to the video store. At $12.95 per month for 50 games (assuming they already own a Sega Genesis console), it's a strong value proposition.

Sega's advertising message to parents is totally geared toward value and convenience. For example, it emphasizes there are "no more late fees for games," and "There are $3,000 worth of video games available for $12.95 per month." And it's been working because that middle income demographic segment is buying the Sega Channel.

For game title developers and publishers (and everyone else in the entertainment enrichment chain), it's not a matter of whether or not games are here to stay—because they are—but rather, what delivery medium (or media) makes the most sense to maximize the value of that particular game title franchise.

In essence, the challenge before Sega Channel and other electronic game distributors is to find a promotional and merchandising voice as an industry that is as clear and effective as retail has been over the decades, so the business can grow into something beyond novelty status.

The World Wide Web

Everybody agrees that content delivered over networks to the PC or TV are going to be an attractive distribution avenue and a much-needed aftermarket for interactive title developers. Developers are not only looking for an electronic exploitation window beyond retail (and maybe even distribution), but determining what network strategy to employ is where industry consensus begins to diverge.

At present, there are four network distribution alternatives:

- Set-up and maintain a proprietary web site to court the global Internet audience
- Create a stand-alone cable TV service that targets the twitch-dominated set-top box segment
- License franchise properties to one (or all) of the online content aggregators (like AOL, CompuServe, etc.)
- Provide connectivity for users via one-on-one phone lines and modems.

Even with multiple options, the respective merits of each individual strategy are less important than what electronic distribution can mean for publishers eager to maximize the value of a particular game title franchise. With shelf space at retail in chronic short supply and costs rising to get product into the channel (let alone keep it there), interactive publishers have long sought alternative windows of distribution over which to amortize development costs.

What's got the industry buzzing now, however, is that online services and the Internet are becoming part of the "culture" so quickly, and they are creating entirely new virtual "viewing" communities and an entertainment consumption metaphor.

With most set-top boxes and PCs destined to be hooked up to some type of network over time, electronic distribution could have the same dynamic effect on interactive content in the '90s as the VCR had on Hollywood back in the early '80s, which is to completely revolutionize the revenue model.

Today, the film industry typically generates 60% of its retail dollar through various aftermarket windows (i.e. other than theatrical), from video, PPV, premium cable and generic cable TV, to broadcast television (not to mention foreign licensing opportunities). Titles such as *Terminator 2*, *Batman* and any Disney vault or first-run product is going to achieve substantial sales in overseas markets. In that case, production negatives can therefore be amortized across a series of windows that could take several years to fully realize. In fact, Hollywood is unlikely to fund any project that doesn't have a strong chance of generating substantial international revenues.

Even most domestic network "shows" don't reach profitability in first-run distribution but do so only after syndication and foreign licensing revenues get factored into the mix. That could take years, as the franchise moves through its first run syndication, foreign and then second run syndication licensing window. Shows like *Three's Company* are in fourth and fifth run syndication and are cash cows for Distributor World Vision (a unit of Spelling Entertainment).

As the game business matures, Jeff Einstein of Crossover Technologies predicts the Internet model for interactive content will evolve into something resembling the basic TV model, with development based on the marketshare (distribution) that a publisher can pocket upfront like any other pre-licensing deal and combine it with corporate sponsorship—namely, ad revenues.

Crossover Technologies is focused primarily on designing games for the WWW because "the same guys that wind up paying for content on TV, broadcast and radio are the same ones who will pay for the convenience of the Internet," according to Einstein. And definable communities attract ad dollars. "The advent of advertising on the web will encourage segmentation, the development of communities and services to meet the needs of those communities," according to Einstein.

One strategy to "break" an interactive-based web site is to sign a distribution deal with an established online provider that functions somewhat like a cyber or video "barker." It offers players a minimum layer of access and also directs traffic to a web site. If it's a pure Internet play, then aggressive PR campaigns in the game trades are useful, as well as cross-branding on cable TV or broadcast.

If the title is a game, educational title or enthusiast product, user interest can also be generated by aligning the product with a high-traffic web site that has cross-promotional (hyperlink) capabilities.

Online Revenue Models

At the heart of any electronic distribution strategy is and revenue generation, either on the Web or via a cable channel. The current Web model is one based on a hybrid of advertiser-supported and pay-as-you play sites. The software is made available to the game player, and then he/she is charged access fees to hook up with other game players. That strategy is being employed by S.F.-based Domark Software.

Domark spokesperson Paul Baldwin says the company's Confirmed Kill title "is going to be the world's largest Internet game, capable of supporting up to 500 players simultaneously." The company is making a downloadable version of game available for free (a software-led marketing approach that paid off big for Id Software and its *Doom* title). After an Internet launch, the title will be available at retail (with enhancements) six months later.

Id also employed another intelligent marketing strategy, according to Baldwin. The company let some of its game code "get out," so players

Chapter 7

(and hackers) could create their own experiences (i.e. new dungeons and pathways). This type of "open-to-programming" lure is a good way to create a "buzz" on the net, according to Baldwin, and drive up site activity.

Plus, says Baldwin, the "net" is a great beta test site. Domark's web service is transactional, and players will pay $10 per month in network fees, plus another $2 per hour for multiplayer game access.

CASE STUDY

Web-based Multiplayer Gaming Strategies

A survey of selected established and proposed online game network providers reveals that flexible pricing strategies, ubiquitous access and key content acquisition are three areas expected to differentiate multiple service entrants from one another as the market begins to grow and eventually mature. In the short-term (through the year 2000), nobody expects online distribution to threaten boxed media (i.e. packaged) assets, but there is a sense that network gameplay will more and more become an expectation in consumers' minds after the initial purchase decision is made, no matter where that transaction actually takes place.

On the network side, there are basically two online models, though each one can (and often does) have multiple variations. Those basic models include: 1) Proprietary dial-up networks (i.e. Dwango, Total Entertainment Network), targeting hard-core twitch game enthusiasts; and 2) Web-based game services (i.e. MPath, Catapult Entertainment and INN's Cyber Park), accessible via ISPs (Internet Service Providers, like Netcom) and OSPs (Online Service Providers, like America Online).

For example, MPath is partnered with the ISP PSINet in a distribution and content aggregation play. That alliance can guarantee its users

ON-LINE GAME NETWORK PRO-FORMA REVENUE–DISCOUNTED CASH FLOW MODEL
Web-Based ISP/OSP-Delivered Game Service Scenario

Year	1	2	3	4	5
Net Service Users	7,500	20,000	35,000	55,000	75,000
Average gameplay hrs/wk	2.5	3.0	3.5	4.0	4.5
Average gameplay hrs/mo	10.0	12.0	14.0	16.0	18.0
"Pay for time" fee/hr	2.00	1.50	1.25	1.00	0.75
"Pay for time" fees/mo	20.00	18.00	17.50	16.00	13.50
Gross revenue/mo	150,000	360,000	612,500	880,000	1,012,500
Gross revenue/yr	1,800,000	4,320,000	7,350,000	10,560,000	12,150,000
COGS#	1,350,000	2,808,000	4,410,000	5,280,000	5,710,500
Gross Profit Margin	25.0%	35.0%	40.0%	50.0%	53.0%
Gross Profit	450,000	1,512,000	2,940,000	5,280,000	6,439,500
Operating Expenses	337,500	982,800	1,617,000	2,376,000	2,575,800
Start-Up costs	-2,500,000	0.0	0.0	0.0	0.0
Operating Income	-2,387,500	529,200	1,323,000	2,904,000	3,863,700
Depreciation /Amortization	358,125	84,672	158,760	290,400	347,733
Cash Flow	-2,029,375	613,872	1,481,760	3,194,400	4,211,433
Cash Flow margin	-112.7%	14.2%	20.2%	30.3%	34.7%
Cumulative cash flow	-2,029,375	-1,415,503	66,257	3,260,657	7,472,090
Discount Rate	**10.0%**	**10.0%**	**10.0%**	**10.0%**	**10.0%**

Cumulative Discount cash flow	4,572,501
5th Year Cash flow multiple	8.5x
Implied 5th year enterprise value	38,866,257

\# = Cost of Goods Sold (COGS) includes royalty payments to title developers and network (i.e. server/software) expenses.

& = Network users are "average" paying users, net of estimated "churn" @ 20%.

Source: Paul A. Palumbo

network latency of about 150 milliseconds, which is a strong promotional inducement for game players interested in high-impact titles.

In that type of business model, the ISP is compensated by a monthly flat rate from game players who access the Web through their dial-up POP sites, mostly because of a guaranteed level of game play. MPath, in turn, generates revenue by charging players about $2.50 per hour for usage. MPath maintains its own network servers and strikes all the content deals. Gross profit (revenue minus cost of goods sold—COGS) is then split equally (similar to the premium pay TV model) between MPath

Chapter 7

and game title developers or rights holders.

Based on an analysis of the Web-based model (see model above), positive cash flow is generated when about 35,000 regular members begin logging onto the site. Adding approximately 20,000 "net" new members per year implies that the entire venture could have a private market value of close to $40 million by year five. "Net" members equals the number of new subscibers minus the churn. The churn being subscribers dropping the service. That assumes start-up costs of $2.5 million, cash flow margins ramping up to about 35%, and an 8.5x cash flow multiple applied to cumulative discounted cash flow. For comparison, that's about half the implied value of a small (niche) premium cable TV network like the Sundance Channel.

Whether those are sufficient numbers to prick the interest of Madison Avenue—which would further increase revenue and value—or maybe even IPO-happy Wall Street underwriters remains an open question. But creating qualified communities is what the Web hype is all about. Kristen Asleson, VP of Marketing for MPath, says the Web game site concept is similar to a neighborhood tavern or game arcade that cultivates a dedicated clientele. Sites have to create a sense of: "This is where I belong. This is where I like to hang-out," says Asleson.

Pricing Pressure

Even so, the pro-forma Web-based model assumes there is going to be intense competition for leisure gameplay dollars, which will drive down price points. The good news is cash flow margins in the Web model benefit from the fact that there are no telecommunications charges to absorb on the part of the site provider, which can make up as much as 30% to 40% of cost of goods sold (COGS).

Proprietary networks, like INN and Dwango, typically pay about 33% of each revenue dollar generated (not including monthly service fees) for telecom charges. Nevertheless, INN says its users average about 5 hours per week, and it can still be cash flow positive (without corporate sponsorship) if it keeps a tight reign on telecom charges.

Looking at the proprietary network model, those services typically charge gamers a flat subscription rate per month ($7.95 for Dwango, $9.95 for INN), which helps cover those additional costs and includes five free hours of usage. Additional hours are then billed at about $2.95 per hour, with increments of time sold on a sliding cost scale.

New Models Emerge

Dean DeBiase, CEO of The Imagination Network, says the company's network is changing its model. DeBiase says, "INN doesn't believe in a future where an online gaming service can be sustained when you charge members on a separate monthly statement." He says INN is moving toward an Internet retail presence, with pricing models ranging from a "pay-per-play scenario, all the way down to free." That type of service would be characterized by its Cyber Park venture, which will potentially be available to millions of online members through agreements with an ISP or an OSP, like AOL.

In that case, says DeBiase, "All the billing and functionality is transferred to the connectivity provider." Then, he says, "It becomes a wholesale transaction between supplier and provider," which is similar to the relationship between theatrical exhibitors, cable TV MSOs or TV networks and Hollywood studios (or their distribution subsidiaries) for filmed entertainment product. The key, says DeBiase, is "There must be pricing flexibility because we are moving from a hard-core audience to a mainstream audience." Cyber Park will have a number of different "flavors," depending on which gateway the service is accessed through. DeBiase suggests, "The new game model is how many potential users are you exposed to via network relationships, and how many sessions can you generate with casual users, not proprietary members."

Dwango is also evolving. President and CEO Bob Huntley noted that the company introduced its Windows 95 Internet client software at E3, which allows gamers to access the service through any ISP they choose. At present, Huntley says Dwango's business model is quite stable because costs are very "fixed." With a relatively fixed model, Huntley

Chapter 7

says, "The company knows where to put its money."

Dwango has also locked up a hyper-linking deal with Pathfinder. The service is going to have a "hot button" on Time Warner's Pathfinder homepage in the not-too-distant future, one of the hottest sites on the WWW. Huntley says an association with the largest content aggregators, whether sites on the Web or networks like AOL, makes a lot of sense for game networks to better drive up usage and awareness.

Online Opportunities and 16-bit Hardware

Catapult Entertainment is unique in the group, however, because the company has just gone beta with its PC software for Web gaming, but it continues to operate a network for 16-bit enthusiasts. And it's generating "positive cash flow right now," according to Adam Grosser, President and CEO of Catapult. Grosser says its 16-bit network service (using the X-Band modem for Sega and Nintendo game boxes) is still adding 50-100 subscribers per day, and the number of connections made into the network on a typical weekday is between 80,000 and 120,000.

The biggest problem the company had with building subscribers for the 16-bit network, though, was gamers with a Sega Genesis machine didn't really think of it in terms of a connectivity device, whereas PCs are, by default, connectivity-enabled nowadays, and those users have a sense about what it means to be online, according to Grosser. The irony is that the company thought it would be dead by now. "There is clearly a desire for it to stay there," added Grosser, considering that churn is averaging only about 2%. The company's 16-bit customers spend about 16 hours per month online, with 50% of Catapult's user base logging on every week.

Catapult's Web-based service will bea very low flat monthly fee, on the order of $1 to $2. But to actually enter one of the tournaments, there will be an entry fee. The hook, says Grosser, is "If players think they have a chance to achieve something meaningful (i.e. win the prize), the transaction is tolerable." Similar to INN, Catapult's Web service will likely be a nominal flat rate model, or with hybrid *a la carte* pricing tiers. Grosser says, "The company does not believe that the time-based pricing model works for games because a reasonable experience with a game takes 30 minutes." At those usage levels, he says, "The economics don't work out."

Exclusive Content and Royalty Rates

The issue of striking exclusive content deals with developers to create provider loyalty and brand differentiation met with mixed reaction from the market survey. Mpath, for example, does not ask for exclusive rights. But the company does work with software developers to co-market in order to create consumer awareness of a particular game available on its Mplayer service. MPath's model is to develop entire game design document specs (Brian Moriarity is the company's massively, multiplayer game design specialist) and then farm them out to developers. Those developers then box the assets for retail distribution along with the MPlayer software kit.

Bob Huntley sees the industry as moving toward a non-exclusive model, which he equates with the theatrical mode. "Movies don't play across one theater chain, but many, in an effort to maximize eyeball reach," he says.

A non-exclusive deal with a developer can generate anywhere from 15% to 25% of online revenue flowing back upstream to the rights holder. But there are other options for developers. In the case of key content, there may be pieces of provider equity put up as a long-term lure for developers that also serves as a guaranteed source of online distribution. There may also be as much as 100% of the revenue offered to developers for a hot title just to generate site traffic. According to providers, no one is offering upfront licensing guarantees right now because revenues just aren't there yet.

Adam Grosser believes exclusive content "in many ways, will be a key differentiator." While the company claims to have the lowest latency network, Grosser says, "The difference between 150 milliseconds and 110 milliseconds probably isn't a huge selling feature, compared with the ability to play a game like *Quake* versus the ability not to play *Quake*."

Chapter 7

He goes on to say, "Exclusive content, over time, will become very important. In the very near term (i.e. two years), it's probably not that important because none of the publishers view online as a dramatically compelling revenue stream when compared to their boxed asset equivalents." Grosser says he can "easily see a network provider like Catapult providing funding for key content." Catapult will not, however, be in the business of producing.

INN already has exclusive access to Sierra On-line (now CUC's) content for approximately the first year it is available on the network. DeBiase says the company does use that as a promotional leverage point, and INN is shooting for about 10% of its inventoried product to be on an exclusive basis.

It probably comes down to a judgment call on the part of network providers, however, whether to put promotional capital into content deals or directly into market awareness muscle. Either way, it's an opportunity for developers who need partners to share internal costs and help to get the product message out.

The All-Purpose Entertainment Appliance

The debate over which platform will emerge as the all-purpose entertainment and information device of choice in the home may not be resolved in the retail marketplace, but Dataquest predicts PCs and TVs will coexist, with each box showing signs of a winner. According to Dataquest analyst Bruce Ryon, "TV sets will win the installed base battle, but the failure of the MPEG movie title market attests to the fact that people do not want to sit and watch full-length movies on the PC." Ryon forecasts, "TVs will win the passive entertainment race, and PCs will win the interactivity battle."

Dataquest predicts PCs will win the revenue generating value, but the company qualifies that statement. Consider that TVs are replaced, on average, about every 10 years, while PCs are upgraded approximately every four years. So the often-quoted statistic about PC outpacing TV shipments is somewhat misleading.

Online Network Franchise

Ryon says, "There is not going to be a war to be won, but a lot of battles to be won." He speculates that the real value is going to be won by the so-called "information worker" because that demographic segment has the money to buy advanced entertainment and communication boxes. Here's the issue. A Dataquest research sample of 10,000 homes found that home PCs were installed in slightly less than 30% of U.S. households, but growing rapidly.

What's fueling growth, though, is corporate downsizing. "Many of those positions were middle management that started home consulting businesses," says Ryon. In addition, "one of the ways that people can be more competitive is to have a PC at home, which allows them to extend working hours."

Dataquest analysts believe the growth of the PC as a gaming device is being enhanced by the explosion of online and the Internet. "The PC has just been designed for home use over the past five years, and now a real trend toward the home markets and interactive is driving that trend," says Ryon.

Ryon claims Interactive TV was essentially "killed" because the cost factor did not match the projected demand. Infrastructure required about a 10 year return on investment, and many companies are looking for a 2-3 year ROI. As a result, he predicts the PC and the Internet are the new market for interactive TV. But that market is going to primarily reside in the information worker household. As for other basic trends, Ryon said both PCs and TVs will be game capable and education capable.

As for games, PCs win with better resolution and performance, but consoles win in social environments. There has also been a leveling off of TV viewing hours and an increase in PC use. Ryon said the main reason game consoles still exist (about 10 million units by the end of 1996) in large quantities is price.

"For $150, gamers can get a lot of good action, and game consoles also tend to be much more conducive to social interaction." Ryon notes that households willing to spend $2,000 for a PC will also spend $150 for a dedicated game box to maximize entertainment investment.

Chapter 7

The opening for PC CD-ROM, according to Dataquest, was that set-top boxes have about a 4 year re-prescription cycle. "The 16-bit is transitioning to the 32-bit market, and that allowed the PC to come into the market," says Ryon.

Ryon believes another key factor in the rise of the PC as a game platform is "there is a lot of secondary storage and RAM." That has meant a lot for titles, since there has been a 75% compound rate of growth in the number of PC CD-ROM units shipped over the last three years, based on Dataquest estimates.

The "Buzz" in Cyberspace

The recent spate of on-line game spectaculars and multiplayer gaming environments are proving to be successful strategies in building communities of users that can generate revenue streams necessary to make a sustainable business in cyberspace, and maximize the value of franchise titles. For example, Catapult Entertainment has sponsored several national gaming tournaments for its 16-bit console-based network, and The Sega Channel has used EA's sports (i.e. Madden Football) to generate a player enthusiasm and create an event atmosphere.

There are numerous ways that event (i.e. game tournament) communities can be built, but it always comes down to leveraging a "brand" (i.e. Madden's football franchise) forward or porting existing product to a new medium (i.e. Total Entertainment Network's online service). But the true hallmark of these gaming or pure entertainment environments is that they are competitive by nature and are therefore designed to create a "social interaction" or social contract that is technology-based.

Online Network Franchise

CASE STUDY

Outer Limts Franchise Goes Online
MGM and Worlds, Inc.

MGM and Worlds Inc. are taking the popular Outer Limits franchise and creating a unique online gaming experience around it. While embracing the chaotic and organic nature of the Web, Outer Limits can be cross-promoted across a variety of media, including cable TV and broadcast TV. This helps drive online click traffic, according to Ron Frankel, VP and GM for MGM Interactive.

Supporting click traffic at the Web site, is the MGM parent. MGM has received orders for 44 more Outer Limits episodes, which originally aired on Showtime. Those episodes are also in broadcast syndication, which will further enhance the brand's value. MGM promotes the series on cable through broadcast affiliates, and those advertisements always list the show's Web site address (www.mgm.com).

Ken Locker, VP of Entertainment for Worlds Inc. says, "Cooperative gaming is the niche position that MGM and Worlds Inc. are taking because it requires players to work together to get to the next level, and at the same time it's communal"—for example, a joint search for clues to enter a new level. The company had planned to close its *Worlds Chat* site, but users told the company they would pay to keep it up and running. Locker believes *Outer Limits* can make money in one of two ways: 1) By the subscription model (i.e. pay for time); or 2) Via the broadcast model (advertiser-supported). The broadcast model delivers players and therefore, corporate sponsorship.

Chapter 7

But, MGM's Frankel says the gaming environment may not support the subscription model, and the venture will simply sell the client CD-ROM at retail. Locker believes, "The CD-ROM client could be bundled in along with Internet access provider software and the site accessed when multiplayer play was desired.

CASE STUDY

Online Distribution Network
Dwango

Dwango's dial-up online gaming service has taken an even more radical approach to event programming by hosting tournaments over its dedicated and proprietary game network. Bob Huntley, President of Dwango says the company's whole model is built on two principles: it's important to make a local call to play and provide a "twitch" gaming service that could maintain low latency and data transfer rates demanded for real-time gaming. This required the installation of point of presence sites across the country.

Dwango is adopting the subscription model and recently established a new pricing structure. According to Huntley, monthly access is now $7.95 per month and worth five hours of play (about $1.50 per hour). Lobby or chat time is free. The company is still selling blocks of time, however, with 10 hours at $19.95, 20 hours at $34.95 and 40 hours at $59.95. Dwango's business plan calls for setting up an additional 130 POP sites (in areas with a population of 250,000) over the next two years.

Dwango partnered with Microsoft, id Software and GT Interactive to host a gaming tournament based on the id's *Hexen* title, an extension of the *Doom* franchise. While a full-scale marketing strategy was not used, the partners were able to stimulate substantial player interest and word-of-mouth buzz by mass mailing details of the tournament to registered users of *Doom*. The next "event," says Huntley, will be a partnership with InterCorp and will exploit the company's Witchhaven franchise. The tournament will be based on the theme of the St. Valentine's Day Massacre.

Even so, community-building is nothing new. The broadcast and cable TV models have survived and thrived on that model for years, albeit with a heavy dose of ad sponsorship. The key difference in cyberspace is niche communities cannot only be courted, but the early response indicates users are willing to pay for the convenience and gaming excitement that these "event" environments offer. That fact should give title developers something to smile about.

It's also good for specialty retail because "event" buzz typically drives more foot traffic at storefronts, which makes up the bulk of software sales, and it will continue to do so for years to come.

CHAPTER 8
merchandising

In today's market, it's a much safer market play for developers to establish publishing and distribution arrangements with larger, more established publishing companies that have both proprietary marketing and sales forces. It's the same evolution Hollywood studios have gone through over the years, and it aligns production with powerful distribution assets.

But, even a large publishing house does not necessarily have all the business relationships to fully maximize the value of a franchise property. There is a lot of market volatility and a significant degree of market consolidation rippling through the industry.

For that reason, developers intent on creating original characters and stories should attempt to retain as much control over copyrights as possible because that's where the long-term return on investment numbers is generated.

It's a difficult balance, however. Interactive publishers don't have the skill sets to go into Hollywood and make a feature film out of proprietary character. The reverse is also true (witness Acclaim Entertainment's alliance with Warner Bros. to develop the game title *Batman Forever*). There are always going to have to be multiple partnerships and alliances woven together to exploit a title through multiple windows.

Chapter 8

CASE STUDY

Disney Creates Merchandising History
Pixar's Toy Story

Walt Disney is really the merchandising model to emulate for title developers. The company has fine tuned the business of franchise exploitation to a fine art. For example, the release of *Toy Story* was unique because it was the first time Disney used a World Wide Web site (http://www.toystory.com) as a cross-promotional tool to coincide with a film's release. It was also the first time Disney released a motion picture title day-and-date with its video game counterpart.

The video game was made available at retail (including toy stores, mass merchants, computer superstores and software boutiques) day-and-date with the release of the film and was designed for play on Sega Genesis and Nintendo Super NES platforms.

For Disney, lining up merchandising partners is a little like setting a holiday dinner table and deciding which candelabra is more appropriate. Basically, Disney assembles a group of potential licensees and presents the properties to them, and each deal is then negotiated separately. Disney's other merchandising partners for Toy Story included Burger King, Frito Lay, Minute Maid, Nestle and Payless ShoeSource. It's quite a line up.

Otherwise, the merchandising of *Toy Story* is the typical full promotional program press honed to exquisite detail by Disney over the years. What's ironic is that *Toy Story* might end up being one of the company's biggest merchandising successes of all time, despite the fact that it did not have the promotional push given to *Pocahontas* and *The Lion King*. Disney's greatest retail merchandising success (so far) is *The Lion King*, which generated over $1 billion in worldwide retail sales within six months of its theatrical release and is well beyond that figure now.

Merchandising

For an average Hollywood licensee, royalties range of about 7%-15%. Disney properties, however, typically go well above those figures. Toronto-based Thinkway Toys is Disney's partner for doll merchandising of *Toy Story* characters, and sales of Cowboy Woody and Buzz Lightyear figures sold out fast. Disney ships merchandise to its network of 450 studio stores worldwide and other retail outlets.

Nestle USA recently signed a 10-year merchandising agreement with Disney to do promotions for such items as *Pocahontas* and *Lion King* chocolate bars. According to Nestle, the chocolate bars are great impulse buy products. There is also the *Toy Story* soundtrack, featuring songs written and performed by Randy Newman.

These are a few of the secrets to interactive moving into mainstream revenue success.

Licensing

While some high-profile, heavily promoted interactive titles can indeed break into profitability through the retail window exclusively, this is not the case with the vast majority of titles.

Developers and publishers increasingly must look to ancillary, after-market windows to help defray the costs of production and reach the maximum number of "eyeballs." Licensing is a Hollywood tradition that has turned into a huge revenue stream for savvy rights holders. Hollywood licensees typically average royalty rates of about 7% to 15% that flows back to licensors, but Disney properties typically go north of those figures.

Interactive title developers simply cannot afford to ignore lucrative merchandising windows that other entertainment media are driven through. According to Karen Raugust, editor of *The Licensing Letter*, entertainment-character products as a whole in 1994 had gross retail sales for the U.S. and Canada markets alone of $17.2 billion--up 9% over the previous year.

Chapter 8

SALES OF LICENSED MERCHANDISE
1982-1994 (In $Billions)

Year	Total	% Chg.
1982	20.5	—
1983	27.0	31.7%
1984	40.0	48.1%
1985	50.0	25.0%
1986	55.0	10.0%
1987	56.0	1.8%
1988	60.0	7.1%
1989	64.0	6.7%
1990	65.0	1.6%
1991	63.0	-3.1%
1992	61.0	-3.2%
1993	68.0	11.5%
1994	70.0	2.9%

Source: Analysis of EPM Communications, Inc. data.

In 1995, that figure should go even higher when all the merchandising efforts behind *Apollo 13*, *Casper*, *Batman Forever*, *Jumanji*, *Cutthroat Island*, *The X-Files*, *Mortal Kombat* and *Toy Story* are finally tallied up.

On a worldwide basis, movie studios and other entertainment giants generate about 25% of the $98 billion in retail merchandising of licensed products. The U.S. and Canada accounted for the largest piece of that retail segment in 1994, with about $70 billion in gross sales (see bar graph). In fact, merchandising of film characters really was started by Disney back in 1929, with *Steamboat Willy*.

But the market really took off in 1977, when licensing of *Star Wars* figures turned into a merchandising gold mine for LucasArts. According to Len Reiter of Bradford Licensing, a deal is "usually based on an advance paid to rights holders against a minimum guarantee, and the guarantee is against royalties."

Today, one of the boom markets going forward into the 21st century is shaping up to be mixing Hollywood creative talent with the computer industry's penchant for workstation productivity and quality.

Merchandising

Moreover, retailers get excited about those type of day-and-date deals, too, because a picture creates a lot of foot traffic (and sales), once the title hits the theatrical exploitation window. With a film like *Toy Story*, there was a tremendous amount of "hype" built up by virtue of the Disney name and its promotional budget.

For example, *The Lion King* generated over $1 billion in worldwide merchandising revenue within six months of its theatrical release. Whenever any interactive publisher looks at original content, they consider that, in success, how the company might be able to translate a character into another aftermarket.

But, Raugust says many interactive developers simply haven't had the time to seriously begin licensing thrusts because they are still focused on cranking out marketable titles to sustain their business. And beyond that, unless a title has "sales of a minimum of 1 million units, they don't really have a realistic shot at a licensing deal."

Reiter says, "There is no substitute for software that is selling successfully." He further suggests,"If there is a ceiling for the software getting incremental exposure, then publishers need to find ways to get additional exposure to the mass market; but licensing is probably the last step in that exploitation chain."

One thing that the industry has not been doing is a concerted marketing effort on a per-title basis. For the most part, what we've seen is that publishers will take a title as part of their marketing campaign and place five or six titles on the same page. Advertisers, publishers and developers must go after a specific demographic in the marketplace that can be qualified, quantified and compelled to try the product.

Developers must know who their audience is, where those eyeballs reside, and how best to deliver messages to those eyeballs. Without communities of interest and a reasonable promotional budget, it will be very hard to create a street buzz about a specific title.

APPENDIX

Appendix

Madeline and the Magnificent Puppet Show
-CASE STUDY-

Publisher:	Creative Wonders
Development Company:	Vortex Media Arts
Content Rights:	DIC Entertainment
Budget:	$500,000
Break-even (units):	60,000
Platforms:	PC/MAC
Retail Price:	$49.95

Description: *Madeline* is a line of French children's books which was first published in the 1930's. DIC Entertainment bought the rights to the project from the author in 1993 and produced a highly acclaimed animated series for Home Box Office and The Family Channel.

The Deal

In 1993, Michael Pole was an executive producer for Creative Wonders, a division of Electronic Arts. Michael believed that the edutainment market needed a recognized, franchizable property which could be marketed to girls in the 7-12 year old age bracket. He approached DIC to acquire the electronic rights to *Madeline*. Creative Wonders secured the franchise for a low up-front fee (plus royalties) by assuring DIC that the produced title would contain the highest quality design elements.

How was such a deal possible? Consider that current licensing fees for branded media characters range from $100,000 to $250,000. Production budgets for high-end, children's edutainment titles range from between $400,000 and $700,000. Obviously, a licensing fee in the six figures would leave little money for the publisher to develop a title with quality production values and still turn a profit. Creative Wonders had to perform a "song & dance" negotiation. It had to convince DIC that the long-term benefit of licensing its content at a lower, up-front licensing fee outweighed the short term, lower cash infusion. Such benefits included:

Association with multimedia software of award-winning caliber

Branding the Madeline name into a new market— multimedia

Free, collateral publicity for DIC's television program from publisher's media campaign for the title

In instances where companies are willing to become partners— as Creative Wonders did with DIC for the *Madeline* title— a publisher & licensee can produce a top-notch title in a cost-effective manner.

There are companies that have made a name for themselves by acquiring branded content— particularly SunSoft and Acclaim. In instances where they paid too much money for licensing rights, they often had little money left over to properly develop the title. Consequently, the title did not always perform up to expectations— both in its gameplay and retail sales results. While the interactive market is in its infancy, high licensing fees do not benefit the publisher nor or licensee. The formula for success lies in a true partnership— the licensee, publisher and developer working together as a lean production entity— while sharing in the back-end rewards when a quality title wows the consumer.

Development

Michael had a prior relationship with a company called Lil' Gangster Entertainment— a development company known for creating high quality animation for top interactive title publishers in Hollywood such as Virgin Interactive, Electronic Arts and Disney Interactive. Michael felt Lil' Gangster could handle the animation work on *Madeline*, but felt the firm lacked the technology to produce the entire title in-house. When Lil' Gangster merged with a technology company, Creative Vision (the creator of Buzz Aldrin's Race Into Space), the new development house

Appendix

was able to secure the *Madeline* deal with Creative Wonders. The merged entity, now called Vortex Media Arts, has gone on to land production deals with Fox Interactive (*Digital Springfield*), Hasbro (*Tonka Construction*) and Electronic Arts (*Bump in the Night*).

Production Considerations

With the money saved by acquiring the rights to *Madeline* at a low, up-front licensing fee, Creative Wonders was able to allocate a fair amount of money to the "on-screen" elements of the project. Many of the artists now working for Vortex had prior experience with the *Madeline* character during production on the animation series at DIC. This lowered the "learning curve" for the title's design work. Additionally, the production team utilized an established engine (a custom authoring tool set) previously created by Creative Vision. This meant that the technology "learning curve" was also kept to a minimum. The unique combination of these business and design caveats allowed Creative Wonders to publish a top-caliber title at a substantial lower cost than usual.

This is one example of how the interactive industry is streamlining its production process to mirror the "best practices" of the Hollywood movie business— where partnerships between previously unrelated companies creates powerful new alliances and products.

Promotion/Marketing

Given that *Madeline* was previously known as a book and being developed as an animated cartoon series, *Madeline* was very recognizable to retailers (it didn't hurt that many national sales reps now in the interactive software industry are former book and toy reps either). With a little extra cash in the marketing budget, Creative Wonders was free to distribute eye-catching, stand-alone displays which were proudly placed in the front section of many retail stores. The display— a combination of toy, software, dolls, books and videos— were presented just in time for the Christmas buying season.

Case Studies

It is important to note that the in-store promotions would have fallen flat if the title itself wasn't everything that the buying public expected from a branded character such as *Madeline*. The *Madeline* deal ultimately paid off for DIC in the back-end. Based on the praise generated for the multimedia title, combined with ABC's need to pick up quality children's programming, the network picked up the animated version of *Madeline* from DIC and aired it all season.

Bob Dylan: Highway 61 Interactive -CASE STUDY-

Publisher:	Graphix Zone
Development Company:	Graphix Zone
Content Rights:	Columbia Records
Budget:	$650,000
Break-even units:	45,000
Units sold as of June 1996:	93,000
Platforms:	PC/MAC
Retail Price:	$59.95

Description: Highway 61 Interactive is a compilation of the events and major works of singer/songwriter Bob Dylan woven into an exploration of Bob Dylan's music. The strategy behind the CD-ROM was to present the artist in a way that the user comes away with a greater appreciation for the artist's work.

Acquisition/Rights

The major issue with any music CD-ROM is to clear the publishing and performance rights. That was made slightly more complicated in the case of the *Dylan* CD-ROM because some concert footage had to be secured from private sources and agreements had to be secured for those properties based on the amount of material used, with an

Appendix

assessment of what that material might be worth in the format presented.

In the case of *Dylan*, however, most of the publishing and performance rights were held by Columbia Records, which made research much easier. Once given the "OK" by the artist and record label, it was then easy to go about determining what shape the licensing agreement would take.

Developer/Partner

Graphix Zone produced and published the D*ylan* title. In addition, the company produced original video for the project. Graphix Zone created everything but the music, which was compiled for the disc by Bob Dylan. The product was assembled using the Apple Media Tool and original source code.

Promotion/Marketing

The artist, Bob Dylan, is well known to music retailers, mass merchants and consumers of all age groups. Therefore the title was easily positioned in a number of retail outlets (record stores, mass merchants, specialty video and computer superstores). When a well-known artist is the basis of a CD-ROM title, marketing experts know how to exploit the artist's name to maximize press coverage and ultimately, sales.

The *Dylan* title was launched with a "premire" party at Bob Dylan's New York studio, which was attended by Roger McGuinn and Al Kooper (key channel partners). Launch parties were thrown in a number of cities with additional channel partners in attendence. The parties provided the "story" for the PR machine to kick into gear—churning out advance release "hype" for radio station promotions and music trade press coverage. This free publicity provided the sales force with the necessary "hook" to sell the title into the channel. By informing the press and key music organizations well in advance of the title release, Graphix Zone was able to sustain the press campaign until the title's natural release date. Graphix Zone was able to continue this PR push by entering the title in numerous multimedia contests—winning 25 of them. The most prestigious award won was *Byte Magazine's Top 10 CD-ROMs of All Time* award. The title went on to garner positive reviews in newspapers and periodicals across the country, helping to expand retail sales efforts.

On the Road with B.B. King
-CASE STUDY-

Publisher:	MCA
Development Company:	Media X
Content Rights:	MCA
Budget:	$625,000
Break-even (units):	55,000
Platforms:	PC/MAC
Retail Price:	$49.95

Description: B.B. King seemed a particularly good subject for a CD-ROM because of his personality—he is the quintessential charming story teller with southern charm. He is also an icon in the blues community. From a marketing perspective, it just doesn't get any better. His appeal flows across all genders, all races, and all ages.

Development

Alex Melnyk was MCA Music's VP of Interactive who helped launch the *B.B. King* title. Before deciding on B.B. King as the focus for MCA's first music CD-ROM title, she looked at several possible properties and characters upon which to enter the interactive universe.

Appendix

Her feeling was that the world wasn't quite ready for a full-blown online title, mainly because of bandwidth considerations. She felt that CD-ROMs which were based on strong musical identities with a body of work of which to draw upon, would be the best bet for MCA's first time out of the interactive chute. Of all of the different properties that MCA owns, a *B.B. King* title seemed to have the most potential.

Acquisition/Rights

MCA has some very stable artists which are known as "bread and butter artists." They no longer sell millions of albums each year, but they generate a fair amount of sales revenue year-in and year-out. *B.B. King,* a legend in his own time, is one such artist. The acquisition of rights were a painless process since MCA and B.B. King had a long, healthy relationship doing business with each other.

Developer/Partner

MCA initially put together a production team, and was sorely disappointed by the team's first effort. After six months of disappointing results, MCA pulled the plug and start all over again with a new development team.

The new development team, Media X, did something pretty remarkable. They took a miserable project and completely re-created everything. Alex Melnyk hired a writer named Michael Shaun Conaway, who wrote the treatment, the script and the branching in five days.

The developers then arranged for the blue screen video shoots and other production details with B.B. King. B.B., a CD-ROM aficionado, was very involved in the whole development process. He was even involved in reviewing the projects scripts and treatments. Media X and Melnyk sifted through every information resource they could find relating to B.B. King and his work, including museums and library archives. They gathered together the necessary material, clearing all of the music, publishing and media rights. In short, they went from inheriting a dismal project to delivering a finished gold master in less than six months, including new video shoots, content acquisition and programming. Media X really saved the day in terms of their ability to contribute to both the creative process as well as doing a bang up job putting the title together.

Promotion/Marketing

The *B.B. King* title was placed in music stores over software channels by a ratio of 60:40. One of the most prominent in-store displays was made possible through a deal with the Tower Records chain. The title also lent itself extremely well to the book channel since the disc contained a rich history of B.B.'s music, as well as a history of the music early scene. MCA did a truckload of audience research and found out everything there was to know about B.B.'s fans, his record sales (where his music sold well and not so well), what kind of channels they sold through, and his concert demographics.

The company also worked very closely with BB's manager (Sid Feinberg, who has been B.B.'s manager for 30-odd years). MCA took the time to get know B.B.'s audience and then utilized that knowledge to their advantage.

It has been said by many that record label marketing leaves a lot to be desired. It tends to follow the software model and yet it is selling what is fundamentally an entertainment product. Working within a tight budget forced MCA to get creative with both its marketing campaign and marketing buck. The music giant even created stickers and slapped them on the bin cards in the B.B. King Blues and R&B sections of record stores. The stickers say things like "now available, B.B. King has gone interactive," pointing the customer to the CD-ROM.

Luckliy for MCA, B.B. was ringing in a "big" year. He won the coveted Kennedy Award, appeared on The David Letterman Show,

Appendix

celebrated his 70th birthday year, and celebrated the 25th anniversary of his single biggest hit, "The Thrill is Gone." MCA even installed a web site two weeks before product launch (www.mca.com).

**PATENTS AND CORPORATE LITIGATION:
PRACTICAL OBSERVATIONS**
Allen S. Melser
Popham, Haik, Schnobrich & Kaufman
1450 G Street, N.W., Suite 800
Washington, D.C. 20005-5717
(202) 824-8013
melsera@popham.com

Synopsis

Those who have experienced a patent litigation know that the drain on monetary and human resources is enormous. This is due in large part to the complex nature of patent litigation and the volume of paperwork necessary to put on a patent case. A major portion of a patent litigation is directed toward invalidating the patent in suit. Many of the activities that take place prior to the issue date of the patent are of great importance to both the patent owner and the accused infringer. Therefore, the beginning of this article presents a general discussion of what a patent is, how a patent is obtained, and some of the considerations that go into filing and prosecuting a patent application. The rest of the article generally covers the considerations that must be taken into account by in-house counsel when faced with trial preparation, infringement risk analysis, damage analysis, cost containment, discovery, and dealing with witnesses.

About the Author

Allen S. Melser is an intellectual property attorney whose practice concentrates on procuring, maintaining and enforcing domestic and foreign patent rights. He heads Popham Haik's intellectual property and technology law group.

© 1995 Allen S. Melser

"Patents and Corporate Litigation: Practical Observations" courtesy of Allen S. Melser © 1996

Appendix

I. INTRODUCTION

Those who have experienced patent litigation know that the drain on monetary and human resources is enormous. This is due in large part to the complex nature of patent litigation and the volume of paperwork necessary to put on a patent case. A major portion of a patent litigation is directed toward invalidating the patent in suit. Many of the activities that take place prior to the issue date of the patent are of great importance to both the patent owner and the accused infringer.

II. THE NATURE OF PATENT RIGHTS

A U.S. patent is a right granted by the Federal government to prevent others from making, using, or selling the invention covered by the patent in the United States. The right is enforceable in any Federal district court, even if the infringer discovered the invention by innocent means, such as his own experimentation. A U.S. patent is not enforceable outside the United States. Three types of patents are granted: (1) design, (2) utility, and (3) plant.

A design patent covers the ornamental appearance of an item, and is primarily of value in protecting the aesthetic aspects of articles of manufacture, such as furniture, ashtrays, and similar items. However, design patents can also be of value of protecting the ornamental appearance of more mundane items such as tools and machines. Recently, design patents have been granted for icons on video display screens.

A utility patent protects the mechanical, electrical, chemical, and/or functional aspects of an invention. A utility patent includes a detailed written description of the invention (referred to as the "specification") and at least one, and usually more, "claims" consisting of a concise listing of structural components and functional limitations (or method steps) of the invention. The claim(s) define the scope of

"Patents and Corporate Litigation: Practical Observations" courtesy of Allen S. Melser © 1996

coverage of the patent. Utility patents are usually more difficult and costly to obtain than design patents.

A plant patent covers any distinct and new variety of plant, including cultivated spores, mutants, hybrids, and newly found seedlings, other than a tuber, propagated plant or a plant found in an uncultivated state.

A patent application should be filed as soon as possible after the invention has been completed <u>and before there is any unrestricted public disclosure to others</u> or publication. This is often necessary to obtain foreign patent protection, because many countries, including those in the European community, subscribe to an absolute novelty standard.

The filing of a patent application does not give any legal rights other than the right to mark the invention "Patent Pending". Competitors can copy an invention up to the date of issuance of the patent.

All patent applications must be filed in the name of, and signed by, the <u>actual true inventor(s)</u>. All assignments or transfers of patent rights should be recorded in the U.S. Patent and Trademark Office ("PTO").

Among other things, a valid U.S. patent cannot be obtained if:

(1) The invention is so close to publicly known devices (disclosures of prior known publications, patents, and the like) as to be obvious to a person of ordinary skill in the art to which the patent is directed; or

(2) The application is filed more than one year following public use or placing on sale of the invention in the United States or disclosure of the invention in a publication anywhere in the world.

"Patents and Corporate Litigation: Practical Observations" courtesy of Allen S. Melser © 1996

Appendix

Before proceeding with a patent application, it is usually desirable to conduct a preliminary patentability search through the public records of the PTO in an effort to uncover prior patents relevant to the subject invention. The search indicates the scope of protection that may be obtained and prevents filing of a useless application where the prior patents indicate that the invention already exists.

If the search is favorable, a patent application is prepared and submitted to the inventor(s) for inspection and signing prior to filing in the PTO. Most patent applications are rejected at least once by the PTO, and applicants should expect to file one or more responses to such rejections.

In circumstances where large scale use, manufacture, and/or sale of an invention is contemplated, it is highly desirable that the question of possible <u>infringement</u> of currently enforceable patents owned by third parties also be investigated at the same time that the probable patentability is investigated. The questions of patentability and possible infringement present different legal considerations; however, there is considerable overlap between patentability and infringement issues. Conducting a simultaneous search covering both the patentability and possible infringement aspects is considerably more economical than separate searches at different times. Investigation of the possible infringement aspects is quite time consuming and relatively expensive as compared with a patentability investigation.

A patent attorney can also counsel companies with regard to setting up proper contractual obligations with employees to ensure that the employer obtains title to inventions of employees and that employees follow necessary procedures for protecting the employer's patent and trade secret rights.

"Patents and Corporate Litigation: Practical Observations" courtesy of Allen S. Melser © 1996

III. PATENT LITIGATION

A. Initial Considerations

Recent patent infringement decisions granting high damage awards serve to remind corporate management that patents are important and valuable corporate assets. For a small company, one key patent may be the entire basis for staying in business. On the other side of the coin, a company's legal staff must be ready to defend the entity from claims of others. Corporate counsel cannot and should not wait for problems to occur. A company holding patents must remain vigilant and ready to protect these assets. At the same time, staff attorneys must be ready to defend against charges of infringement. These processes require constant monitoring and control. The trick is to both protect the business' intellectual property and keep the company from becoming a defendant in a patent suit.

A patent infringement defendant may assert a counterclaim alleging infringement of a different patent. Another alternative is attempting to invalidate the plaintiff's patent. The choices are numerous and corporate counsel must be aware of the dangers and pitfalls of patent practice.

A company's attorney does not want to first discover a conflict over patent rights by receiving a cease and desist letter from a law firm representing a patent owner. In-house counsel should analyze patent infringement liability whenever new equipment is developed.

B. Infringement Risk Analysis

If a business is accused of infringement, legal counsel should assess the risk presented by the claim of infringement. This assessment usually takes the form of a review of the "best case" and "worst case" scenarios. Under a "best case" scenario, the company considers the issues of liability, defenses, counterclaims, and claims

"Patents and Corporate Litigation: Practical Observations" courtesy of Allen S. Melser © 1996

Appendix

against the plaintiff and third parties in the most favorable light possible under the circumstances of the case. In general, the best case scenario provides a framework for determining how the company might aggressively litigate to achieve optimum results. One of the most difficult parts of this determination will be analyzing the company's ability to handle the litigation process. Generally, in-house attorneys are paid to keep a company out of a courtroom. However, if the other side is bound and determined to go to war, the time for diplomacy may be over and the company should consider hiring experienced trial counsel.

Hiring outside trial attorneys should also be considered after analyzing the worst case scenario, in which the company assumes liability. Penalties and hardships may include the issuance of an injunction against the company and damages, costs, and fees commensurate with an increased, possibly treble, damage award.

Although time consuming, the study of liability for patent infringement is essential for a complete appreciation of the risks of litigation. Often, the worst case scenario can be summarized as an injunction coupled with the greatest monetary award possible under the circumstances of the dispute. The worst possible injunction is usually one which compels complete and immediate cessation of the infringing activity and a delivering up of all infringing materials or inventory. The monetary award may include damages, prejudgment interest, a punitory increase in the award, and the patent owner's attorneys' fees and costs. These elements are designed to restore a patent owner to the financial position it would have occupied had the infringer not engaged in the unlawful conduct. An accurate study of the worst case scenario is especially important today, because the growing trend is to try patent infringement cases before juries, rather than before a judge.

"Patents and Corporate Litigation: Practical Observations" courtesy of Allen S. Melser © 1996

C. Damage Analysis

Damage analysis is at the heart of determining, from a business perspective, what the company's response will be to cease and desist letter from a patent owner. There is no simple standard rule of damages, but rather a flexible array of applications to fit the proofs available to the damaged party. Theories of recovery include lost profits, established royalty, reasonable royalty, and compensation for miscellaneous expenses and injuries as a result of the infringement.

D. Role of In-House Counsel

When discussing the interplay between in-house corporate counsel and trial counsel, the duties and responsibilities of each must be well-defined to avoid confusion. Some decisions should be made long before any specific litigation is contemplated, such as (1) what the company should do before threatening to sue, (2) whether negotiation is a valid alternative to litigation, and (3) whether it is more important to strengthen the company's case or to attack the other party's arguments. If inside counsel cannot make these decisions, outside help is clearly needed.

Once outside counsel is selected, the attorneys must work together preparing defenses and/or counterclaims. One approach is to leave the responsibility for preparing the corporation's case with in-house counsel. Assign the lawyer or lawyers hired for the instant dispute the task of attacking the other side. In general, corporate counsel makes substantive decisions and sets policy. Trial counsel handles tactics and strategy.

Under this division of labor, in an action defending a patent's validity, a business' legal staff will spend time collecting supporting material for the patent in question, and documenting non-infringement of an opposing party's patent. If a corporation hires outside assistance in an action to shut down an infringer, the

"Patents and Corporate Litigation: Practical Observations" courtesy of Allen S. Melser © 1996

Appendix

should be handled by in-house corporate counsel or outside counsel. One reason suggested for avoiding outside counsel in a settlement situation is to cut down on the amount of back and forth and cross-checking involved between attorney and client in any settlement negotiation. By the same token, outside counsel can act as a buffer between the disputing parties.

The decision whether to negotiate instead of litigate should be made by in-house counsel. While it is true that some trial attorneys are by nature adversarial and confrontational, outside help can also be employed effectively in settlement talks. Therefore, part of this process involves a decision as to what kind of outside counsel should be engaged. Some patent firms made their reputations as tigers in the courtroom, while others are very good at hammering out settlement agreements and avoiding a winner-take-all battle.

F.　Discovery

An entire volume could be written on the problems of discovery in patent litigation. The issues are often complex and confusing. Even if outside counsel is not responsible for preparing material regarding the client's products or processes, outside counsel must be fully briefed regarding facts, figures, and other technical data. Corporate counsel must be ready to provide their outside counterparts with all the information necessary. Whether outside counsel's responsibility is attacking the validity of the other side's patent while in a defensive posture or proving infringement in an offensive action, they will need to know all the details surrounding their client's operations. A well-informed litigator can prepare better questions and employ more effective tactics.

One strategy is to give trial counsel responsibility for handling all contact with the court and with the other side. Discovery requests are received and then passed onto the client's legal staff for answers. In-house counsel prepares the material, which

"Patents and Corporate Litigation: Practical Observations" courtesy of Allen S. Melser © 1996

is returned to the trial attorneys. At the same time, a litigation team prepares material to be served on the opposing party. The corporate lawyers give the requests and questions a once-over and return them to the outside attorneys for service.

Conducting and defending depositions involve the use of skills only developed through practice. Experienced trial lawyers can use depositions as a way of intimidating prospective witnesses, asking clever questions, and allowing self-doubt to creep into the deponent's thoughts. A party to a patent infringement case wants this kind of attorney on his side, or perhaps more importantly, a party to a patent suit wants an advocate that can deal with that kind of attorney on the other side.

G. Witnesses

Every trial attorney has heard advice like, "let the witness tell a story," and patent litigation is no different. A tale of invention and discovery can be interesting and exciting -- if you have a credible and articulate witness and a lawyer who can keep the narrative going without boring his audience or violating rules of evidence. Although expert witnesses are essential for some phases of a patent infringement trial, a simple fact witness will often be more effective.

Patent litigators should use experts to cover highly technical or confusing topics, keeping in mind the fact that the other side has experts too. The second word of the term "expert witness" is just as, if not more important than the first. All the technical expertise or scientific knowledge in the world counts for nothing if the witness cannot respond to questioning in a convincing manner. Professional patent litigators should have a list of experts ready to testify on patent matters. Attorneys litigating for a living know who can react to tough cross-examination from an opposing counsel. A trained litigator will also be able to judge the potential of prospective witnesses already familiar with the case. In-house counsel knows what point or ideas need to be brought out or explained. Outside counsel knows what kind of person will do the job.

"Patents and Corporate Litigation: Practical Observations" courtesy of Allen S. Melser © 1996

Appendix

The task a courtroom expert is to present and explain with complex and often confusing data in a simple straightforward manner to lead the trier of fact to an inevitable conclusion. It almost goes without saying that any witness testifying as to prior art must be familiar with the field. When proving patent validity, experts should define and pay tribute to the inventive concept of the patent in question. Naturally, a witness testifying to defend an infringement claim is expected to demonstrate the obvious qualities or the non-originality of the subject patent. Without this kind of testimony, it may be difficult to prove the novelty and beneficial aspects of a particular apparatus or method.

At some point, probably sooner than later, experts become boring. Any change of pace can reawaken juror or judicial interest. The tricks of the trade are really no different than any other kind of litigation. Visual aids, charts, and diagrams can be helpful. Complicated mechanisms or processes make a lot more sense if the witness can demonstrate what she is talking about.

A corporation's witnesses, often employees, would be best prepared by outside counsel. Unaffiliated counsel is less likely to make assumptions common between co-workers. Everyone who works for a company producing specialized products, from the receptionist to the legal staff, will have some knowledge of the goods in question. An outsider brings fresh perspective to the situation and knows what kind of questions someone unfamiliar with the device or idea on trial would ask. Conversely, inside counsel should be responsible for explaining the product or idea to experts procured by trial counsel.

IV. CONCLUSION

The foregoing represents a broad overview of patents and patent litigation. It is the hope of the author that this article will give the reader a better understanding of the complex issues that arise in patent litigation and a feel for the desirable interaction between in-house counsel and outside trial counsel.

"Patents and Corporate Litigation: Practical Observations" courtesy of Allen S. Melser © 1996

Software Development and Publishing Agreement

SOFTWARE DEVELOPMENT AND PUBLISHING AGREEMENT

THIS SOFTWARE DEVELOPMENT AND PUBLISHING AGREEMENT is made as of _____ (the "Effective Date") by and between THE PUBLISHER, INC., a Delaware corporation with offices at _____ ("Publisher") and MULTIMEDIA DEVELOPER, INC., a Delaware corporation with offices at _____ ("Developer").

RECITALS

A. Developer wishes to produce a multimedia program based upon mutually acceptable specifications.

B. Publisher wishes to retain Developer to develop the program.

NOW, THEREFORE, in consideration of the promises and mutual covenants and agreements set forth herein, Publisher and Developer agree as follows:

Section 1
Definitions

1.1 **Program**. "Program" means the software program with the working title "_____" described in the Specifications.

1.2 **Specification**. "Specifications" for the Program shall be as set forth in Schedule "A" of this Agreement.

1.3 **Source Materials**. "Source Materials" means the source code, documentation, notes and other materials and content produced or created by Developer during the development of the Program, in such internally documented form as is actually used by Developer for development and maintenance of the Program, together with (i) all software tools, development aids and technical documentation created by or for Developer, as they may be modified, corrected or added to from time to time, that are necessary or helpful in the modification and maintenance of the Program, and (ii) the name of a person or persons knowledgeable about and familiar with the source code whom Publisher may contact with questions thereon.

1.4 **Development and Payment Schedule**. "Development Schedule" shall be as set forth in Schedule "B" to this Agreement which lists the deliverable items contracted for ("Deliverables") and the deadlines for their delivery. "Payment Schedule" shall be as also set forth in Schedule "B".

1.5 **Alpha Copy**. "Alpha Copy" means a version of the Program which includes all interface art, all navigational programming, all navigational voice-overs, all music, and

-1-

"Software Developer and Publishing Agreement," courtesy of Thomas J. Cervantez and the law firm of Pillsbury, Madison & Sutro, LLP © 1996

Appendix

representative examples of all content including movies, still photos and text displays.

1.6 <u>Beta Copy</u>. "Beta Copy means a working version of the Program recorded in executable form on the specified medium with any necessary supporting software and data, which has been fully tested by Developer prior to delivery and which Developer believes in good faith to be bug free and to fully implement all functions called for in the Specifications.

1.7 <u>Final Copy</u>. "Final Copy" means a non-copy protected and unencrypted disk master of the Program, recorded in executable form on the specified medium with any necessary supporting software and data, as to which all development work hereunder, and corrections to the Beta Copy, have been completed and which, prior to the delivery thereof to Publisher, Developer believes in good faith to conform in all respects to the Specifications.

1.8 <u>Collateral Materials</u>. "Collateral Materials" means any art work, graphics or written copy for packaging, disk labels, manuals and related materials, if any, which are developed by Developer for use in association with the Program. Developer shall be under no obligation to produce Collateral Materials.

1.9 <u>Licensed Product</u>. "Licensed Product" means an object code copy of the Program together with packaging, manuals and associated materials which are either independently developed by Publisher or which incorporate Collateral Materials.

1.10 <u>Net Receipts</u>. "Net Receipts" means gross receipts actually received by Publisher from the sale or sublicense of Licensed Products less Cost of Goods, credits for discounts, refunds, replacements and returns, or credits allowed to purchasers for the return of Licensed Products or as reimbursement for damaged Licensed Products, including returns for stock balancing purposes. No license fee shall be payable on units of the Licensed Products which are sold at, or less than, Publisher' cost.

1.11 <u>Trademarks</u>. "Trademarks" means the words _____, and or a replacement trademark.

1.12 <u>Conversion</u>. "Conversion" means the Program as modified for use on a computer, video game or delivery technology other than the DOS or Macintosh platform (e.g., Windows, Sega Genesis System, 3DO).

1.13 <u>Cost of Goods</u>. "Cost of Goods" means the actual cost, to Publisher, of program media, manuals and other collateral materials, packaging materials and shipping costs for the Licensed Product. The Cost of Goods is comprised of the components set forth in Schedule "E". Schedule "E" contains the

"Software Developer and Publishing Agreement," courtesy of Thomas J. Cervantez and the law firm of Pillsbury, Madison & Sutro, LLP © 1996

Software Development and Publishing Agreement

Cost of Goods which will be used for the first year of the Effective Date of this Agreement. Upon each anniversary of the Effective Date, the Cost of Goods shall be reviewed and adjusted to reflect Publisher' actual Cost of Goods for the Licensed Product.

1.14 <u>Story Boards</u>. "Story Boards" means graphic depictions of audiovisual displays and the sequence of those displays in hard copy or electronic form. For purposes of this definition, Story Boards also include screen shots and graphics which demonstrate the overall look and feel of the Program.

Section 2

<u>Development and Delivery of Deliverables</u>

2.1 <u>Development; Progress Reports</u>.

(a) Developer shall, in good faith and using commercially reasonable efforts, develop each Deliverable in accordance with the Specifications. Developer shall deliver Deliverables which conform with the Specifications. Once the Specifications and Story Boards are accepted, such acceptance not to be unreasonably withheld, Publisher may request modifications or additions to the Specifications and/or Story Boards. If the requested modifications will require demonstrable additional expenses to be incurred by Developer, the parties will negotiate in good faith any required modifications to the development fees set forth in Schedule "B".

(b) All development work will be performed by Developer or its employees at Developer's offices. Developer agrees that no development work shall be performed by independent contractors without a suitable assignment of rights agreement.

(c) Following execution of this Agreement during which any development and/or testing hereunder remains uncompleted, upon Publisher' reasonable request, Developer shall contact, or meet with Publisher' representative, and report all tasks completed and problems encountered relating to development and testing of the Program. During such discussion or meeting, Developer shall advise Publisher in detail of any recommended changes with respect to remaining phases of development in view of Developer's experience with the completed development. In addition, Developer shall contact Publisher' representative promptly by telephone upon discovery of any event or problem that will materially delay development work, and thereafter, if requested, promptly confirm such report in writing.

2.2 <u>Delivery</u>. Developer shall deliver all Deliverables for the Program within the times specified in the Development Schedule and in accordance with the Specifications. In the event a delay in the delivery of a Deliverable occurs for reasons which are solely attributable to Publisher, one (1) day

"Software Developer and Publishing Agreement," courtesy of Thomas J. Cervantez and the law firm of Pillsbury, Madison & Sutro, LLP © 1996

Appendix

shall be added to the due date for delivery of the Deliverable for each day of delay which is attributable to Publisher. Publisher shall be responsible for the delivery of check disks within one business day following receipt of the submission to Publisher. Developer shall schedule said submission no less than twenty-four (24) hours prior to the time said materials are submitted to Publisher. Publisher shall provide reasonable and prompt technical assistance in order for Developer to implement the Media Vision movie compression and play back technology.

2.3 <u>Manner of Delivery</u>. Developer agrees to comply with all reasonable requests of Publisher as to the manner of delivery of all Deliverables, which may include delivery by electronic means.

2.4 <u>Delivery of Source Materials</u>. Simultaneously with the delivery of each Deliverable, and all additions, corrections or enhancements thereto, Developer shall also deliver to Publisher copies of all corresponding Source Materials.

Section 3

<u>Testing and Acceptance; Effect of Rejection</u>

3.1 <u>Testing and Acceptance Procedure</u>. All Deliverables shall be thoroughly tested by Developer and all necessary corrections as a result of such testing shall be made, prior to delivery to Publisher. Upon receipt of a Deliverable, Publisher will, in its reasonable discretion either: (i) determine that the Deliverable conforms to the Specifications, accept the Deliverable and make the milestone payment set forth in Schedule "B"; or, (ii) provide Developer with written notice of the aspects in which the Deliverable does not conform to the Specifications and request that Developer correct said Deliverable.

3.2 <u>Additional QA Passes</u>. If Publisher requests that Developer correct the Deliverable, Developer shall within five (5) calendar days of such notice, or such longer period as Publisher may allow, submit at no additional charge a revised Deliverable in which such errors have been corrected. Upon receipt of the corrected Deliverable Publisher may, in its reasonable discretion: (i) accept the corrected Deliverable and make the milestone payment set forth in Schedule "B."; or, (ii) request that Developer make further corrections to the Deliverable and repeat the correction and review procedure set forth in this Paragraph 3.2. In the event Publisher determines, in its sole discretion, that the Deliverable is still not acceptable after the further corrections, Publisher may terminate this Agreement.

3.3 <u>Check Disk</u>. All check disks needed for the development and testing of each platform of the Program will be produced by Publisher at Publisher' expense.

-4-

"Software Developer and Publishing Agreement," courtesy of Thomas J. Cervantez and the law firm of Pillsbury, Madison & Sutro, LLP © 1996

Section 4

Other Obligations of Developer

4.1 <u>Product Quality</u>. Developer agrees that the Program will be of a high quality consistent with products previously developed by Developer and will be free of defects in material and workmanship in all material respects, and the Program will conform in all respects to the functional and other descriptions contained in the Specifications. Developer agrees to fix at its own expense any errors or defects which may be discovered in the Program for a period of one (1) year after the date of acceptance of the Final Copy by Publisher.

4.2 <u>Product Support</u>. In order to assist Publisher' efforts to provide its customers with technical support, Developer agrees to provide Publisher with reasonable technical support and assistance for a period of one (1) year after Publisher' shipment of the Program at no additional expense to Publisher. Developer further agrees to inform Publisher, and Publisher agrees to inform Developer promptly of any known defects or operational errors in the Program.

Section 5

Development Fees

5.1 <u>Progress Payments</u>. Publisher shall pay Developer according to the payment schedule set forth in Schedule "B" upon Publisher' acceptance of each Deliverable.

5.2 <u>Compliance with Laws</u>. Any and all amounts payable to Developer hereunder shall be subject to all laws and regulations now or hereafter in existence requiring the deduction or withholding of payment for income or other taxes payable by or assessable against Developer. Publisher shall have the right to make such deductions and withholdings and the payment thereof to the governmental agency concerned, and Developer agree that it shall make and prosecute any claims which it may have with respect thereto directly with the governmental agency having jurisdiction over any such matter.

Section 6

Rights Conveyed to Publisher

6.1 <u>Grant</u>. In accordance with the terms and conditions of this Agreement, Developer hereby grants to Publisher, its subsidiaries, parent company and affiliates for the later of (a) five (5) years from the Effective Date, or (b) upon Publisher' discontinuation of its distribution of all platforms of the Program (the "Term"), the sole and exclusive license and rights to modify, create derivative works, including but not limited to sequels, use internally, manufacture, use, reproduce, publicly

-5-

"Software Developer and Publishing Agreement," courtesy of Thomas J. Cervantez and the law firm of Pillsbury, Madison & Sutro, LLP © 1996

Appendix

display, publicly perform, market, distribute and sell copies of the Program and Licensed Products throughout the world, subject to the continuing license fee obligations set forth in this Agreement. The right to create derivative works (other than translations), including but not limited to sequels, shall be subject to the terms set forth in Schedule "D". Discontinuation of the distribution of the Program for purposes of this Section 6.1 means that Publisher no longer makes all of the platforms of Program available to its wholesale or OEM customers. Developer shall provide Publisher with sixty (60) days notice that it considers this Agreement expired for discontinuation of distribution and this Agreement shall be deemed expired unless Publisher makes the Program available for distribution prior to the expiration of said sixty (60) day period. Upon the expiration of the term of this Agreement all rights in the materials licensed from Developer shall revert to Developer except that all rights in materials developed by Publisher as well as title to any finished products manufactured during the Term shall remain with Publisher.

Publisher acknowledges that some of the material to be incorporated into the Program by Developer will be licensed and that said license may restrict the use of that licensed material so that it cannot be used in all types of derivative works, modifications or sequels (other than conversions, translations or similar type derivations of the work) of the program or in any advertising for the program. Publisher agrees that Developer may nevertheless use such licensed material in the program and Publisher, its subsidiaries, parent company, affiliates and sublicenses will abide by the license agreements made by Developer. Developer represents that it will not use any material that is not able to be fully utilized in the Program and any and all versions and conversions of the Program. Developer will provide Publisher with copies of all license agreements for all materials that Developer does not own that are incorporated into the Program with the Beta Copy when delivered.

6.2 <u>Trademarks</u>. Developer grants Publisher the right to reproduce, use and publish materials bearing the Trademarks in association with the Licensed Product in accordance with the product approval and quality control procedures set forth in this Agreement.

6.3 <u>Sublicenses</u>. Developer hereby grants Publisher the right to sublicense any and all of the rights set forth in Sections 6.1 and 6.2.

6.4 <u>Sequels and Other Derivative Works</u>. Except as specifically set forth herein, Developer shall have no right to produce updates, sequels or other derivative works of the Program during the Term. Publisher shall have the right to produce updates, translations, sequels, and other derivative

"Software Developer and Publishing Agreement," courtesy of Thomas J. Cervantez and the law firm of Pillsbury, Madison & Sutro, LLP © 1996

works of the Program during the Term pursuant to the terms set forth in Schedule "D".

6.5 <u>Conversions</u>. Pursuant to the terms set forth in Schedule "D", Publisher shall have the right to produce Conversions of the Program during the Term subject to Developers right of first refusal to develop the Conversions. During the first six (6) months following the initial commercial shipment of the Program, Developer shall not have the right to request that Publisher produce a specific Conversion of the Program. After the expiration of said six (6) month period, Developer shall have the right to request that Publisher develop such Conversion. If Publisher fails to agree to develop said Conversion within six (6) months after its receipt of a written request to prepare the Conversion, Developer shall have the right to produce and distribute the Conversion. Developer shall not have the right to use the packaging, collateral materials, trademarks or other materials developed by Publisher in Developer's promotion or distribution of the Conversion in the absence of a separate license agreement with Publisher for the use of said materials. The right to develop the Conversion shall be personal to Developer and shall not be assigned or sublicensed to a third party but Developer shall have the right to sublicense the distribution of object code versions of said Conversions.

6.6 <u>Competing Products</u>. During the Term, Developer agrees to not develop, license or distribute other programs which perform substantially the same functions as the Program (e.g., an interactive multimedia work that contains the type of sports covered and the way in which they are covered as detailed in the Treatment dated July 26, 1993.), including but not limited to programs which would not otherwise infringe upon or violate Publisher' intellectual property rights.

Section 7

<u>License Fees; Promotional Copies</u>

7.1 <u>Rate</u>. In consideration for the rights granted Publisher under Section 6 of this Agreement, and for the other obligations imposed upon Developer, Publisher shall pay to Developer the license fees and advances against license fees set forth in Schedules "B" and "C".

7.2 <u>Payment Schedule</u>. Except for the advances set forth in Schedule "B", license fees or other payments due under this Agreement shall be paid within forty-five (45) days after the end of each calendar quarter in which Publisher receives Net Receipts, accompanied by a statement setting forth the basis for the payment.

7.3 <u>Records</u>. Publisher agrees to keep accurate books of account and records at its principal place of business covering

"Software Developer and Publishing Agreement," courtesy of Thomas J. Cervantez and the law firm of Pillsbury, Madison & Sutro, LLP © 1996

Appendix

all transactions subject to a license fee or other payment under this Section 7. Upon reasonable notice of not less than fourteen (14) days, but in no event more than twice per year, Developer shall have the right to inspect such books of account and records to confirm that the correct amount owing Developer under this Section 7 has been paid. Publisher shall maintain such books of account and records which support each statement for at least two (2) years after the date of the statement.

7.4 <u>Compliance with Tax Laws</u>. Any and all amounts payable to Developer hereunder shall be subject to all laws and regulations now or hereafter in existence requiring the deduction or withholding of payment for income or other taxes payable by or assessable against Developer. Publisher shall have the right to make such deductions and withholdings and the payment thereof to the governmental agency concerned, and Developer agree that it shall make and prosecute any claims which it may have with respect thereto directly with the governmental agency having jurisdiction over any such matter.

7.5 <u>Promotional Copies</u>. Publisher will provide Developer with 25 copies of each platform of the Program in retail packaging at no charge within 14 days of shipping. In addition, Developer shall have the right to purchase 250 copies of each platform of the Program in retail packaging at $_____ per copy. Said promotional copies are not for resale and shall be conspicuously marked "Promotional Copy--Not For Resale." No license fees shall be payable to Developer for said promotional copies.

Section 8

<u>Proprietary Rights; Acknowledgments</u>

8.1 <u>Ownership</u>. Title to all property rights including but not limited to copyrights, patents, trade secrets, trade names, and trademarks in the Programs, and the Collateral Materials licensed under this Agreement are and shall remain the exclusive property of Developer. All copies of the Licensed Products made by or for Publisher, as well as any and all program and collateral materials developed by Publisher or for its benefit shall be and remain the property of Publisher subject to Developer's copyright ownership of the Program and Collateral Materials. Publisher shall have the right to mark these Publisher developed materials with appropriate Publisher copyright and trademark notices.

8.2 <u>Acknowledgments</u>.

(a) Publisher agrees to show the following Developer trademark and copyright notices on packaging, in the manuals and disk labels for the Licensed Products as set forth: Copyright 1996 Multimedia Developer, Inc. All Rights Reserved.

-8-

"Software Developer and Publishing Agreement," courtesy of Thomas J. Cervantez and the law firm of Pillsbury, Madison & Sutro, LLP © 1996

(b) The Program credit screen, external box (or OEM sleeve) the CD Rom disk itself as well as the jewel case insert or CD sleeve and documentation will include the following credit which reads: "Conceived and Produced by Multimedia Developer, Inc."

The external box (or OEM sleeve), the CD Rom disk itself as well as the jewel case insert will include a representation of Developer's logo (at a size of no less than 80% of the logo which currently appears on Developer's business card) which will appear in conjunction with Publisher' logos and publishing credits. Detailed credits, including the listing of staff, names of content owners, etc. will appear in a mutually acceptable credits screen located in a mutually acceptable location in the program ("Credits Screen").

(c) The parties will acknowledge each other's role in the creation of the Program in any press release or other promotional materials it produces which is solely devoted to the Program or programs developed by Developer. Subject to Publisher approval of the statements, which approval shall not be unreasonably withheld, Developer shall have the right to promote its role in developing the Program via its own marketing communications.

8.3 <u>Approvals</u>. Publisher acknowledges and agrees that the Licensed Products shall be subject to Developer's prior approval as to any use of the Trademarks, which approval shall not be unreasonably withheld. Developer will endeavor to approve or disapprove submitted materials within three (3) working days after receipt and shall be deemed to have granted approval if a response is not received by Publisher within five (5) working days after Developer's receipt of the submitted materials.

8.4 <u>Publisher Developed Materials</u>. Publisher may adopt its own artwork, copy and packaging in marketing and promoting the Licensed Products subject to Developer's approval which shall not be unreasonably withheld, and Publisher is under no duty to use the artwork, copy and packaging of previously published versions of the Licensed Products in marketing, promoting or selling the Licensed Products.

8.5 <u>Trademark and Copyright Status</u>. Developer shall provide Publisher with information concerning any trademark searches which it has conducted and trademark registrations which it has secured for the Programs or Trademarks in any country in the Territory. Similarly, Developer agrees to provide Publisher with information concerning the current status of any copyright registrations which it has filed or copyright registrations which it has secured for the Programs. Developer shall advise Publisher if it has any reason to believe that the Programs or Trademarks are not available for use in any country in the Territory.

"Software Developer and Publishing Agreement," courtesy of Thomas J. Cervantez and the law firm of Pillsbury, Madison & Sutro, LLP © 1996

Appendix

8.6 <u>Sponsorships</u>. Developer shall have the right to include in the Credit Screen for the Program the names of various sponsors who have provided services or materials to Developer in exchange for an acknowledgment. No paid advertisements shall be included in the Program without the mutual agreement of the parties. The credit shall take the form of the statement "Special Thanks to" or similar language. The inclusion, locations of the placement, and form of the acknowledgment shall be subject to Publisher' prior written approval, which approval shall not be unreasonably withheld. Unless Publisher accepts or rejects the acknowledgment within five (5) days of its receipt, the proposed acknowledgment shall be deemed accepted.

Section 9

Confidentiality

9.1 <u>Confidential Information</u>. The terms of this Agreement, the Source Materials and any other source code, computer program listings, techniques, algorithms and processes and technical and marketing plans or other sensitive business information, including all materials containing said information, which are supplied by the Publisher to Developer or developed by Developer in the course of developing the Program shall be deemed confidential information ("Confidential Information").

9.2 <u>Restrictions on Use</u>. The recipient of the Confidential Information ("Recipient") agrees that except as authorized in writing by the party disclosing the Confidential Information ("Disclosing Party"): (i) Recipient will preserve and protect the confidentiality of all Confidential Information; (ii) Recipient will not disclose to any third party, the existence, source, content or substance of the Confidential Information or make copies of Confidential Information; (iii) Recipient will not deliver Confidential Information to any third party, or permit the Confidential Information to be removed from Recipient's premises; (iv) Recipient will not use Confidential Information in any way other than to develop the Program as provided in this Agreement; (v) Recipient will not disclose, use or copy any third party information or materials received in confidence by developer for purposes of work performed under this Agreement; and (vi) Recipient shall require that each of its employees who work on or have access to the materials which are the subject of this Agreement sign a suitable confidentiality and work-for-hire agreement and be advised of the confidentiality and other applicable provisions of this Agreement.

9.3 <u>Limitations</u>. Information shall not be considered to be Confidential Information if it (i) is already or otherwise becomes publicly known through no act of Recipient; (ii) is lawfully received from third parties subject to no restriction

-10-

"Software Developer and Publishing Agreement," courtesy of Thomas J. Cervantez and the law firm of Pillsbury, Madison & Sutro, LLP © 1996

of confidentiality; (iii) can be shown by Recipient to have been independently developed by it; (iv) is authorized in writing by the Disclosing Party to be disclosed, copied or used; or (v) is required to be disclosed in the context of an administrative or judicial proceeding.

9.4 <u>Return of Source Materials</u>. Upon Publisher' acceptance of the Final Copy of the Program, Developer shall provide Publisher with one complete copy of the Source Materials, as well as any other materials provided to Developer, or created by Developer under this Agreement. Not later than seven (7) days after the termination of this Agreement for any reason, or if sooner requested by Publisher, Developer will return to Publisher all originals and copies of any Confidential Information provided by Publisher to Developer as well as any Source Materials for which Developer has received compensation under this Agreement.

9.5 <u>Third Party Confidential Information</u>. Developer acknowledges that its association with Publisher is in no way conditioned or based upon its knowledge or disclosure to Publisher of confidential information or trade secrets of others, and agrees that Developer will not disclose to Publisher or induce Publisher to use any confidential information or trade secrets belonging to any third party. Developer agrees to advise Publisher of any agreements or other circumstances which may give rise to such a confidential relationship.

Section 10

<u>Warranties Covenants and Indemnification</u>

10.1 <u>Warranties and Covenants of Developer</u>. Developer represents, warrants and covenants to Publisher the following:

(a) Developer has the full power to enter into this Agreement and perform the services provided for herein, and that such ability is not limited or restricted by any agreements or understandings between Developer and other persons or companies;

(b) Any information or materials developed for, or any advice provided to Publisher, shall not rely or in any way be based upon confidential or proprietary information or trade secrets obtained or derived by Developer from sources other than Publisher unless Developer has received specific authorization in writing to use such proprietary information or trade secrets;

(c) The code and other materials and information added by Developer, and the modifications made by Developer to the program materials provided by Publisher do not infringe upon or misappropriate, any copyright, patent right, trade secret or other proprietary rights of any third party.

-11-

"Software Developer and Publishing Agreement," courtesy of Thomas J. Cervantez and the law firm of Pillsbury, Madison & Sutro, LLP © 1996

Appendix

10.2 <u>Developer's Indemnity</u>. Developer agrees to indemnify, hold harmless and defend Publisher from all claims, defense costs (including reasonable attorneys' fees), judgments and other expenses arising out of or an account of such claims, including without limitation claims of:

(a) alleged infringement or violation of any trademark, copyright, trade secret, patent or other proprietary right with respect to the Program or Collateral Materials;

(b) any use of confidential or proprietary information or trade secrets Developer have obtained from sources other than Publisher;

(c) the breach of any covenant or warranty set forth in Section 10.1 above.

10.3 <u>Conditions to Indemnity</u>. Developer's obligation to indemnify is conditioned on Publisher' notifying Developer promptly of any claim as to which indemnification will be sought and providing Developer reasonable cooperation in the defense and settlement thereof.

10.4 <u>Publisher' Indemnification</u>. Publisher agrees to indemnify, hold harmless and defend Developer from all claims, defense costs (including reasonable attorneys' fees), judgments and other expenses arising out of the breach of the following Covenants and Warranties:

(a) Publisher possesses full power and authority to enter into this Agreement and to fulfill its obligations hereunder.

(b) The performance of the terms of this Agreement and of Publisher' obligations hereunder shall not breach any separate agreement by which Publisher is bound.

10.5 <u>Conditions to Indemnity</u>. Publisher' obligation to indemnify is conditioned on Developer's notifying Publisher promptly of any claim as to which indemnification will be sought and providing Publisher reasonable cooperation in the defense and settlement thereof.

Section 11

Termination

11.1 <u>Termination</u>. In the event of a termination of this Agreement by Publisher pursuant to Paragraph 3.2 hereof, Publisher will have no further obligations or liabilities under this Agreement. Publisher will have the right, in addition to all of its other rights, to require Developer to deliver to Publisher all of Developer's work in progress, including one copy thereof, as well as any other materials provided to Developer, or created by Developer under this Agreement.

"Software Developer and Publishing Agreement," courtesy of Thomas J. Cervantez and the law firm of Pillsbury, Madison & Sutro, LLP © 1996

Payment of any Development Schedule milestones under Schedule "B" which have been met shall be deemed payment in full for all obligations of Publisher under this Agreement, including full payment for the licenses granted herein for all source code, object code, documentation, notes, graphics and all other materials and work relating to the portion of the Program which has been completed as of the time of termination. Alternatively, in Publisher sole discretion, Publisher may elect to return all materials developed under this Agreement by Developer and all rights granted to Developer under this Agreement upon Developer's repayment to Publisher of all payments made by Publisher to Developer under this Agreement.

11.2 <u>Termination by Developer</u>. Developer shall have the right to terminate this Agreement because of a material breach by Publisher which remains uncured for thirty (30) days after Publisher' receipt of written notice of the nature of breach. If Developer terminates this Agreement because of an uncured material breach by Publisher, all licenses granted to Publisher shall terminate and revert to Developer. If Developer is able to publish, license, or otherwise commercially exploit or transfer its rights in the Program, Developer shall repay to Publisher all development fees (advances) previously paid to Developer under this Agreement at the rate of fifty cents ($.50) for each dollar ($1.00) which Developer receives from such disposition until all of the monies previously paid by Publisher to Developer are repaid.

Section 12

<u>Governing Law and Dispute Resolution</u>

12.1 <u>Arbitration</u>. The parties agree to submit any dispute arising out of or in connection with this Agreement to binding arbitration in San Francisco, California before the American Arbitration Association pursuant to the provisions of this Section 12.1, and, to the extent not inconsistent with this Section 12.1, the rules of the American Arbitration Association. The parties agree that such arbitration will be in lieu of either party's rights to assert any claim, demand or suit in any court action, (provided that either party may elect either binding arbitration or a court action with respect to a breach by the other party of such party's proprietary rights, including without limitation any trade secrets, copyrights or trademarks). Any arbitration under this Agreement shall be before one arbitrator. Discovery shall be allowed in such arbitration pursuant to the Federal Rules of Civil Procedure, except that no more than three (3) depositions and one set each of interrogatories and requests for admissions and documents shall be allowed. Any arbitration shall be final and binding and the arbitrator's order will be enforceable in any court of competent jurisdiction. The arbitrator will be chosen within 30 days of the submission of any issue to arbitration, the discovery (if any) shall be completed within 60 days thereafter, the hearing

"Software Developer and Publishing Agreement," courtesy of Thomas J. Cervantez and the law firm of Pillsbury, Madison & Sutro, LLP © 1996

Appendix

shall occur within 30 days thereafter and the arbitrator must render its decision, in writing, within 30 days after the end of such hearing.

12.2 <u>Governing Law</u>. The validity, construction, and performance of this Agreement shall be governed by the laws of the state of California without regard to principles of conflicts of law.

Section 13

Legal Proceedings

13.1 Publisher agrees to promptly notify Developer of any infringement of Developer's proprietary rights that comes to Publisher' attention and to co-operate with Developer in any action brought by Developer to investigate or remedy any such infringement of these rights. Publisher may at its own cost take all such steps as may be necessary to protect the original copyright and all other intellectual property rights existing in the Program, Licensed Products and Collateral Materials. Any recovery shall be shared equally after deducting costs and expenses incurred by both parties.

Section 14

Miscellaneous Provisions

14.1 <u>Notices</u>. For purposes of all notices and other communications required or permitted to be given hereunder, the addresses of the parties hereto shall be as indicated below. All notices shall be in writing and shall be deemed to have been duly given if sent by facsimile, the receipt of which is confirmed by return facsimile, or sent by first class registered or certified mail or equivalent, return receipt requested, addressed to the Parties at their addresses set forth below:

If to Developer: Multimedia Developer, Inc.
                     _____
                     Attention: President

If to Publisher: Publisher Inc.
                     _____
                     Attention: VP Legal

14.2 <u>Designated Person to Send and Receive Material</u>. The Parties agree that all materials exchanged between the parties for formal approval shall be communicated between single designated persons, or a single alternate designated person for each Party. Neither Party shall have any obligation to consider for approval or respond to materials submitted other than through the Designated Persons. Each Party shall have the right

-14-

"Software Developer and Publishing Agreement," courtesy of Thomas J. Cervantez and the law firm of Pillsbury, Madison & Sutro, LLP © 1996

to change its Designated Persons from time to time and to so notify the other.

14.3 <u>Entire Agreement</u>. This Agreement, including the attached Schedules which are incorporated herein by reference as though fully set out, contains the entire understanding and agreement of the Parties with respect to the subject matter contained herein, supersedes all prior oral or written understandings and agreements relating thereto except as expressly otherwise provided, and may not be altered, modified or waived in whole or in part, except in writing, signed by duly authorized representatives of the Parties.

14.4 <u>Force Majeure</u>. Neither Party shall be held responsible for damages caused by any delay or default due to any contingency beyond its control preventing or interfering with performance hereunder.

14.5 <u>Severability</u>. If any provision of this Agreement shall be held by a court of competent jurisdiction to be contrary to any law, the remaining provisions shall remain in full force and effect as if said provision never existed.

14.6 <u>Contract Assignment</u>. This Agreement is personal to Developer. Developer may not sell, transfer, sublicense, hypothecate or assign its rights and duties under this Agreement without the written consent of Publisher. No rights hereunder shall devolve by operation of law or otherwise upon any receiver, liquidator, trustee, or other party. This Agreement shall inure to the benefit of Publisher, its successors and assigns.

14.7 <u>Waiver and Amendments</u>. No waiver, amendment, or modification of any provision of this Agreement shall be effective unless consented to by both Parties in writing. No failure or delay by either Party in exercising any rights, power, or remedy under this Agreement shall operate as a waiver of any such right, power, or remedy.

14.8 <u>Agency</u>. The Parties are separate and independent legal entities. Developer is performing services for Publisher as an independent contractor. Nothing contained in this Agreement shall be deemed to constitute either Developer or Publisher an agent, representative, partner, joint venturer or employee of the other party for any purpose. Neither Party has the authority to bind the other or to incur any liability on behalf of the other, nor to direct the employees of the other.

14.9 <u>Titles and Headings</u>. The titles and headings of each section are intended for convenience only and shall not be used in construing or interpreting the meaning of any particular clause or section.

-15-

"Software Developer and Publishing Agreement," courtesy of Thomas J. Cervantez and the law firm of Pillsbury, Madison & Sutro, LLP © 1996

Appendix

14.10 <u>Contract Interpretation</u>. Ambiguities, inconsistencies, or conflicts in this Agreement shall not be strictly construed against the drafter of the language but will be resolved by applying the most reasonable interpretation under the circumstances, giving full consideration to the Parties' intentions at the time this Agreement is entered into.

14.11 <u>No Third Party Rights</u>. This Agreement is not for the benefit of any third party, and shall not be considered to grant any right or remedy to any third party whether or not referred to in this Agreement.

14.12 <u>Singular and Plural Terms</u>. Where the context of this Agreement requires, singular terms shall be considered plural, and plural terms shall be considered singular.

14.13 <u>Limitation on Liability; Remedies</u>. Except as provided in Section 10 above, neither party shall be liable to the other party for any incidental, consequential, special, or punitive damages of any kind or nature, including, without limitation, the breach of this Agreement or any termination of this Agreement, whether such liability is asserted on the basis of contract, tort (including negligence or strict liability), or otherwise, even if either party has warned or been warned of the possibility of any such loss or damage.

IN WITNESS WHEREOF, this Agreement is executed as of the Effective Date set forth above.

MULTIMEDIA DEVELOPER, INC.   THE PUBLISHER, INC.

By: _____   By: _____
    (printed name)   (printed name)

Its: _____   Its: _____

"Software Developer and Publishing Agreement," courtesy of Thomas J. Cervantez and the law firm of Pillsbury, Madison & Sutro, LLP © 1996

SCHEDULE A
SPECIFICATIONS

In addition to the preliminary Specifications attached, the Program shall include no less than forty-five (45) minutes of synchronized sound motion video. The full Specifications, which shall be separately delivered to Publisher, are hereby incorporated by this reference.

"Software Developer and Publishing Agreement," courtesy of Thomas J. Cervantez and the law firm of Pillsbury, Madison & Sutro, LLP © 1996

Appendix

SCHEDULE B
DEVELOPMENT AND PAYMENT SCHEDULE
Page 1 of 2

EXTREMES--WINDOWS VERSION

Item		Due Date	Payment Upon Acceptance
1	Execution of formal agreement		
2	Delivery of final Specifications and substantial completion of Story Boards		
3	Alpha Copy--WINDOWS		
4	Beta Copy--WINDOWS		
5	Final Copy--WINDOWS		
6	The earlier of Publisher' shipment of finished Program or sixty (60) after Publisher' acceptance of the Final Copy.		
		TOTAL	

All development fee shall be payable upon acceptance of the milestone by Publisher and shall be fully recoupable against any license fees payable under this Agreement. All development fees shall be non-refundable once the Deliverable has been accepted by Publisher.

-18-

"Software Developer and Publishing Agreement," courtesy of Thomas J. Cervantez and the law firm of Pillsbury, Madison & Sutro, LLP © 1996

Software Development and Publishing Agreement

SCHEDULE B
DEVELOPMENT AND PAYMENT SCHEDULE
Page 2 of 2

EXTREMES -- MACINTOSH VERSION

Item		Due Date	Payment Upon Acceptance
1	Execution of formal agreement		
2	Delivery of final Specification and substantial completion of Story Boards		
3	Alpha Copy--MAC		
4	Beta Copy--MAC		
5	Final Copy--MAC		
6	The earlier of Publisher' shipment of finished Program or sixty (60) after Publisher' acceptance of the Final Copy.		
		TOTAL	

All development fee shall be payable upon acceptance of the milestone by Publisher and shall be fully recoupable against any license fees payable under this Agreement. All development fees shall be non-refundable once the Deliverable has been accepted by Publisher.

-19-

"Software Developer and Publishing Agreement," courtesy of Thomas J. Cervantez and the law firm of Pillsbury, Madison & Sutro, LLP © 1996

Appendix

SCHEDULE C
LICENSE FEES

Publisher shall pay Developer ___ % of Publisher' Net Receipts from the sale or license of the Licensed Products for which Developer has provided an acceptable Final Copy.

"Software Developer and Publishing Agreement," courtesy of Thomas J. Cervantez and the law firm of Pillsbury, Madison & Sutro, LLP © 1996

SCHEDULE D
CONVERSIONS

Publisher has the exclusive right to develop and publish the Program on all delivery platforms subject to the continuing royalty obligation set forth in this Agreement and Developer's right of first refusal to prepare the following Conversions on the following terms:

1. <u>VIS or Sony MMCD</u>. Developer agrees that upon request by Publisher, Developer will grant Publisher the exclusive rights for the VIS or Sony MMCD version in one of three ways, at the discretion of Developer:

(a) perform the conversion itself, paying Developer an additional royalty advance of _____ per title per platform for its redesign and content preparation work; or,

(b) pay Developer a royalty advance of _____ per title per platform, in consideration for its content conversion;

(c) pay Developer a royalty advance of _____ per title per platform, in consideration of which Developer shall be responsible for all programming in addition to platform redesign, content preparation and conversion.

Developer may not select option (b) or (c) if it cannot finish and deliver the completed work to Publisher in a reasonable period of time to accommodate Publisher' release schedule.

2. <u>3DO, Nintendo CD or Sega CD formats</u>. If Publisher elects to publish any of the titles on any one of these platforms, Developer will grant Publisher the exclusive rights for the 3DO, Nintendo CD or Sega CD version in one of three ways, at the discretion of Developer:

(a) perform the conversion itself, paying Developer an additional royalty advance of _____ per title per platform for its redesign and content preparation work; or

(b) pay Developer a royalty advance of _____ per title per platform, in consideration for its content conversion;

(c) pay Developer a royalty advance of _____ per title per platform, in consideration of which Developer shall be responsible for all programming in addition to platform redesign, content preparation and conversion.

"Software Developer and Publishing Agreement," courtesy of Thomas J. Cervantez and the law firm of Pillsbury, Madison & Sutro, LLP © 1996

Appendix

If Publisher elects to produce the Program on a second or third of these three platforms (3DO, Nintendo CD or Sega CD), Developer agrees to perform the additional selected 1 of 3 levels of work for a reduced royalty advance, to be determined by both parties in a manner consistent with the pricing of previous versions.

Developer may not select option (b) or (c) if it cannot finish and deliver the completed work to Publisher in a reasonable period of time to accommodate Publisher' release schedule.

The conversion of the Program for any other platform not set forth herein, and the preparation of derivative works (other than translations), including but not limited to sequels, shall be negotiated in good faith on a case by case basis at terms no less favorable to Publisher than the terms set forth in this Agreement. Royalty obligations for all derivative works, including but not limited to sequels and conversions shall be as set forth in Schedule "C". Publisher shall have the right to create foreign language translations of the Program without providing Developer with the right of first refusal to prepare such translations, however, Developer shall have the right to approve any foreign language translation versions prior to distribution, said approval not to be unreasonably withheld and said approval shall be limited to any errors or omissions in content.

-22-

"Software Developer and Publishing Agreement," courtesy of Thomas J. Cervantez and the law firm of Pillsbury, Madison & Sutro, LLP © 1996

Software Development and Publishing Agreement

SCHEDULE E
COST OF GOODS

$_____ for retail version of the Licensed Product.
$_____ for the OEM version of the Licensed Product.

"Software Developer and Publishing Agreement," courtesy of Thomas J. Cervantez and the law firm of Pillsbury, Madison & Sutro, LLP © 1996

Appendix

INTELLECTUAL PROPERTY RIGHTS AFFECTING MULTIMEDIA PROJECTS

Allen S. Melser
Becky L. Troutman
Popham, Haik, Schnobrich & Kaufman, Ltd.
Washington, D.C. 20005
(202) 824-8013
melsera@popham.com
troutmanb@popham.com

Synopsis

Creation of a multimedia project involves several aspects of intellectual property law, including copyright, trademark, patent and trade secret law. A multimedia project author must be aware of the intellectual property issues associated with multimedia to avoid creating disputes with others and to protect intellectual property rights in the multimedia project.

About the Authors

Allen S. Melser is an intellectual property attorney whose practice concentrates on procuring, maintaining and enforcing domestic and foreign patent rights. He heads Popham Haik's intellectual property and technology law group. Becky L. Troutman is an associate at Popham Haik's D.C. office.

© 1995 Allen S. Melser and Becky L. Troutman

"Intellectual Property Rights Affecting Multimedia Projects," courtesy of Allen S. Melser and Becky L. Troutman of the law firm— Popham, Haik, Schnobrich & Kaufman © 1996

Appendix

I. Introduction[1]

It is critical for a multimedia project author to understand the intellectual property issues involved in multimedia development to avoid creating intellectual property disputes with owners of software or content used in the project. A typical multimedia project combines content, such as text, visual images and sound, and software that enables a user to manipulate the content. The content and software are created either by the author of the project or another. Copyright, trademark, patent and trade secret law affect creation and protection of both the content and software aspects of multimedia projects. Other areas of the law, such as right of publicity law, are also important. Avoiding intellectual property disputes requires a thorough analysis of all aspects of the project to identify any software and content that may be a protected intellectual property right of another. Once the owners of protected aspects of the project are identified, the author must secure permission from each owner of each protected aspect to use it in the project.

---

[1] This article is provided with the understanding that it is not intended to provide legal services and that the authors by the article are not rendering legal services. Because each situation is unique, if you have a legal problem, you should seek the advice of experienced counsel.

"Intellectual Property Rights Affecting Multimedia Projects," courtesy of Allen S. Melser and Becky L. Troutman of the law firm— Popham, Haik, Schnobrich & Kaufman © 1996

The author has certain intellectual property rights in the completed multimedia project, any software or content created by the author and any trademarks or service marks used in connection with the project. Protection for these rights should be sought and actively enforced to ensure that they do not become narrowed in scope or lost altogether due to poor policing efforts. This article provides guidelines for identifying software and content that require permission for use in a multimedia project and for securing intellectual property rights in the project.

II. Overview: Laws Relating To Multimedia Projects

An author may use software, images, text or sound created by another or celebrity images in a multimedia project. The author must identify the proper owner or owners of any rights to the software, images, text, sound or celebrity images and secure permission from each owner to use the material. Such material is normally protected by copyright, trademark, patent or trade secret law, the right of publicity, or a combination of these rights.

"Intellectual Property Rights Affecting Multimedia Projects," courtesy of Allen S. Melser and Becky L. Troutman of the law firm— Popham, Haik, Schnobrich & Kaufman © 1996

Appendix

A. Copyright Law

Copyright law protects original works of authorship fixed in any tangible medium of expression.[2] The expression of an idea, not the idea itself, is protected. Both software and content used in multimedia projects are protected by copyright. Examples of such content include text, databases, characters, musical works, sound recordings, photographs, still images, motion pictures and other audiovisual works. In addition, the completed multimedia project and any original software or content created by the project author are protected by copyright.

A work made for hire is either (1) a work prepared by an employee within the scope of his or her employment or (2) a work "specially ordered or commissioned for use as a contribution to a collective work, as a part of a motion picture or other audiovisual work, as a translation, as a supplementary work, as a compilation, as an instructional text, as a test, as answer material for

---

[2] 17 U.S.C.A. § 102 (West Supp. 1995). Works of authorship include literary works; musical works including accompanying words; dramatic works including accompanying music; pantomimes and choreographic works; pictorial, graphic and sculptural works; motion pictures and other audiovisual works; sound recordings; and architectural works.

"Intellectual Property Rights Affecting Multimedia Projects," courtesy of Allen S. Melser and Becky L. Troutman of the law firm— Popham, Haik, Schnobrich & Kaufman © 1996

a test, or as an atlas, if the parties expressly agree in a written instrument signed by them that the work shall be considered a work made for hire."[3]

Copyright protection exists automatically as soon as a work is fixed in tangible form. For works created on or after January 1, 1978, copyright endures for a term of the life of the author plus 50 years after the author's death.[4] Works made for hire have a term of seventy-five years from the year of first publication, or one hundred years from the year of creation, whichever expires first.[5] The author does not have to register the copyright with the U.S. Copyright Office to enjoy protection, and no copyright notice is required for works published after March 1, 1989. However, it is preferable to use a proper copyright notice to inform the public that the work is protected by copyright, to identify the copyright owner, and to show the year of first publication.[6] If the

---

[3] 17 U.S.C.A. § 101 (West Supp. 1995).

[4] 17 U.S.C.A. § 302(a) (West Supp. 1995). For joint works, the copyright term is the life of the last surviving author and fifty years after the last surviving author's death. 35 U.S.C.A. § 302(b) (West Supp. 1995).

[5] 17 U.S.C.A. § 302(c) (West Supp. 1995).

[6] Copyright notice should contain (1) the symbol ©, the word "copyright", or the abbreviation "Copr."; (2) the year of first publication of the work; and (3) the name of the owner of copyright in the work, or an abbreviation by which the name can be

"Intellectual Property Rights Affecting Multimedia Projects," courtesy of Allen S. Melser and Becky L. Troutman of the law firm— Popham, Haik, Schnobrich & Kaufman © 1996

Appendix

work is infringed and it carries a proper notice, a court will not allow a defendant to claim that the infringement was "innocent" (that the infringer did not realize the work was protected). In addition, copyright must be registered to sue infringers,[7] and registration prior to the infringing act is necessary to recover certain statutory damages and attorneys fees.[8]

A work may have more than one copyright associated with it and more than one copyright owner. For example, if Elvis Costello writes the lyrics to a song, David Byrne writes the music, and both Elvis and David make a sound recording of the song, there are three different copyrights and two different owners at issue. Elvis owns copyright in the lyrics, David owns copyright in the music, and Elvis and David are co-owners of the copyright in the sound recording of the song.

---

recognized. For example, "© 1995 Jane Doe" is a proper copyright notice.

[7] 17 U.S.C.A. § 411 (West Supp. 1995).

[8] 17 U.S.C.A. § 412 (West Supp. 1995).

"Intellectual Property Rights Affecting Multimedia Projects," courtesy of Allen S. Melser and Becky L. Troutman of the law firm— Popham, Haik, Schnobrich & Kaufman © 1996

A copyright owner has the exclusive right to do and authorize any of the following:

(1) reproduce the copyrighted work in copies or phonorecords;[9]

(2) prepare derivative works based upon the copyrighted work;

(3) distribute copies or phonorecords of the copyrighted work to the public by sale or other transfer of ownership, or by rental, lease or lending;

(4) publicly perform copyrighted literary, musical, dramatic and choreographic works, pantomimes, motion pictures and other audiovisual works; and

(5) publicly display literary, musical, dramatic and choreographic works, pantomimes, and pictorial, graphic or sculptural works, including individual images of a motion picture or other audiovisual work.[10]

In general, a person who exercises one of the exclusive rights of a copyright owner without the owner's permission infringes the copyright. Infringing acts include copying and modifying content and publicly distributing, performing or displaying a work.

---

[9] The term "phonorecords" is defined broadly in the copyright statute to include "material objects in which sounds, other than those accompanying a motion picture or other audiovisual work, are fixed by any method now known or later developed, and from which the sounds can be perceived, reproduced, or otherwise communicated, either directly or with the aid of a machine or device. The term 'phonorecords' includes the material object in which the sounds are first fixed." 17 U.S.C.A. § 101 (West Supp. 1995).

[10] 17 U.S.C.A. § 106 (West Supp. 1995).

"Intellectual Property Rights Affecting Multimedia Projects," courtesy of Allen S. Melser and Becky L. Troutman of the law firm— Popham, Haik, Schnobrich & Kaufman © 1996

Appendix

B. Trademark Law

A trademark is a word, symbol or slogan used in connection with a product to identify the source of the product and distinguish it from other products. "ADOBE" and "COREL" are well-known trademarks in graphics design. Similarly, a service mark is a word or symbol used in connection with a service to identify the source of the service and distinguish it from others. Examples of service marks include "MCDONALD'S" and "AMTRAK."

Trademark protection is based on use of a mark in commerce. A federally registered mark is protected under federal trademark law.[11] The trademark registration owner can prevent others from using any mark that is so similar to the registered mark as to cause a likelihood of consumer confusion as to the source or sponsorship of the goods or services of the parties.[12] A court will consider several factors in determining whether there is a likelihood of confusion, including:

(1) Priority of use;

(2) Strength of the plaintiff's mark;

---

[11] Even if a mark is not federally registered, it is protected under common law. In addition, a trademark owner may obtain a state trademark registration and be protected under state trademark law.

[12] 15 U.S.C.A. § 1114 (West Supp. 1995).

"Intellectual Property Rights Affecting Multimedia Projects," courtesy of Allen S. Melser and Becky L. Troutman of the law firm— Popham, Haik, Schnobrich & Kaufman © 1996

(3) Similarity of the parties' marks, goods, channels of trade, channels of advertising and consumers; and

(4) Evidence of actual confusion.

C. Patent Law

Patent law protects ideas. Specifically, patent law protects any process, machine, manufacture, composition of matter, or any improvement thereof that is new, useful and nonobvious.[13] For example, it is possible to obtain a patent covering a process including a series of operative steps performed by a software program incorporated into a multimedia project if the legal requirements of novelty, utility and nonobviousness are met.

A patent owner has the right to exclude others from making, using or selling the patented invention in the United States. The patent owner can also prevent others from importing infringing products into the United States. Patents granted on applications filed on or after June 8, 1995, have a term of 20 years from the application filing date.[14]

---

[13] 35 U.S.C.A. §§ 101-103 (West Supp. 1995).

[14] Patents granted on applications filed before June 8, 1995 have a term of 17 years from the patent issue date.

"Intellectual Property Rights Affecting Multimedia Projects," courtesy of Allen S. Melser and Becky L. Troutman of the law firm— Popham, Haik, Schnobrich & Kaufman © 1996

Appendix

Where a multimedia project uses software written by a third party, the project author should (1) obtain permission from the owner of the copyright in the software and (2) investigate whether the software is patented. If so, the author will need permission to use both the patented and the copyrighted aspects of the program.

D. Trade Secret Law

Most states have a trade secret law that protects any formula, pattern, program process, plan, device, tool, mechanism, compound or compilation of information that is (1) kept secret and (2) gives the trade secret owner an advantage over its competitors. A classic example of a trade secret is the formula for Coca-Cola. Trade secret protection can last indefinitely if secrecy is preserved. However, trade secret protection does not prevent others from discovering the trade secret by legitimate means, such as independent research. Typically, multimedia technology, such as data processing techniques, and software are protected under trade secret law if proper steps are taken to keep the technology and software secret.

"Intellectual Property Rights Affecting Multimedia Projects," courtesy of Allen S. Melser and Becky L. Troutman of the law firm— Popham, Haik, Schnobrich & Kaufman © 1996

E. Right Of Publicity

The "right of publicity" is a public celebrity's right to control use of his or her personality, name and likeness for profit. For example, John Travolta can object to unauthorized use of his image in a multimedia project based on his right of publicity in his personality, name and likeness. The right of publicity may survive an individual's death if the individual built up commercial value in his or her personality and exploited it during his or her lifetime.

III. Creating A Multimedia Work

The following hypothetical multimedia project raises several intellectual property issues.

> Allen plans to create a multimedia project called "ALLEN'S WORLD." ALLEN'S WORLD includes a software program, "MIXIT," owned by Cybervinyl Inc. that is used in conjunction with several programs written by Allen to allow users to manipulate various content choices and create their own custom music videos.
>
> Allen would like to either use Paul Simon's recording of the song "Graceland" or hire use a version of "Graceland" recorded by James Brown as the theme song for ALLEN'S WORLD. Flashing images of Elvis Presley will appear on the opening screen for ALLEN'S WORLD during James' rendition of "Graceland."

"Intellectual Property Rights Affecting Multimedia Projects," courtesy of Allen S. Melser and Becky L. Troutman of the law firm— Popham, Haik, Schnobrich & Kaufman © 1996

Appendix

The user will then be given a choice of songs upon which to base the custom video. Allen would like the user to be able to select either REM's "It's the End of the World As We Know It," The Rolling Stones' "Start Me Up," or one of several pieces written and recorded by Yanni for the ALLEN'S WORLD project.

Once the user has selected a song, a content menu of various images and text appears. The user selects and manipulates the images and text to create the video. The content menu includes clips from the motion pictures "Pulp Fiction" and "Dr. Strangelove."

In addition, the user can choose textual passages from Richard Lattimore's translation of Homer's The Iliad, several of Maya Angelou's poems and text written for ALLEN'S WORLD by John Grisham.

When the user logs off of ALLEN'S WORLD, an image of Bugs Bunny in a top hat and tails dances across the final screen and says "That's All Folks!"[15]

As you can see, Allen is going to be busy obtaining permission to use the various content elements for ALLEN'S WORLD. First, he will need permission from Cybervinyl Inc. to use its Mixit program. Also, he should investigate whether use of the MIXIT program or use of his own programs in conjunction with MIXIT will present any patent infringement problems.

---

[15] For Warner Bros. purists, the authors recognize that Porky Pig normally stutters the slogan "That's All Folks!" However, for purposes of this hypothetical, Bugs Bunny works better than Porky in top hat and tails.

12

"Intellectual Property Rights Affecting Multimedia Projects," courtesy of Allen S. Melser and Becky L. Troutman of the law firm— Popham, Haik, Schnobrich & Kaufman © 1996

Intellectual Property Rights

To use Paul Simon's recording of "Graceland," Allen will need permission from both Paul Simon, the copyright owner of the lyrics, and The Everly Brothers, who jointly own the copyright in the "Graceland" sound recording with Paul Simon. If The Everly Brothers have assigned their copyright rights in the "Graceland" sound recording to Paul Simon, then Allen will only need permission from Paul.

To use James Brown's "Graceland" recording, Allen will need permission from Paul Simon, the copyright owner of the song lyrics and music. Allen will also need permission from James Brown, who will own the copyright in his sound recording of "Graceland." Similarly, Allen will need permission from REM and The Rolling Stones to use their sound recordings of "It's the End of the World As We Know It" and "Start Me Up."

Allen's contract with Yanni for the lyrics and music Yanni writes and records for ALLEN'S WORLD should qualify as a works made for hire, because Allen has hired Yanni to create the works for use as a contribution to a collective work as part of an audiovisual work. The contract must specifically state that Yanni's pieces are works made for hire, and should also provide for

"Intellectual Property Rights Affecting Multimedia Projects," courtesy of Allen S. Melser and Becky L. Troutman of the law firm— Popham, Haik, Schnobrich & Kaufman © 1996

Appendix

assignment of Yanni's copyright rights to Allen. If no agreement is executed, Yanni will be an independent contractor who owns the copyright to the song lyrics, music and sound recordings, and Allen will need Yanni's permission to use the sound recordings.

Use of the flashing Elvis image creates a right of publicity problem. Elvis' right of publicity has survived, because he built up commercial value in his personality and exploited it during his lifetime. Therefore, Allen will need permission from Elvis' estate to use the flashing Elvis image at the beginning of ALLEN'S WORLD. Allen will also need to determine the copyright owners of the clips from "Pulp Fiction" and "Dr. Strangelove" and obtain permission from the owners to use the clips.

Although Homer's <u>The Iliad</u> is in the public domain, Richard Lattimore owns the copyright in his particular translation of <u>The Iliad</u>. Therefore, Allen will have to obtain permission from Richard Lattimore to use excerpts from his translation, as well as permission from Maya Angelou to use excerpts from her poems. The text written by John Grisham for ALLEN'S WORLD is similar to the Yanni situation. Allen's contract with Mr. Grisham must specify that the

"Intellectual Property Rights Affecting Multimedia Projects," courtesy of Allen S. Melser and Becky L. Troutman of the law firm— Popham, Haik, Schnobrich & Kaufman © 1996

text is a work made for hire and provide for assignment of Mr. Grisham's copyright rights to Allen to ensure that Allen owns the copyright in the text. If no such agreement is in place, Mr. Grisham will own the copyright and Allen will need his permission to use the text.

Use of the Bugs Bunny image and the slogan "That's All Folks!" may create both copyright and trademark problems for Allen. He will need permission from the copyright owner of the Bugs Bunny character to use Bugs in ALLEN'S WORLD. Bugs Bunny may also be protected under trademark law. If so, Allen needs to determine whether the trademark and copyright owner are the same entity to ensure that he has obtained all of the necessary licenses to use the Bugs Bunny character. The slogan "That's All Folks!" also may be subject to trademark protection. If so, Allen will need a separate license to use the slogan.

IV. Maximizing Intellectual Property Protection For A Multimedia Project

A completed multimedia project is protected under a combination of copyright, trademark, patent and trade secret law. The overall project is protected by copyright law, as well as any software or content created by the

"Intellectual Property Rights Affecting Multimedia Projects," courtesy of Allen S. Melser and Becky L. Troutman of the law firm— Popham, Haik, Schnobrich & Kaufman © 1996

Appendix

author. For example, in the above hypothetical, the completed ALLEN'S WORLD project is copyrighted, as well as the software programs written by Allen for use in conjunction with Cybervinyl Inc.'s MIXIT program. Allen's programs may also be patentable if the steps or processes performed by the programs meet the statutory requirements of novelty, utility and nonobviousness. Otherwise, certain aspects of the programs, such as interval data processing techniques, are covered by trade secret if proper steps are taken to keep them secret.

Allen could have some trouble using and registering the mark "ALLEN'S WORLD" for his project. It is important to carefully select and register a unique trademark to identify a multimedia project in order to obtain the broadest scope of protection possible. Under U.S. law, a sliding scale of protection is afforded to marks having different levels of uniqueness. There are four levels: generic, descriptive, suggestive and arbitrary marks.

A generic mark is merely a common name for a type of product. Generic marks are not registrable. Examples of generic marks include "SAFARI" for

"Intellectual Property Rights Affecting Multimedia Projects," courtesy of Allen S. Melser and Becky L. Troutman of the law firm— Popham, Haik, Schnobrich & Kaufman © 1996

hats and clothing[16] and "FIRST NATIONAL BANK" for a bank.[17] "ESCALATOR" is an example of a mark that has become generic.

A descriptive mark directly indicates qualities or characteristics of a product or service to a consumer. Little or no thought process or imagination is required to determine what qualities or characteristics the mark designates. For example, "TASTY SALAD DRESSING" for salad dressing is merely descriptive, rather than generic.[17] "LA" for beer with low alcohol content[18] and "CUSTOM-BLENDED" for gasoline[19] have also been held to be merely descriptive. A descriptive mark cannot be registered unless it has acquired secondary meaning to consumers as designating a particular source of the goods designated by the mark. Therefore, it is normally difficult to obtain registration for descriptive marks.

---

[16] *Abercrombie & Fitch Co. v. Hunting World, Inc.*, 189 U.S.P.Q. 759, 766 (2d Cir. 1976).

[17] *First National Bank and Trust Co. of Columbia, Mo. v. First Nationwide Bank*, 15 U.S.P.Q.2d 1457, 1461 (W.D. Mo. 1990).

[17] *Henri's Food Prods. Inc. v. Tasty Snacks Inc.*, 2 U.S.P.Q.2d 1856, 1858 (7th Cir. 1987).

[18] *G. Heileman Brewing Co. v. Anheuser-Busch Inc.*, 10 U.S.P.Q.2d 1801, 1811 (7th Cir. 1989).

[19] *In re Sun Oil Co.*, 165 U.S.P.Q. 718, 719 (C.C.P.A. 1970).

"Intellectual Property Rights Affecting Multimedia Projects," courtesy of Allen S. Melser and Becky L. Troutman of the law firm— Popham, Haik, Schnobrich & Kaufman © 1996

Appendix

A suggestive mark requires thought or imagination to link the mark to the product it designates. Examples of marks held to be suggestive rather than descriptive include "RUFFLES" for ridged potato chips[20] and "360°" for shoes with pivotal cleats.[21] In general, suggestive marks are relatively easy to register.

Arbitrary marks, such as "KODAK," are typically coined terms that have nothing to do with the product they designate and are normally easily registered. Such marks are afforded the broadest scope of protection possible.

Under U.S. law, a personal name mark is normally considered merely descriptive unless and until it has acquired secondary meaning. Therefore, Allen is likely to have difficulty registering the mark "ALLEN'S WORLD." He may wish to select a more arbitrary mark that has a greater likelihood of being registerable and will be afforded a broader scope of protection by the courts.

The owners rights in the movie WAYNE'S WORLD or other third parties may object to use and registration of the ALLEN'S WORLD mark. For

---

[20] *Frito-Lay Inc. v. The Bachman Co.*, 14 U.S.P.Q.2d 1027, 1033-1034 (S.D.N.Y. 1989).

[21] *Tanel Copr. v. Reebok Int'l. Ltd.*, 16 U.S.P.Q.2d 2034, 2037 (D. Mass. 1990).

"Intellectual Property Rights Affecting Multimedia Projects," courtesy of Allen S. Melser and Becky L. Troutman of the law firm— Popham, Haik, Schnobrich & Kaufman © 1996

example, If the WAYNE'S WORLD people can establish that use of the ALLEN'S WORLD mark is likely to confuse the public as to the source or sponsorship of the ALLEN'S WORLD project, then they will be able to prevent Allen's use and registration of the mark. The WAYNE'S WORLD people could also assert a claim of trademark dilution against Allen by asserting that use of the ALLEN'S WORLD mark dilutes the distinctive quality of the WAYNE'S WORLD mark, regardless of whether any consumer confusion is likely.

V. Conclusion

Allen may be in big trouble if he proceeds with the ALLEN'S WORLD project without identifying the aspects of the project that require permission from copyright, trademark, patent and trade secret owners and obtaining permission from the owners. Once the project is completed, Allen should take appropriate steps to secure and maintain his rights in all protectable aspects of the completed work, including copyrightable and/or patentable software, copyrightable content, trademarks used in connection with the project and trade secrets.

"Intellectual Property Rights Affecting Multimedia Projects," courtesy of Allen S. Melser and Becky L. Troutman of the law firm— Popham, Haik, Schnobrich & Kaufman © 1996

Appendix

Affiliated Label Agreement

AFFILIATED LABEL AGREEMENT

THIS AFFILIATED LABEL AGREEMENT (this "Agreement") is entered into effective _____ __, 199_, between <u>PUBLISHER COMPANY</u> ("Publisher"), a California corporation with principal offices at _____, and <u>DEVELOPER COMPANY</u> ("Developer"), a California corporation with its principal place of business at _____.

W I T N E S S E T H:

WHEREAS, Developer desires to enter into an agreement with Publisher pursuant to which Developer shall grant Publisher rights to resell and distribute Developer's products (the "Products"), as defined below, to Publisher's customers in all the countries of the world (the "Territory"); and

WHEREAS, Publisher desires to purchase from Developer the Products for resale and distribution in the Territory;

NOW, THEREFORE, in consideration of the mutual covenants herein contained, the parties agree as follows:

1. <u>Grants</u>. During the term hereof, Developer grants to Publisher and its subsidiaries the exclusive first right of refusal to sell and distribute the Products to any Customer in the Territory. As used herein, the term "Products" shall mean all software programs developed and/or published by Developer for its own general distribution during the term of this Agreement on all computer-based, cartridge-based or multimedia platforms. Products currently available are specified in <u>Exhibit A</u>, "Current Products."

2. <u>Channels</u>. Developer has the right to sell to [describe applicable distribution channel].

3. <u>Price and Payment</u>.

3.1 The purchase price for the Products is f.o.b. Publisher's designated point of receipt, currently _____, which may be changed from time to time to a different designated point of receipt within the United States by written notice from Publisher. All risk of loss prior to receipt by Publisher of the Products shall be borne by Developer and thereafter shall be borne by Publisher. Publisher shall be responsible for all shipping costs beyond its designated point of receipt. Notwithstanding that risk of loss shall pass to Publisher upon delivery of the Products, legal and beneficial ownership shall remain vested in Developer until such time as Developer has received payment for such Products. Such payment shall not be construed to include the accounting reserve as defined in Section 3.7 below. Developer shall retain a purchase money security interest in all Products and their identifiable proceeds securing the payment of all obligations arising hereunder. It shall be clear, however, that Publisher shall be entitled to sell the Products in the ordinary course of business.

3.2 Payment for Products shall be due sixty (60) days after the later of (i) delivery at Publisher's designated point of receipt or (ii) the invoice date.

"Affiliated Label Agreement" courtesy of Thomas J. Cervantez of the law firm— Pillsbury, Madison & Sutro, LLP © 1996

Appendix

3.3 Developer and Publisher shall agree mutually on the expected retail price of all Products. For all Products with an expected retail price of $____, Publisher's purchase price shall be $____, unless a different price is mutually agreed between the parties and set forth in an amendment hereto.

3.4 In the event Publisher is offered certain special sales opportunities which require Publisher to sell Products at a discount from its distributor price, Publisher shall contact Developer and solicit its agreement to participate. Participation in such an opportunity shall require a different purchase price, to be agreed between the parties.

3.5 In the event that Publisher and Developer should mutually agree to lower the purchase price of any Product, Developer shall credit to Publisher the difference between the new purchase price to Publisher and the former purchase price, for all units of the affected Products that are in Publisher's inventory and the inventory of Publisher's customers to whom Publisher has provided price protection, provided that Publisher supplies reasonable proof of inventory levels within thirty (30) days of the agreement to lower the price.

3.6 Publisher may maintain an accounting reserve to protect Publisher from overpayment to Developer on each SKU of Products that are returned to Developer by Publisher.

> (i) Publisher may withhold from each payment an amount equal to _____ percent (____%) of such payment.
>
> (ii) Ninety (90) days from the date of each payment, all amounts withheld from that payment shall be refunded to Developer except that:
>
> (iii) For Products rightfully returned by Publisher to Developer, Publisher shall reduce any amounts due to be refunded to Developer in accordance with Section 3.7(ii) by an amount equal to the amount paid for such Products by Publisher.
>
> (iv) All payments shall be made in U.S. dollars by check to Developer at the address shown in the Preamble to this Agreement or such other address as Developer may advise from time to time.

3.7 Developer shall use all reasonable efforts to maintain a sufficient inventory level to provide delivery of an order of any Product up to _____ (_____) units within ten (10) working days of the placement of such order by Publisher. Publisher purchase orders shall specify for each SKU: (i) the Products ordered by title and Developer's stock number, (ii) the quantities ordered, (iii) the price per unit and in the aggregate, (iv) the requested ship date and (v) the aggregate purchase price for the order. For all orders, Publisher shall provide Developer with as much advance notice as is reasonably possible.

3.8 In the event of a partial shipment by Developer to Publisher, Publisher shall be required to pay only for the units actually received. The portion not shipped shall be deemed a separate order.

"Affiliated Label Agreement" courtesy of Thomas J. Cervantez of the law firm— Pillsbury, Madison & Sutro, LLP © 1996

Affiliated Label Agreement

3.9 Publisher shall allow 30 days to receive the initial order of a title and 20 days to receive any re-order. If the Product is not delivered during the time spans specified above, then Publisher may cancel the order.

4. Reporting and Audit.

4.1 Publisher shall provide to Developer, within thirty (30) days of the end of each calendar month, the following standard reports: (i) monthly sales of Products (showing unit and dollar sales by SKU); and (ii) monthly returns (showing unit and dollar values by SKU). In addition, Publisher shall provide details of all cooperative advertising activities which may have been undertaken by Publisher during the reporting period. Publisher shall also share with Developer the regular sales information which it receives from distributors and retailers regarding the Products.

4.2 In conjunction with this Agreement, Publisher shall keep and maintain full and accurate books and records relating to the sale of the Products during the term of the Agreement and for two (2) years thereafter.

4.3 Developer shall have the right, not more than once per year during the term and for one year following its termination, to have an independent certified public accountant approved by Publisher inspect those business records of Publisher which relate to the sale of the Products for the purpose of verifying the accuracy of the information provided by Publisher to Developer hereunder, provided that Developer gives thirty (30) days written notice prior to the inspection, that the CPA sign Publisher's then-current non-disclosure agreement and that all inspections are conducted during Publisher's regular business hours and on Publisher's premises. The expenses of such audits shall be borne by Developer, except that Publisher shall be charged for the expense of any such audit that discloses a discrepancy of five percent (5%) or more in favor of Publisher between the amounts paid to Developer and the amounts due according to the terms hereof. The amount of any underpayment disclosed by such audit shall be paid promptly to Developer, together with interest at ten percent per annum.

5. Term and Termination.

5.1 This Agreement shall continue in full force and effect for an initial term ("Initial Term") of one year, and shall thereafter be renewed automatically for additional periods of one year ("Renewal Terms") unless canceled or terminated as set forth below.

5.2 Unless either party notifies the other, in writing, at least ninety (90) days prior to the expiration of the Initial or any Renewal Term, that it desires to terminate this Agreement at the end of such Term, this Agreement shall automatically renew for an additional Renewal Term.

5.3 In the event of a breach by either party of its obligations as provided in this Agreement, the non-breaching party may, in its sole discretion, terminate this Agreement, provided that no such termination shall be effected unless the non-breaching party first gives the breaching party thirty (30) days prior written notice of its intent to terminate, which notice sets forth a description of the breach, and the breaching party fails to cure such breach within the 30-day period.

"Affiliated Label Agreement" courtesy of Thomas J. Cervantez of the law firm— Pillsbury, Madison & Sutro, LLP © 1996

Appendix

5.4 In the event that either party discontinues business operations or files or has filed against it a voluntary or involuntary bankruptcy petition, the other party shall be entitled to terminate this Agreement immediately upon written notice.

5.5 Upon expiration of this Agreement, or upon its termination by either party, Publisher shall prepare an accurate inventory statement of the Products and deliver such statement to Developer within ten (10) days following the effective date of such termination or expiration. Developer shall have the option, exercisable by notice to Publisher within ten (10) days following Developer's receipt of the inventory statement, to repurchase all or any part of Publisher's inventory of Products. Repurchased Products shall be shipped FOB Publisher's warehouse and payment shall be made on delivery to Developer's designated carrier. Developer shall be entitled to set off any sum due to Publisher with respect to such repurchase against any sum due from Publisher's purchase of Products. Amounts held in reserve by Publisher against returned Products, except amounts in excess of Publisher's exposure to its Customers, may not be offset or deducted from amounts due to Publisher for repurchased Products.

Should Developer not exercise such right, then Publisher and each of its customers shall have the right to continue to sell their inventory of Products until their supply is exhausted or for a period of nine (9) months after termination, whichever occurs first. During this sell-off period Developer shall not be required to fill any new orders. If Developer should terminate the Agreement, then Publisher shall have the right to return all of its inventory for a six-month period, at the original purchase price, to be paid within 30 days of invoice date.

5.6 Upon termination of this Agreement for any cause, all rights granted hereunder to Publisher shall revert to Developer except as provided in this Agreement. In addition, upon termination of this Agreement and of any sell-off period authorized hereunder. Publisher shall promptly return to Developer, or otherwise dispose of as Developer may request, any documents or papers whatsoever relating to Developer's business and/or the Products (with the exclusion of information and documents relating to Publisher's customers, financial or accounting information).

6. Overstock Adjustment/Stock Balancing.

6.1 At Publisher's request, from time to time but not before ninety (90) days following Publisher's receipt of the initial order for any title of Products and not more than nine (9) months following receipt of the copies of the title of Products to be returned. Developer shall credit Publisher based either on a "Close Out" sale price or the return to Developer of all copies of any title of a Product purchased during the preceding nine (9) months. The decision as to whether to close out the Product or to return it to Developer shall be made mutually by the parties. Upon the Close Out sale by Publisher or receipt of such returns. Developer shall issue a credit to Publisher based on the amount previously paid by Publisher to Developer for such returned Products less the greater of the actual Close Out price or the actual manufacturing cost for the Products. Such credit may be applied by Publisher to future or past purchases, but only after the depletion of the accounting reserve established in Section 3.7. Publisher shall pay all transportation charges from Publisher's warehouse to Developer's warehouse associated with the return, and risk of loss shall pass to Developer upon receipt at Developer's warehouse.

6.2 If a Product is returned to Developer under Section 6.1 above, then with respect to such Product Developer shall not be subject to the restrictions in Section 1.1. Developer shall have

-4-

"Affiliated Label Agreement" courtesy of Thomas J. Cervantez
of the law firm— Pillsbury, Madison & Sutro, LLP © 1996

Affiliated Label Agreement

the right to resell such Product without restriction, but Developer shall bear the full responsibility for price protection to resellers.

6.3 For stock balance items, Publisher shall provide at no charge new shrink wrapping or other means of securing on items which are otherwise in acceptable condition for resale by Publisher. Any units requiring more than new shrink wrapping shall be returned by Publisher, at Developer's cost, to Developer's warehouse for full refund or credit.

6.4 Developer acknowledges that Publisher shall have no responsibility for any Product previously purchased from Developer by any third party.

7. Marketing Support/Cooperative Advertising.

7.1 Developer shall furnish to Publisher, promptly upon request, two hundred (200) each, not for resale demonstration copies of each SKU of the Products, additional end-user manuals and any other promotional material as may be available for distribution to Publisher's reselling customers for the purpose of supporting sales. All such material shall be provided at no cost to Publisher.

7.2 Publisher may, from time to time, be offered cooperative advertising opportunities for the Products by Publisher's reselling customers. Publisher may decide to participate in such advertising opportunities and commit funds for such purpose. Such cooperative advertising expenditures may be deducted by Publisher from amounts otherwise owed to Developer hereunder, providing that, unless authorized by Developer, such expenditures shall not in any quarter exceed five percent (5%) of net revenues received by Publisher for Products sold by Publisher in such quarter.

7.3 All Products shall be clearly marked on the front of the outside of the Product as to machine, medium, and other important requirements (e.g., memory), as well as an easily identifiable indication that the Product is distributed by Publisher, Developer shall, at its expense, shrink wrap or otherwise properly secure all Product, and incorporate bar code information and ISBN numbers on the packaging. No modification of the Product or its packaging shall be made by Publisher without Developer's prior approval.

7.4 Developer shall provide, for marketing, promotional and advertising purposes, free of charge, to Publisher all packaging artwork, screen shots, reprints of any advertising placed by Developer and any other marketing, sales or press materials as well as all technical information relative to the Products that is reasonably requested by Publisher.

7.5 At least thirty (30) days prior to initial shipment of each Product, Developer shall develop and provide to Publisher, at no additional cost, reasonable quantities of sell sheets for each such Product. Such sell sheets shall include major features, functions and capabilities of the Products, screen shots, a picture of the packaging and the principal technical requirements.

7.6 Publisher shall include each of the Products in any Publisher sales and marketing trade literature and direct mail marketing materials which are designed and printed after the Products are available to Publisher, and in which the substantial majority of the Publisher product line is included. The Products shall be included in the next and subsequent copies of Publisher's product catalogues which are made available to end user customers. In the event that Publisher offers free

"Affiliated Label Agreement" courtesy of Thomas J. Cervantez of the law firm— Pillsbury, Madison & Sutro, LLP © 1996

Appendix

or reduced-price software products to its customers as part of a promotion, Publisher shall use reasonable efforts to give Developer the option to have the Products included, at Developer's expense, in such promotion on a basis similar to the other products included in such promotion.

7.7 Publisher shall be permitted to issue an initial press release announcing the commencement of this Affiliated Label Agreement. Thereafter, all responsibilities to communicate with the press relative to the Products shall rest with Developer.

8. Product Quality and Support.

8.1 Publisher shall perform a quality assurance test on all Products. Developer shall provide to Publisher a completed version of the end-user manual and operating instructions alone with a copy of the Product at least one month prior to the intended release date of each machine format. Publisher shall prepare and deliver to Developer a written list of all errors which it finds during such testing. It shall be understood that Publisher shall make reasonable efforts to check that the Product operates in accordance with the end user manual and that there are no fatal program errors which cause the Product to cease operation or "crash." All identified errors shall be corrected by Developer, at no cost to Publisher, before manufacturing of the final Products shall begin. The foregoing shall not be deemed to affect Developer's responsibilities pursuant to Section 14 below, nor will it place any responsibility on Publisher regarding the quality of the Products manufactured.

8.2 Developer shall promptly inform Publisher of any known defects or operational errors in any of the Products. Developer shall issue a credit to Publisher at the original purchase price, for all Products that are determined by Publisher or Publisher's reselling customers to be materially defective, which are properly returned to Developer as defective products, and which Developer reasonably agrees are defective. Defective Products are defined as Products with material defects in any of the following: media, programming, packaging, documentation and other components.

8.3 If a Product is released with a major defect which causes massive returns, Publisher shall have the right to return all of the units of such Product which it has purchased from Developer, for a full refund, to be paid promptly.

8.4 Publisher shall have the right to inspect each order of Products it receives. Such inspection shall be limited to two percent (2%) of the units received in each order unless defects are found in the inspected units, in which case Publisher may inspect all units in the order. If the inspected unit is found to be acceptable, Publisher shall repackage and Developer shall provide to Publisher, at no additional cost, whatever stickers or other portions of the original package may be required for such repackaging. Publisher may return to Developer, for replacement or credit, at Publisher's election (i) each materially defective unit or (ii) if Publisher finds defect rates in any one order of greater than three percent (3%), all of the units in such order.

8.5 Developer shall provide a telephone number and technical support for end users to call during Developer's normal business hours in order to have their technical questions about the Products answered. This telephone number shall be featured prominently on all packaging and materials.

9. Advance Notice. Developer shall provide to Publisher, from time to time and upon request, a complete list of all Products manufactured or sold by or intended to be manufactured or

"Affiliated Label Agreement" courtesy of Thomas J. Cervantez of the law firm— Pillsbury, Madison & Sutro, LLP © 1996

sold by Developer. Developer shall give Publisher at least sixty (60) days' prior notice of any change in the Products, including but not limited to price, availability and packaging.

10. Publisher Responsibilities.

10.1 Publisher shall make a comparable effort to present the Products to all of Publisher's customers and offer them for sale as it does for its own products.

10.2 Publisher shall provide the opportunity for Developer to participate along with Publisher at both the _____ Trade Shows. The costs associated with such participation shall be passed on to Developer at Publisher's actual cost. Developer shall provide personnel to demonstrate the Products.

10.3 Publisher shall make a comparable effort to negotiate agreements to bundle, couple, distribute or sell the Products with other computer games and/or other products as it does for its own products.

10.4 Publisher shall include the Products in its "hints and tips" 900 line service to end users.

10.5 Publisher shall not be required to provide end user customer support.

10.6 Publisher shall be responsible for and shall bear all costs associated with bad debt and uncollectible payments due from Publisher customers with respect to the sale of the Products.

10.7 Publisher shall not register nor use any of the business trade names, trademarks, emblems or designs relating to the Products except as provided for in this Agreement or with Developer's written consent and in accordance with any directions given by Developer.

10.8 Publisher shall not alter, remove, conceal or otherwise interfere with any markings or nameplates or other indication of the source of origin of the Products.

10.9 Publisher shall immediately bring to Developer's attention any improper or wrongful use in the Territory of Developer's patents, trademarks, emblems, designs, models, copyright or other rights known to Publisher which may come to its notice in the execution of its duties, and use reasonable efforts to assist Developer, at Developer's expense, in taking steps to defend such rights.

10.10 Publisher covenants with Developer that at all times it shall:

(i) not make any representation or give any warranties other than those expressly authorized in writing by Developer with respect to the Products;

(ii) ensure that it employs suitable sales representatives to deal efficiently with the sale of the Products;

(iii) ensure that the Products are in good external condition when dispatched from its premises.

-7-

"Affiliated Label Agreement" courtesy of Thomas J. Cervantez of the law firm— Pillsbury, Madison & Sutro, LLP © 1996

Appendix

11. <u>Developer Responsibilities</u>.

11.1 Developer shall provide all packaging and other materials used and shipped in the finished Products.

11.2 Developer shall pay for the design, preparation and placement of all consumer advertising.

11.3 Developer shall be responsible for manufacturing activities including but not limited to providing inventory, warehousing and delivery of finished goods to Publisher.

11.4 Developer shall notify Publisher of its manufacturing cost prior to receipt of Publisher's initial order for each Product.

11.5 Developer agrees to spend on an annual basis on the marketing of the Products, between _____ percent (__%) and _____ percent (__%) of Publisher's net revenues on the sale of Products. Such figure shall include amounts spent on cooperative advertising as set forth in Section 7.2.

11.6 Developer agrees that, during the term of the Agreement, it shall refer to Publisher all enquiries about sales of the Products within the Territory.

11.7 Developer shall be responsible for performing all public relations efforts except as provided in Section 7.

11.8 Developer shall be responsible for all freight, duty and shipping costs for the Products to Publisher's Designated Point of Receipt. In addition, Developer shall be responsible for all such costs when Publisher returns product, either mint or defective, to Developer from Publisher's Designated Point of Receipt.

11.9 Developer shall provide a representative who shall function as a single point of contact for Publisher. The representative shall cooperate with and work closely with all personnel at Publisher involved in the sales and distribution of the Products. All marketing, public relations and manufacturing activities shall be coordinated within the Territory by this representative.

12. <u>Responsibilities of Both Parties</u>. Each party covenants with the other that it will at all times during the term of this Agreement observe and perform the terms and conditions set out in this Agreement and in particular shall:

(a) ensure its employees at all times use their reasonable endeavors to cooperate with and assist each other for the mutual benefit of the parties;

(b) in all matters act legally and faithfully to the other;

(c) unless otherwise provided for in this Agreement not incur any liability on behalf of the other nor in any way pledge or purport to pledge the other's credit;

"Affiliated Label Agreement" courtesy of Thomas J. Cervantez of the law firm— Pillsbury, Madison & Sutro, LLP © 1996

Affiliated Label Agreement

(d) immediately pass to the other details of any complaints received from customers in the Territory in connection with the Products or any difficulties which arise in implementing the terms of this Agreement;

(e) use its reasonable endeavors to promote and extend the sale of the Products throughout the Territory.

13. Confidentiality.

13.1 Each of the parties acknowledges and agrees that certain information which it may receive from the other party shall be proprietary to the disclosing party. Such information includes, without limitation: (i) the fact that the disclosing party intends to develop or market any particular hardware or software product; (ii) the designs, schematics, specifications and all other technical information of or concerning the Products; (iii) any non-public information concerning the business or finances of the disclosing party; and (iv) any other information the disclosure of which might harm or destroy a competitive advantage of the disclosing party. All of the types of information reflected in clauses (i) through (iv) of this Subsection shall be collectively referred to hereinafter as the "Proprietary Information."

13.2 Each of the parties agrees that it shall not, directly or indirectly, either during or subsequent to the term of this Agreement: (i) disclose any Proprietary Information of the other party, other than to its own employees who participate directly in the performance of the receiving party's obligations under this Agreement; (ii) copy or use any Proprietary Information of the other party except for the purpose of fulfilling its obligations hereunder; or (iii) publish any Proprietary Information of the other party without the prior written consent of such party. The degree of care employed by each of the parties to protect and safeguard the Proprietary Information of the other party shall be no less protective than the degree of care used by such party to protect its own confidential information of like importance.

13.3 The parties acknowledge and agree that this Agreement and the subject matter and terms and conditions of this Agreement fall within the scope of Proprietary Information identified in Subsection 13.1 above.

13.4 The obligations set forth in this Section 13 shall not be applicable to any information which:

(a) the receiving party is authorized by the disclosing party in writing to disclose, copy or use;

(b) is generally known or becomes part of the public domain through no fault of the receiving party;

(c) is disclosed by the disclosing party to third parties without restriction on subsequent disclosure;

(d) is provided to the receiving party by a third party without breach of any separate nondisclosure agreement; or

"Affiliated Label Agreement" courtesy of Thomas J. Cervantez of the law firm— Pillsbury, Madison & Sutro, LLP © 1996

Appendix

(e) is required to be disclosed in the context of any administrative or judicial proceeding.

14. Warranty and Indemnity.

14.1 Publisher acknowledges and agrees that the Products which Developer sells to Publisher in furtherance of this Agreement shall be sold without any express or implied warranties being granted or otherwise extended to Publisher, including, without limitation, any implied warranties of merchantability or of fitness for any purpose. Developer agrees, however, that it shall extend a limited warranty to all end user purchasers of any of the Products that the physical media incorporated in the Products purchased by any such end users shall, for a period of ninety (90) days from the date of consumer purchase, be free from defects in materials and workmanship under normal use and service. Developer's liability thereunder shall be limited to the obligation, at Developer's option, to repair or replace any units of the Products which are determined to be defective and which are returned to Developer at the original consumer purchaser's expense within the applicable warranty period. Developer's limited express warranty described herein shall not apply to any units of the Products which are damaged as a result of any accident, negligence, use in any application for which such Products were not designed or intended, modification without the prior consent of Developer, or by any other causes unrelated to defective material or workmanship.

14.2 Developer warrants that it either owns all rights, title and interest in and to the Products or that it otherwise has the right to grant all of the rights granted hereunder, and that to the best of its knowledge neither the Products nor the rights granted hereunder violate the personal or proprietary rights of any person or entity. Developer agrees to indemnify and hold Publisher and its customers harmless from and against any and all losses, damages, costs and expenses, including reasonable attorneys' fees, arising out of any of Developer's representations and warranties including without limitation: (i) alleged failure of any Product to perform to specification or in a customary and reasonable manner as specified or advertised by Developer; (ii) alleged breach of express or implied warranty by Developer with respect to any Product; (iii) alleged infringement or violation of any trademark, copyright, trade secret, patent, or other proprietary right with respect to any Product; and (iv) unfair trade practice, trade libel or misrepresentation based on any promotional material, packaging, documentation or other materials provided by Developer with respect to any Product.

14.3 Developer's obligation to indemnify is conditioned on Publisher's notifying Developer of any claim as to which indemnification will be sought, promptly after Publisher first becomes aware of such claim and, in the event Developer elects to defend, providing Developer with reasonable cooperation in the defense and settlement thereof; provided, however, that any failure of Publisher to give such prompt notice shall not affect any of its rights hereunder, unless such failure materially and adversely affects the ability of Developer to defend such claim. In the case of a final determination that a Product is infringing, and at Developer's option, Developer shall:

(a) procure a license from any claimant with respect to the infringing Product that will enable Publisher to continue marketing the Product;

(b) modify the Product so as to make it non-infringing without materially changing the theme or play of the Product; or

"Affiliated Label Agreement" courtesy of Thomas J. Cervantez of the law firm— Pillsbury, Madison & Sutro, LLP © 1996

(c) buy back from Publisher all inventory of Publisher and Publisher's reselling customers at Publisher's original purchase price from Developer, and pay all shipping, insurance and customs duties associated with its return to Developer.

14.4 Each party warrants to the other that:

(a) it is not under any disability, restriction or prohibition with respect to its right to enter into this Agreement and its rights or obligations to perform each and every term and provision hereof;

(b) during the Term of the Agreement it shall not make any agreement with any third party which is inconsistent with or is in conflict with this Agreement.

14.5 Each of the parties (the "Indemnifying Party") shall indemnify the other (the "Indemnified Party") and hold it harmless from any and all damages, costs, losses and expenses, including reasonable legal fees, arising out of or in connection with a material breach by the Indemnifying Party of any provisions of this Agreement.

15. Limitation of Liability. EXCEPT FOR THE INDEMNIFICATION OBLIGATIONS OF EITHER PARTY AS EXPRESSLY SET FORTH IN SECTION 14 ABOVE, NEITHER PARTY SHALL BE RESPONSIBLE OR LIABLE TO THE OTHER FOR ANY INCIDENTAL, CONSEQUENTIAL, SPECIAL OR PUNITIVE DAMAGES ARISING OUT OF THIS AGREEMENT OR ITS TERMINATION OR THE BREACH OF ANY OF ITS PROVISIONS, WHETHER FOR BREACH OF WARRANTY OR ANY OBLIGATION ARISING THEREFROM OR OTHERWISE, WHETHER LIABILITY IS ASSERTED IN CONTRACT OR TORT (INCLUDING NEGLIGENCE AND PRODUCT LIABILITY), AND IRRESPECTIVE OF WHETHER THE PARTIES HAVE BEEN ADVISED OF THE POSSIBILITY OF ANY SUCH DAMAGE.

16. Assignment. This Agreement may not be assigned by either party without first obtaining the written consent of the other party (which consent shall not be unreasonably withheld), except as part of the sale or transfer of all or substantially all of the party's entire business or the merger or consolidation of the party into any other company or entity (a "Change of Ownership"). This Agreement shall be binding upon and shall inure to the benefit of Publisher and Developer and their respective successors and assignees permitted hereunder.

17. Independent Contractors. Developer shall be deemed to have the status of an independent contractor, and nothing in this Agreement shall be deemed to place the parties in the relationship of an employer-employee, principal-agent, partners or joint ventures. Developer shall be responsible for any withholding taxes, payroll taxes, disability insurance payments, unemployment taxes and other similar taxes or charge on the payments received by Developer hereunder.

18. General.

18.1 All notices, demands and communications hereunder shall be in writing and shall be deemed given if personally delivered or sent to a party by certified mail, return receipt requested,

"Affiliated Label Agreement" courtesy of Thomas J. Cervantez of the law firm— Pillsbury, Madison & Sutro, LLP © 1996

to the address set forth in the preamble to this Agreement, or to such other addresses as the parties shall notify each other from time to time.

18.2 Any delay in the performance by Developer or Publisher of any of its obligations hereunder which are caused by any strike, fire, explosion, accident, delay by carrier, act of God or any other delay beyond such party's reasonable control (collectively, an "Event of Force Majeure") shall be excused for a period of time equal to such delay if, promptly after such party becomes aware of the effects of such Event of Force Majeure, it provides the other party with written notice of such delay and such Event of Force Majeure.

Notwithstanding the above, (a) if an Event of Force Majeure makes it impossible for Developer or its manufacturer to manufacture the Products for a period of more than 90 days, then Publisher shall have the right to find an alternative source of manufacture for the period of the Force Majeure, and (b) if an Event of Force Majeure makes it impossible for Publisher to sell the Products for a period of more than 90 days, then Developer shall have the right to find an alternative method of selling the Products within the Territory for the period of the Force Majeure.

18.3 This Agreement and any Exhibits or Addenda hereto represent the entire agreement between the parties regarding the subject matter hereof and supersede all prior agreements and understandings between the parties, and may not be changed or modified except if done so by written agreement between the parties.

18.4 No waiver of any right, obligation or default shall be implied but must be in Kiting and signed by the party against whom the waiver is sought to be enforced. One or more waivers of any rights obligation or default shall not be construed as a waiver of any subsequent right, obligation or default.

18.5 Any provision or provisions of this Agreement which shall prove to be invalid, void or illegal shall in no way affect, impair or invalidate any of the other provisions, and the remaining provisions hereof shall remain in full force and effect.

18.6 This Agreement shall be governed by and construed under the laws of the State of California applicable to contracts executed and intended to be performed entirely within the State of California by residents of the State of California.

18.7 In the event of any arbitration or litigation arising hereunder between the parties, the prevailing party shall be entitled to recover from the non-prevailing party reasonable attorneys' fees incurred therein. The parties agree to submit any disputes hereunder to binding arbitration in _____ County, California, in accordance with the rules of the American Arbitration Association.

"Affiliated Label Agreement" courtesy of Thomas J. Cervantez of the law firm— Pillsbury, Madison & Sutro, LLP © 1996

Affiliated Label Agreement

18.8 The following Sections shall survive the expiration or termination of this Agreement: 4.3, 5.5, 5.6, 13, 14, 15, 18.6, 18.7 and 18.8.

IN WITNESS WHEREOF, the parties hereto have executed and delivered this Agreement effective as of _____ __, 1996.

PUBLISHER COMPANY   DEVELOPER COMPANY

By _____   By _____

Its _____   Its _____

"Affiliated Label Agreement" courtesy of Thomas J. Cervantez of the law firm— Pillsbury, Madison & Sutro, LLP © 1996

Appendix

EXHIBIT A

DEVELOPER PRODUCTS AND PRICING

Product	Publisher Price

*"Affiliated Label Agreement" courtesy of Thomas J. Cervantez
of the law firm— Pillsbury, Madison & Sutro, LLP © 1996*

DISTRIBUTORS

ABCO Distributors
400 Route 59
Monsey, NY 10952
Ph: 914-368-1930

Academic Distributing
P.O. Box 1360
Dewey, AZ 86227
Ph: 520-632-7176
  Gary Rogers .... Buyer

Ace Computers
8 E. Camp McDonald Rd.
Prospect Heights, IL 60070
Ph: 708-253-9400
  John Samborski .... Buyer

Acecom Inc.
3350 Scott Blvd.
Building 27
Santa Clara, CA 95054
Ph: 408-980-1881
  Ken Kim .... Buyer

ACMA Computers Inc.
47988 Fremont Blvd.
Fremont, CA 94538
Ph: 510-623-1212
  Christine Hsingh .... Buyer

Advanced Electronics Inc.
1965 Lycoming Creek Rd.
Suite 201
Williamsport, PA 17701
Ph: 717-327-1091
  Kurt Haupt .... Buyer

Agama Computers
9401 Orion Ave.
North Hills, CA 91343
Ph: 818-891-6710
  Jacques Milon .... Buyer

Allegro Tech. Inc.
274 Wahconah St.
Suite B
Pittsfield, MA 01201
Ph: 413-443-9443
  Bill Nichols .... Buyer

Almo Distributing Inc.
9815 Roosevelt Blvd.
Philadelphia, PA 19114
Ph: 215-698-4000
  Dennis Billodeau .... Buyer

AMAX Engineering Corp.
3288 Laurelview Ct.
Fremont, CA 94538
Ph: 510-651-8886
  Christine Lee-Hsing .... Buyer

Amcom Business Centers Corp.
1028 Saunders Ln.
West Chester, PA 19380
Ph: 610-918-9000
  Pat Rucker .... Buyer

American International Distribution Corp.
2 Winter Sport Ln.
P.O. Box 80
Williston, VT 05495
Ph: 800-678-2432

AmeriQuest Technologies Inc.
3 Emperial Promenade
Santa Ana, CA 92707
Ph: 714-437-0099

Appendix

Anson Computer
15318 E. Valley Blvd.
City of Industry, CA 91746
Ph: 818-333-8558

Anti Gravity Products
456 Lincoln Blvd.
Santa Monica, CA 90402
Ph: 310-393-6650

The ASCII Group Inc.
7475 Wisconsin Ave.
Suite 350
Bethesda, MD 20814-3412
Ph: 301-718-2600
 Jill Kerr .... Buyer

ASI
48289 Fremont Blvd.
Fremont, CA 94538
Ph: 510-226-8000
 Mike .... Buyer

ATV VarServ
950 Keynote Circle
Cleveland, OH 44131
Ph: 800-843-5010

AVT
26 W. Highland Ave.
Atlantic Highlands, NJ 07716
Ph: 908-872-9090

AW Industries
8415 Ardmore Rd.
Landover, MD 20785
Ph: 301-322-1000
 Charles Privote .... Buyer

Baker & Taylor Software
3850 Royal Ave.
Simi Valley, CA 93063
Ph: 805-552-9800

Big Byte Media
18425 Napa St.
Northridge, CA 91325
Ph: 818-700-2983
 Ricky Berggren .... Marketing Manager

CAL-ABCO
6041 Variel Ave.
Woodland Hills, CA 91367
Ph: 818-704-9100
 Bobby Strauss .... Buyer

Camelot Corp.
17770 Preston Rd.
Dallas, TX 75252
Ph: 214-733-3005
 Danny Wettrich .... CEO

Casey-Johnston Sales Inc.
37300 Central Ct.
Newark, CA 94560
Ph: 510-745-9991
 Donald Johnston, Jr. .... Buyer

CD- Interactive Inc.
3611 S. Harbor Blvd.
Suite 105
Santa Ana, CA 92704-6928
Ph: 714-378-4020
 Dennis Acebo .... VP, Marketing

Columbia House Co.
1211 Avenue of the Americas
New York, NY 10020-1090
Ph: 212-596-2703
 Harriet Yassky .... VP, Aquisition

CompuAdd Computer Corp.
12303 Technology Blvd.
Austin, TX 78727
Ph: 512-250-2000

Distributors

CompuStar
1283F Old Mountain View Rd.
Sunnyvale, CA 94089
Ph: 408-747-0366

    Neveen Mourad .... Vice President- Sale

Comsource
16-5 Middle Country Rd.
Coram, NY 11727
Ph: 516-696-2906

    Gene Smith

Connecticut Computer Graphics Distributors
75 Glen Rd.
Sandy Hook, CT 06482
Ph: 800-422-8416

    John Rohmer .... Buyer

Consan Inc.
7676 Executive DR.
Eden Prairie, MN 55344
Ph: 612-949-0053

    Becky Thomason ....Buyer

Continental Technologies Inc.
300 McGaw Dr.
Edison, NJ 08837
Ph: 908-225-1166

Cranel Inc.
8999 Gemini Pkwy.
Columbus, OH 43240
Ph: 614-431-8000

    Carl Reichert .... Vice President

Creative Data Products Inc.
P.O. Box 361630
Milpitas, CA 95036-1630
Ph: 408-448-3773

    Larry Friss .... Vice President

D&H Distributing Co.
2525 N. 7th St.
Harrisburg, PA 17110
Ph: 717-236-8001

    Gary Brothers .... Vice President

Data Storage Marketing Inc.
5718 Central Ave.
Boulder, CO 80301
Ph: 303-442-4747

    Tom Ward .... President

Datalink Corp.
7423 Washington Ave. S
Minneapolis, MN 55439
Ph: 612-944-3462

    Brent Miller .... Inside Sales

Datamini Systems
6223 Richmond Ave.
Suite 102
Houston, TX 77057
Ph: 713-784-1666

    Arif Hussnian .... Buyer

Davidson & Associates
19840 Pioneer Ave.
Torrance, CA 90503
Ph: 310-793-0600

Decision Support Systems Inc.
11800 Sunrise Valley Dr.
15th Floor
Reston, VA 22091
Ph: 703-715-9500

    Mort Rezaee .... Buyer

Digital Entertainment
7400 49th Ave. N
New Hope, MN 55428
Ph: 612-535-8333

    Ian Andrew Perl .... Vice President- Sales

Appendix

Direct Source Distributing
4548 McEwen Farmers Branch
Dallas, TX 75244
Ph: 214-387-8338

DTR Business Systems
1160 Centre Dr.
Suite A
Walnut, CA 91789
Ph: 800-598-5721
  Jack Hilburn .... Buyer

Duthie Associates
3310 West End Ave.
Nashville, TN 37203
Ph: 615-386-3061

Educational Resources
1550 Executive Dr.
Elgin, IL 60123
Ph: 708-888-8300
  Patricia Laystrom .... Vice President- Sales

Educational Technology Specialists Inc.
243 Foam St.
Monterey, CA 93940
Ph: 408-372-8100
  Tone Larsen .... Marketing Manager

Educorp Computer Services
7434 Trade St.
San Diego, CA 92121
Ph: 619-536-9999
  Suzi Nawabi .... VP, Marketing

Electrograph Systems
175 Commerce Dr.
Hauppauge, NY 11788
Ph: 516-436-5050
  Sam Taylor .... Buyer

Electronic Vision, Inc.
5 Depot St.
Athens, OH 45701
Ph: 614-592-2433

EMJ America Inc.
301 Gregson Dr.
Cary, NC 27511
Ph: 919-460-8861
  Shelley Darden .... Buyer

En.Gen Inc.
2727 W. Baseline
Tempe, AZ 85283
Ph: 602-438-1110
  Rick Jeralds .... Buyers

Eternal Graphics Inc.
1016 Airpark Dr.
Sugar Grove, IL 60554
Ph: 708-556-3339
  Jerry Proefrock .... Buyer

Evershine, Inc.
1101 Monterey Pass Rd.
Monterey Park, CA 91754
Ph: 213-265-2228

Fifth Dimension
2500 Don Reid Dr.
Ottawa, ONT K1H 8P5
Canada

First Computer Corp.
341 Shore Dr.
Hinsdale, IL 60521
Ph: 708-920-1050
  Gary Hirsch .... Vice President

Gates/Arrow
39 Pelham Ridge Dr.
Greenville, SC 29615
Ph: 800-332-2222
  Rhonda Corn .... Buyer

Distributors

Gates/FA Distributing Inc.
121 Interstate Blvd
Greenville, SC 29615
Ph: 803-234-0736

    Andrew Heyman .... Vice President

GBC Technologies Inc.
100 GBC Ct.
Berlin, NJ 08009
Ph: 609-767-2500

    Rob Schwartz .... Buyer

Globelle Corp.
6410 W. Old Shakapee Rd.
Minneapolis, MN 55420
Ph: 800-745-7000

    Mark Todd .... Buyer

GPN
Box 80669
Lincoln, NE 68501-0669
Ph: 402-472-2007

    Larry Aerni .... Marketing Director

Great Beyond International Inc.
2255 Lois Dr.
Suite 2
Rolling Meadows, IL 60008
Ph: 708-734-1282

    Mark Lin .... Buyer

GT Interactive Software Corp.
16 E 40th St.
New York, NY 10016
Ph: 212-726-6500

    Todd Steckbeck .... Vice President- Sales

Hall-Mark Computer Products
3011 S. 52nd St.
Tempe, AZ 85282
Ph: 602-414-6500

    Stan Phillips .... Buyer

Handleman Co.
500 Kirts Blvd.
Troy, MI 48084
Ph: 810-362-4400

    Don Bucher .... Buyer

HB
9630 Clarewood
Building B1
Houston, TX 77036
Ph: 713-776-4750

    Nick Walker.......................... Buyer

Hi-Link Computer
973 Hope St.
Stamford, CT 06907
Ph: 203-975-9335

    Jerry Lin .... Buyer

High Technology Distributing Co.
20520 Nordhoff St.
Chatsworth, CA 91311
Ph: 818-772-8001

    Steve Matsuyama .... Buyer

Inacom Corp.
10810 Farnam Dr.
Omaha, NE 68154
Ph: 402-392-3900

    Michael A. Steffan .... Vice President

Infotel Distributing
6990 US Route 36 E
Fletcher, OH 45326
Ph: 800-537-1423

    Mark Runkle .... President

Ingram Micro Inc.
1600 E. St. Andrew Pl.
Santa Ana, CA 92705
Ph: 714-566-1000

    Sanat Dutta.......................... Executive Vice President

Appendix

Inland Associates Inc.
15021 W. 117th St.
Olathe, KS 66062
Ph: 913-764-7977

    Peggy Meader .... President

Intelligent Electronics Inc.
411 Eagleview Blvd.
Exton, PA 19341
Ph: 610-458-5500

    Gregory Pratt .... COO

International Computer Graphics Inc.
30481 Whipple Rd.
Union City, CA 94587
Ph: 510-471-7000

    Mike Ahmar .... President

IST Inc.
3444 DeLaCruz Blvd.
Santa Clara, CA 95054
Ph: 408-653-1000

    I. Ahmad .... Buyer

Kenfil Inc.
16745 Saticoy St.
Van Nuys, CA 91406
Ph: 818-785-1181

    Irwin A. Bransky .... President

Kenitec Computer & Technologies
99 Route 70 North
Maywood, NJ 07607
Ph: 800-536-4832

    Mike Lowe .... Buyer

L.A. Data Systems
1825 Surveyor
Simi Valley, CA 93063
Ph: 805-526-1603

    Jeff Cook .... Buyer

Laser Resources Inc.
20620 Leapwood Ave.
Suite F
Carson, CA 90746
Ph: 310-324-4444

    Bob Helphant .... Buyer

Law Cypress Distributing Co.
5883 Eden Park Pl.
San Jose, CA 95138
Ph: 408-363-4700

    David Law .... President

Leadman Electronics USA
2980 Golden Ave.
Santa Clara, CA 95051
Ph: 408-738-1751

Liuski International Inc.
6585 Crescent Dr.
Norcross, GA 30071
Ph: 404-447-9454

    Edwin J. Feinberg .... Vice President

LSI Distribution
1900 Jay Ell Dr.
Richardson, TX 75081
Ph: 214-690-6110

M.C.P.S.
1 Coventon Ave.
Garden City, NY 11530
Ph: 516-248-8889

    Tony Lau .... President

MacWarehouse
P.O. Box 3013
1720 Oak St.
Lakewood, NJ 08701
Ph: 908-370-4779

Distributors

Magic Multimedia Inc.
2445 Cleveland Ave.
West Lawn, PA 19609
Ph: 610-678-2300
    Barry Zettlemoyer .... CEO

Marshall Industries
9320 Telstar Ave.
El Monte, CA 91731
Ph: 818-307-6000
    Bob Caldarella ....Corp. Sales Manag

Marvic International
768 E 93rd St.
Brooklyn, NY 11236
Ph: 718-346-7822
    Victor Lee .... Buyer

Max Group
16605 Gale Ave.
City of Industry, CA 91745
Ph: 818-968-6798
    Sue Tsai .... Vice President

MDL Enterprise Inc.
9888 SW Freeway
Houston, TX 77074
Ph: 713-771-6350
    D. Lamm .... Buyer

Media Graphics Distribution
370 Amapola Ave.
Suite 212
Torrance, CA 90501
Ph: 310-782-1532
    Mark Lewis .... Buyer

Media Integration Inc.
2521 S. Rodeo Gulch Rd.
Soquel, CA 95073
Ph: 408-475-9400
    Mike Rynas .... Buyer

Media Lab, Inc.
400 S. McCaslin Blvd.
Louisville, CO 80027
Ph: 303-499-5411

Media Magic, Inc.
4514 Chamblee Dunwoody Rd.
Atlanta, GA 30338
Ph: 404-454-6889

Merisel Inc.
200 Continental Blvd.
El Segundo, CA 90245
Ph: 310-615-3080
    Beth Wright .... Buyer

Micro Central Inc.
P.O. Box 1009
Old Bridge, NJ 08857-1009
Ph: 800-836-4276
    Jay Lopatin .... President

Micro Equipment
6155-G Jimmy Carter Blvd.
Norcross, GA 30071
Ph: 404-447-1726
    Jason Kamaivand .... Buyer

Micro Informatica Corp.
99 SE 5th ST.
Suite 120
Miami, FL 33131
Ph: 305-377-1930

Micro Star Software
2245 Camino Vida Roble
Suite 101
Carlsbad, CA 92009
Ph: 619-931-4949
    Stephen Benedict .... Owner

Appendix

Micro United
2200 E. Golf Rd.
Des Plaines, IL 60016
Ph: 708-297-1200

Micro-Pace Inc.
109 S. Duncan Rd.
Champaign, IL 61821
Ph: 217-356-1884

    Uzee Payton .... Buyer

Microage Inc.
2400 Microage Way
Tempe, AZ 85282
Ph: 602-968-3168

    Gary Palenbaum .... Vendor Dev. Manager

Micromodem
Route 1
Caribou, ME 04736
Ph: 207-493-3300

    Don Robertonson .... Buyer

Mini-Micro Supply Co. Inc.
4900 Patrick Henry
Santa Clara, CA 95054
Ph: 408-327-0388

    Steve Flynn .... Buyer

Most Significant Bits
37207 Colorado Ave.
Avon, OH 44011-1527
Ph: 216-529-1888

    Patricia Miller....................... CEO

Multi-Ad Services
1720 W. Detweiller Dr.
Peoria, IL 61615
Ph: 309-692-1530

Muse Ed Inc.
220 Washington Ave.
Savannah, GA 31405
Ph: 912-238-4657

    William Keith .... VP, Marketing

National CD-ROM
11005 Indian Trail
Suite 101-A
Dallas, TX 75229
Ph: 800-237-6613

Navarre Corp.
7400 49th Ave. N
New Hope, MN 55428
Ph: 612-535-8333

    Rick Vick............................... Senior National Buyer

NIDI Peripherals & Technology Inc.
15209 NE 95th St.
Redmond, WA 98052
Ph: 206-861-6434

    Jack Showalter .... President

Nimax Inc.
7740 Kenamar Ct.
San Diego, CA 92121
Ph: 619-566-4800

    Ms. Kokao .... Buyer

Nimbus Information Systems
State Route 629
Guilford Farm
Ruckersville, VA 22968
Ph: 804-985-1100

    Tamara Crabaugh .... Account Representative

One Source Micro Products Inc.
3305 Lathrop St.
Suite 200
South Bend, IN 46628
Ph: 219-288-7455

    James Ainsley....................... President

Distributors

One Stop Micro Inc.
524 Prospect Ave.
Little Silver, NJ 07739
Ph: 908-741-8888
    Rochelle Firestone.................. Vice President

Online Computer System, Inc.
20251 Century Blvd.
Germontown, MD 20874
Ph: 301-601-2405

Optical Laser Inc.
5862 Bolsa Ave.
Suite 103
Huntington Beach, CA 92649
Ph: 714-379-4400
    Michael S. Raab .... President

PDP Systems Inc.
2140 Bering Dr.
San Jose, CA 95131
Ph: 408-944-0301

PF Micro
3598 Cadillac Ave.
Costa Mesa, CA 92626
Ph: 714-549-4669

PC Wholesale
472 Fox Ct.
Bloomingdale, IL 60108
Ph: 708-307-3636
    Daniel O'Brien .... Vice President

Precision Data Products
5036 Falcon View Ave. SE
Grand Rapids, MI 49512
Ph: 616-698-2242
    Chuck Williams .... Buyer

Print NW/Six Sigma
4918 20th St. E
P.O. Box 1418
Tacoma, WA 98401
Ph: 206-922-9393
    Wendy Carroll .... Vice President- Sales

Promotional Products Fulfillment & Distribution
89 Mills Rd.
Ajax, ON L1S 7L3
Canada
Ph: 800-263-4678

Promotions Distibutor Services Corp.
10303 Norris Ave.
Los Angeles, CA 91331
Ph: 818-834-8800

Quantum Communications
801 W. Mineral Ave.
Littleton, CO 80120-4501
Ph: 303-797-9379
    Rick Pinkham .... President

R.T.I.
13533 I Circle
Omaha, NE 68137
Ph: 800-383-3257
    Steve Lukowski .... Buyer

Random Access Inc.
8000 E. Iliff Ave.
Denver, CO 80231
Ph: 303-745-9600
    Bradley A. Comer .... Vice President

RandomSoft
A Division of Random House Inc.
201 E. 50th St.
New York, NY 10022
Ph: 212-751-2600
    Randi Benton....................... New Media Director

Appendix

Revelation Products Corp.
1220 Valley Forge Rd.
P.O. Box 2225
Valley Forge, PA 19482
Ph: 610-933-5875

Norman Ross Publishing
330 W. 58th St.
New York, NY 10019
Ph: 800-648-8850

    Maja Lakicevic .... Marketing

RTM
13177 Ramona Blvd.
Suite 7
Irwindale, CA 91700
Ph: 818-813-2630

    Christopher Chan .... President

SBM Inc.
7076 Peachtree Industrial Blvd.
Suite 200
Norcross, GA 30071
Ph: 800-662-8277

    Jack Thorton .... President

Sega Ozisoft
729 Bay Rd.
Mill Valley, CA 94941
Ph: 415-383-1501

Seneca Data Distributors Inc.
19 Corporate Circle
East Syracuse, NY 13057
Ph: 315-433-1160

    Kevin Conley .... Executive Vice President

Signet Sales Inc.
2830 Copley Rd.
Akron, OH 44321
Ph: 216-666-6055

    Robert Smith .... President/Buyer

Sirex USA Inc.
132-14 11th Ave.
College Point, NY 11356
Ph: 718-746-7500

Sofsource Inc.
401 N. 17th St.
Suite 4
Las Cruces, NM 88005
Ph: 505-523-6789

    Steven Meyer .... Vice President- Sales

Software Services Group
1218 East Hartman Ave.
Omaha, NE 68110
Ph: 402-453-1699

    Barb K. Kegel .... Vice President

Southern Electronics Distributors
4916 N. Royal Atlanta Dr.
Tucker, GA 30085
Ph: 770-938-4041

    Gerald Diamond .... CEO

The Douglas Stewart Co.
2402 Advance Rd.
Madison, WI 53704
Ph: 608-221-1155

    Jim Hannem

Supercom Inc.
410 S. Abbot Ave.
Milpitas, CA 95035
Ph: 408-456-8888

    Mark Wayler .... Buyer

Systems Supplies
P.O. Box 8332
Grand Rapids, MI 49518
Ph: 616-698-2262

    Chuck Williams .... Buyer

Distributors

Tech Data Corp.
5350 Tech Data Dr.
Clearwater, FL 34620

Ph: 813-539-7429

Jerry Engel .... Buyer

Technology Distributors Inc.
605 Neponset St.
Canton, MA 02021

Ph: 617-575-0357

Pat West .... President

Thinkware
345 Fourth St.
San Francisco, CA 94107

Ph: 415-777-9876

Ray Bachand .... President

Trans America International
10-27 45th Ave.
Long Island City, NY 11101

Ph: 718-786-3366

Tom Jones .... Buyer

Transamerican Computer Wholesalers
4503 Irvington Ave.
Unit 2
Jacksonville, FL 32210

Ph: 800-780-9545

Bob D'Augustinis .... Buyer

Twix Technology Corp.
12005 Forestgate Dr.
Suite 100
Dallas, TX 75243

Ph: 214-238-9888

Robert Staples .... Buyer

Value Software Corp.
2849 Woodbridge Ave.
Suite 6-499
Edison, NJ 08837-3451

Ph: 908-603-7735

VARtek Distributing
1785 S. Metro Pkwy.
Dayton, OH 45459

Ph: 513-438-3550

Bill Richards .... Buyer

Vision Source
19950 Mariner
Torrance, CA 90503

Ph: 310-214-4299

Warner/Elektra/Atlantic Corp: MM Division
185 Berry St.
Suite 130
San Francisco, CA 90107

Ph: 415-281-4230

David Archambault .... VP, Multimedia

Wave Interactive Network
480 Pleasant St
Suite 3
Lee, MA 01238

Ph: 413-243-1600

Nolan Bushnell .... Director

WorldNet Computers
92 Argonaut
Suite 140
Aliso Viejo, CA 92656

Ph: 714-454-1818

Simon Harv .... Buyer

Wynit Inc.
6A 47 Elliocott
East Syracuse, NY 13067

Ph: 315-437-1086

Geoffrey Lewis .... President

Zoltrix
47273 Fremont Blvd.
Fremont, CA 94538

Ph: 510-657-1188

Appendix

Law Firms

LAW FIRMS

Akin, Bump, Strauss, Hauer & Feld
1333 New Hampshire Ave. NW
Washington, D.C. 20036
Ph: 202-887-4000

Arent, Fox, Finter, Plotkin & Kahn
1050 Connecticut Ave. NW
Washington, D.C. 20036-5339
Ph: 202-857-6402

Arnold & Porter
1200 New Hampshire Ave. NW
Washington, D.C. 20036
Ph: 202-872-3736

Baker & McKenzie
2 Embarcadero Center
San Francisco, CA 94111
Ph: 415-576-3000

Bechtel & Cole
1901 L St. NW
Suite 250
Washington, D.C. 20036
Ph: 202-833-4190

Bloom, Dekom, Hergott & Cook
150 S. Rodeo Drive, 3rd Fl.
Beverly Hills, CA 90212
Ph: 310-859-68200

    Richard Thompson .... Attorney

Blooston & Mordkofsky
2120 L St. NW
Suite 300
Washington, DC 20037
Ph: 202-659-0830

Blumenfeld & Cohn
1726 M St. NW
Washington, DC 20036
Ph: 202-955-6300

Brobeck Hale & Dorr International
1301 Ave. of the Americas
New York, NY 10019
Ph: 212-581-1600

Brown, Nietert & Kaufman
1920 N. St. NW
Suite 660
Washington, DC 20036
Ph: 202-887-0600

Budd Larner Gross Rosenbaum Greenberg
150 Houn F. Kennedy Pkwy
CN 1000
Short Hills, NJ 07078
Ph: 201-379-4800

    Donald Jacobs .... Partner

Carr, Morris & Graeff
1120 G. ST. NW
Suite 930
Washington, DC 20005
Ph: 202-789-1000

Chadbourne & Parke
1101 Vermont Ave. NW
Suite 900
Washington, DC 20005
Ph: 202-289-3000

Cohen & Berfield
1129 20th St. NW
Suite 507
Washington, DC 20036
Ph: 202-466-8565

Appendix

Cohn & Marks
1333 New Hampshire Ave. NW
Suite 600
Washington, DC 20036
Ph: 202-293-3860

Cole, Raywid & Braverman
1919 Pennsylvania Ave. NW
Suite 200
Washington, DC 20006
Ph: 202-659-9750

Cooley Godward
5 Palo Alto Sq.
Palo Alto, CA 94306
Ph: 415-843-5000

Covington & Burling
1202 Pennsylvania Ave. NW
Washington, DC 20044
Ph: 202-662-6000
   Gerard J. Waldron

Creative Licensing Corp.
2551 S. Bundy Dr.
Los Angeles, CA 90064
Ph: 310-479-6777

Cutner & Ron, LLC
641 Lexington Ave.
New York, NY 10022
Ph: 212-308-9393

DeSimone Pearson, LC
4330 Bellvue St.
Suite 10
Kansas City, MO 64111
Ph: 816-753-2823
   David J. DeSimone .... Partner

Dickstein, Shapiro & Morin
2101 L St. NW
Washington, DC 20037
Ph: 202-785-9700

Dow Lohnes & Albertson
1255 23rd St. NW
Suite 500
Washington, DC 20037
Ph: 202-857-2732

Dunnington Bartholow & Miller
666 3rd Ave.
New York, NY 10017
Ph: 212-682-8811

Farr & Taranto
2445 M St. NW
Suite 225
Washington, DC 20037
Ph: 202-775-0184

Fenwick & West
2 Palo Alto Square
Suite 800
Palo Alto, CA 94306
Ph: 415-494-0600
   Fred M. Greguras .... Partner

Frankfurt, Garbus, Klein & Selz
488 Madison Ave.
New York, NY 10022
Ph: 212-980-0120

Ginsberg, Feldman & Bress
1250 Connecticut Ave. NW
Washington, DC 20036
Ph: 202-637-9191
   Henry Rivera .... Partner

Gipson, Hoffman & Pancione
1901 Avenue of the Stars
Los Angeles, CA 90067
Ph: 310-556-4660

Law Firms

Goldberg, Godles, Weiner & Wright
1229 19th St. NW
Washington, DC 20036
Ph: 202-429-4900

    W. Kenneth Feree..................Assistant

Gray, Cary, Ware & Freidenrich
400 Hamilton Ave.
Palo Alto, CA 94301-1825
Ph: 415-328-6561

    Mark Radcliffe......................Attorney

Gurman, Hurtis, Blask & Freedman
1400 16th St. NW
Suite 500
Washington, DC 20036
Ph: 202-328-8200

Haley, Bader & Potts
4350 N. Fairfax Dr.
Suite 900
Arlington, VA 22203
Ph: 703-841-0606

Hall Dickler Kent Friedman & Wood
909 3 Ave.
New York, NY 10022
Ph: 212-339-5400

Hobbs, Straul, Dean & Wilder
1819 H. ST. NW
Suite 800
Washington, DC 20006
Ph: 202-783-5100

Holland & Knight
2100 Pennsylvania Ave.
Suite 400
Washington, DC 20037
Ph: 202-955-5550

Hopkins & Sutter
888 16th St. NW
Washington, DC 20003
Ph: 202-835-8098

Irell & Manella
1800 Avenue of the Stars
Los Angeles, CA 90067
Ph: 310-277-1010

Irwin, Campbell & Tannenwald, PC
1320 18th St. NW
Suite 400
Washington, DC 20006
Ph: 202-728-0400

    Alan C. Campbell..................Principal

Jacobson & Colfin P.C.
156 5 Ave.
New York, NY 10010
Ph: 212-691-5630

Kenoff & Machtinger
1999 Avenue of the Stars
Los Angeles, CA 90067
Ph: 310-552-0808

Kirkland & Ellis
655 15th St. NW
Suite 1200
Washington, DC 20005
Ph: 202-879-5176

Koteen & Naftalin
1150 Connecticut Ave. NW
Suite 1000
Washington, DC 20036
Ph: 202-467-5700

Latham & Watkins
633 W. 5th St.
Suite 4000
Los Angeles, CA 90071
Ph: 213-485-1234

Appendix

Leventhal, Senter & Lerman
2000 K St. NW
Suite 600
Washington, DC 20005
Ph: 202-429-8970

Lukas, McGowan, Nece & Gutierrez
1111 19th St. NW
Suite 1200
Washington, DC 20036
Ph: 202-857-3500
    David A. LaFuria...................Partner

Lynch Rousin Novack
300 E. 42nd St.
New York, NY 10017
Ph: 212-682-4001

McBride, Baker & Coles
500 W. Madison
40th Floor
Chicago, IL 60661-2511
Ph: 312-715-5700
    Larry M. Zanger

McFadden, Evans & Sill
1627 Eye St. NW
Suite 810
Washington, DC 20006
Ph: 202-659-4400

Mangum, Smietanka & Johnson
35 E. Wacker Dr.
Chicago, IL 60601
Ph: 312-368-8500

Meyer, Faller & Weisnam, PC
4400 Jennifer St. NW
Suite 380
Washington, DC 20015
Ph: 202-362-1100

Morrison & Foerster
1290 6 Ave.
New York, NY 10104
Ph: 212-468-8000

Mullin, Thuyne, Emmons and Topel, PC
1225 Connecticut Ave. NW
Suite 380
Washington, DC 20036
Ph: 202-659-4700
    Nathaniel F. Emmons............Owner

Nixon, Hargrave, Devans & Doyle
Clinton Square
P.O. Box 1051
Rochester, NY 14603
Ph: 716-546-8000

O'Connor & Hannan, LLP
1919 Pannsylvania Ave. NW
Suite 800
Washington, DC 20006
Ph: 202-887-1400

Ohana Communications
233 E. 70 St.
New York, NY 10021
Ph: 212-737-6906

Paul, Weiss, Rifkind, Wharton & Garrison
1615 L St. NW
Suite 1300
Washington, DC 20036
Ph: 202-223-7340
    Phillip L. Spector..................Partner

Pepper & Corazzini
1776 K St. NW
Washington, DC 20006
Ph: 202-296-0600
    Neal J. Freidman

Law Firms

Popham Haik Schnobrich & Kaufman, LTD
Metropolitan Square Building
655 Fifteenth Street, N.W., Suite 800
Washington, D.C. 20005-5701

Ph: 202-824-8000
Fax 202-824-8199

    Alan Melser..........................Partner

Preston Gates Ellis and Rouvelas Meeds
1735 New York Ave. NW
Suite 500
Washington, DC 20006

Ph: 202-628-1700

    Greg McCarthy

Reed, Smith, Shaw & McClay
1301 K St. NW
Suite 1100
Washington, DC 20005-3317

Ph: 202-463-2970

Renouf & Polivy
1532 16th St. NW
Washington, DC 20036

Ph: 202-265-1807

Rosenfeld, Meyer & Susman
9601 Wilshire Blvd.
Beverly Hills, CA 90210

Ph: 310-858-7700

Ross, Marsh & Foster
1401 H. St. NW
Suite 1000
Washington, DC 20006

Ph: 202-822-8888

Santarelli, Smith & Carroccio
1155 Connecticut Ave.
Suite 900
Washington, DC 20036

Ph: 202-466-6800

Schwartz, Woods & Miller
1350 Connecticut Ave. NW
Suite 300
Washington, DC 20036

Ph: 202-833-1700

The Skornia Law Firm
160 W. Santa Clara St.
Suite 1500
San Jose, CA 95113

Ph: 408-280-2820

    Thomas A. Skornia................Principal

Squire, Sanders & Dempsey
1201 Pennsylvania Ave. SW
Suite 500
Washington, DC 20004

Ph: 202-622-6600

Steptoe & Johnson
1330 Connecticut Ave.
Washington, DC 20036

Ph: 202-429-6479

Strook Strook & Lavan
2029 Centure Park E.
Los Angeles, CA 90067

Ph: 310-556-5800

Swidler & Berlin
3000 K St. NW
Suite 300
Washington, DC 20007

Ph: 202-424-7500

    William B. Wilhelm Jr. ....Assistant Attorney

Tierney & Swift
1001 22nd St. NW
Suite 350
Washington, DC 20037-1803

Ph: 202-293-7979

Appendix

Wei, Gotshal & Manges
2882 Sand Hill Rd.
Menlo Park, CA 94025
Ph: 415-926-6200

Wiley, Rein & Felding
1776 K St. NW
Washington, DC 20006
Ph: 202-429-7000

    Jim Slattery ....Partner

VC FIRMS

21st Century Group
921 N. Pennsylvania Ave.
Winter Park, FL 32789

Ph: (407) 644-7335

    Fern Duquette........................ Managing Partner

Accel Partners
One Embarcadero Center
San Francisco, CA 94111

Ph: (415)989-5656
email: Jim Breyer, jbreyer@accel.com
www: http://www.accel.com

$350M Under Management

    James Breyer........................ General Partner

Accel Partners
One Palmer Square
Princeton, NJ 08542
Ph: (609)683-4500
email: Don Gooding, dgooding@accel.com
www: http://www.accel.com

$350M Under Management

Alpha Partners
545 Middlefield Rd.
Suite 170
Menlo Park, CA 94025

Ph: (415) 854-7024

    Wallace F. Davis................... General Partner

American Strategic Investments
P.O. Box 2941
Beverly Hills, CA 90213

Ph: (213) 278-1898

    Dennis McCarthy .... Managing Director

Asset Management Co.
2275 E. Bayshore Rd.
Suite 150
Palo Alto, CA 94303

Ph: (415) 494-7400

AT&T Ventures
East Hanover, NJ
Ph: (201) 952-1485

$80M Under Management

    Alessandro Piol

Atlas Venture
222 Berkeley Street
Boston, MA 02116

Ph: (617) 859-9290
fax: (617) 859-9292

AVI Management Partners
1 First St.
Suite 12
Los Altos, CA 94022

Ph: (415) 949-9855

    Chuck K. Chan..................... General Partner

Baccharis Venture Partners
2420 Sand Hill Rd.
Suite 100
Menlo Park, CA 94025

Ph: (415) 324-6844

    Mary Bechmann .... PartnerBank

America Capital Corp.
555 California St.
Dept. 3908
San Francisco, CA 94104

Ph: (415) 622-2230

    Patrick J. Topolski .... Vice President

Bay Partners
10600 N. De Anza Blvd.
Cupertino, CA 95014-2031

Ph: (408) 725-2444

    John E. Bosch....................... General Partner

Appendix

Bechtel Investments Inc.
50 Fremont St.
Suite 3700
San Francisco, CA 94105
Ph: (415) 768-0197

    Thomas D. Wilardson .... Principal

The Benefit Capital Companies
P.O. Box 49422
Los Angeles, CA 90049
Ph: (213) 440-2296

    Edward M. Bixler .... President

Canaan Partners
105 Rowayton Avenue
Rowayton, CT 06853
Ph: (203) 855-0400
fax: (203) 854-9117

CEO Venture Fund
4516 Henry St.
Pittsburgh, PA 15213
Ph: (412) 687-3451

De Vries & Co Inc.
800 W. 47th St.
Kansas City, MO 64112
Ph: (816) 756-0055

    Robert J. De Vries .... President

Digital Technology Partners
World Trade Center Suite 235
San Francisco, CA 94111
Ph: (415) 249-3995
fax: (415) 788-2514

Dillon Read Ventures
535 Madison Ave.
New York, NY 10017
Ph: 212-906-7759

Draper Associates
400 Seaport Court, Suite 250
Redwood City, CA 94063

Ph: (415) 599-9000
fax: (415) 599-9726

    Mary Ruth Moran .... Vice President

Drysdale Enterprises
177 Bovet Road, Suite 600
San Mateo, CA 94402
Ph (415) 341-6336
fax: (415) 341-1329

Geocapital Partners
1 Bridge Plaza
Fort Lee, NJ 07024
Ph: (201) 461-9292

    Lawrence Lepard

Gerald Klauer Mattison & Co.
529 5 Ave.
New York, NY 10017
Ph: 212-338-8900

Grace Software Marketing Co.
3091 Mayfield Rd.
Suite 320
Rockefeller Building
Cleveland Heights, OH 44118
Ph: (216) 321-2000

Hambrecht & Quist Venture Partners
One Bush St.
San Francisco, CA 94104
Ph: (415) 576-3300

    G. Mead Wyman .... General Partner

Hancock Venture Partners
Boston, MA
Ph: (617) 348-3713

    Ofer Nemirovsky

Hummer Winblad Venture Partners
5900 Hollis St.
Suite R
Emeryville, CA 94608
Ph: (510) 652-8061

Venture Capital Firms

Interwest Partners

3000 Sand Hill Rd.
Building Three
Suite 255
Menlo Park, CA 94025-7112

Ph: (415) 854-8585

    H. Berry Cash........................ General Partner

Kleiner Perkins Caufield & Byers

2750 Sand Hill Road
Menlo Park, CA 94025

Ph: (415) 233-2750

    John Doerr............................ General Partner

Lawrence Tyrell Ortale & Smith

515 Madison Ave.
New York, NY 10022

Ph: 212-826-9824

Matrix Partners

Boston, MA

Ph: (617) 345-6740

    Andrew Marcuvitz

Mayfield Fund

2800 Sand Hill Road
Menlo Park, CA 94025

Ph: (415) 854-5560
fax (415) 854-5712

    Michael Levinthal

Menlo Ventures

Palo Alto, CA

Ph: (415) 854-8540

Mohr, Davidow Ventures

Menlo Park, CA

Ph: (415) 854-7236

    Jonathan Feiber

New Enterprise Associates

235 Montgomery Street, Suite 1025
San Francisco, CA 94104

Ph: (415) 956-1579
fax (415) 981-4168

New Media Associates

148 Duane st.
New York, NY 10013

Ph: 212-349-2700

North Bridge Venture Partners

404 Wyman Street, Suite 365
Waltham, MA 02181

Ph: (617) 290-0004
Fax (617)290-0999

    Bill Geary

Ohana Communications

233 E. 70 St.
New York, NY 10021

Ph: 212-737-6906

Olympic Venture Partners

2420 Carillion Pt.
Kirkland, WA 98101

Ph: (206) 889-9192

    Gerard Langeler

ONSET Enterprise Associates

301 University Avenue, Suite 250
Palo Alto, CA 94301

Ph: (415) 327-5470
fax: (415) 327-5488

ONSET Venture

8920 Business Park Drive, Suite 140
Austin, TX 78759

Ph: (512) 349-2255
fax: (512) 349-2258

Patricof & Co. Ventures

445 Park Ave.
New York, NY 10022

Ph: 212-753-6300

Appendix

The Phoenix Partners
1000 2nd Ave.
Suite 3600
Seattle, WA 98104
Ph: (206) 624-8968
  Alessandro Piol

Piper Jaffray
1200 5 Ave.
Seattle, WA 98101
  Ph: 206-287-8831

Platinum Venture Partners
Oakbrook Terrace, IL
Ph: 708-620-5000
  Michael Santer

Quaestus Management
Milwaukee, WI
Ph: (414) 287-4500
  Richard Weening

Sacher Capital
375 Park Ave.
New York, NY 10152
  Ph: 212-319-1968

Sage Management Group
2311 Webster St.
San Francisco, CA 94115
Ph: (415) 346-4036
  Charles A. Bauer .... Principal

Sevin Rosen Funds
550 Lytton Avenue, Suite 200
Palo Alto, CA 94301
  Ph: (415) 326-0550

Sigma Partners
Menlo Park, CA
Ph: (415) 854-1300
  Wade Woodson

Sofinnova Inc.
One Market Plaza Steuart Tower, Suite 2630
San Francisco, CA 94105
Ph: (415) 597-5757
fax (415) 597-5750

Sorrento Associates Inc.
4225 Executive Square
Suite 1450
San Diego, CA 92037
Ph: (619) 452-6400
  Mitchell L. Siegler .... Vice President

St. Paul Venture Capital, Inc.
8500 Normandale Lake Blvd., Suite 1940
Bloomington, MN 55437
Ph: (612) 830-7474
fax (612) 830-7475

Morgan Stanley & Co.
555 California St.
San Francisco, CA 94104
Ph: (415) 576-2000

Summit Partners
Boston, MA
Ph: (415) 321-1166
  Walter Kortschak

Sutter Hill Ventures
Palo Alto, CA
Ph: 415-493-5600
  Tench Coxe

Technology Partners
1550 Tiburon Blvd., Suite A
Belvedere, CA 94920
Ph: (415) 435-1935
fax (415) 435-5921
  William Hart .... Managing Partner

Venture Capital Firms

Trident Capital, LP
2480 Sand Hill Rd.
Suite 201
Menlo Park, CA 94025
Ph: (415) 233-4300

Union Venture Corp.
445 S. Figueroa St.
Los Angeles, CA 90071
Ph: (213) 236-4092

    Kenton Pattie......................... Executive Vice President

Unterberg Harris
65 E. 55 St.
New York, NY 10022
Ph: 212-888-5600

Venrock Associates
30 Rockefeller Plaza, Room 5508
New York, NY 10112
Ph: (212) 649-5600

    Ray Rothrock .... Partner

Venrock Associates
755 Page Mill Road, Suite A230
Palo Alto, CA 94304
Ph:(415) 493-5577

Volpe Welte & Co.
1 Maritime Plaza
San Francisco, CA 94111
Ph: 415-956-8120

Walden Group
750 Battery St.
San Francisco, CA 94111
Ph: 415-391-7225

Weiss, Peck & Greer Venture Partners
555 California Street, Suite 4760
San Francisco, CA 94104
Ph: (415) 622-6864

The Windgate Fund, LLC
130 William St.
Suite 807
New York, NY 10038
Ph: (212) 227-0905

Appendix

REPLICATION & PACKAGING FIRMS

3M Prerecorded Optical Media
3M Center
St. Paul, MN 55144
Ph: 612-733-2142

    Dave Iverson ....Production Manager

Acutrack Software Duplication
16592 Rolando Ave.
San Leandro, CA 94578
Ph: 510-278-5441

Advanced Media Concept, Inc.
236 W. 27th Street
NYC, NY 1001
Ph: 212-229-1348

Allied Digital Technologies
1301 Avenue of the Americas
14th Floor
New York, NY 10019
Ph: 212-757-6800

    Steve Granat ....Vice President-Marketing

Americ Disc Inc.
812 Anne St., SW
Leesburg, VA 22075
Ph: 703-777-1872

    Glenn Tompkins ....Regional Sales Manager

American Multimedia Inc.
2609 Tucker St.
Burlington, NC 27215
Ph: 910-229-5554

American Pro Digital Inc.
P.O. Box 550
Rooseveltown, NY 13683-0550
Ph: 315-769-0034

Ashby Champion
43301 Osgood Rd.
Fremont, CA 94539
Ph: 510-651-1934

Astraltech Americas Inc.
5400 Broken Sound Blvd.
Boca Raton, FL 33487
Ph: 407-995-7011

AT&T Software Replication Center
2443 Warrenville Rd.
Lisle, IL 60532
Ph: 800-772-2443

Big Byte Media
18425 Napa St.
Northridge, CA 91325
Ph: 818-700-2983

    Jack Daly ....Vice President

Braun Media Services Inc.
3800 Annapolis Ln.
Plymouth, MN 55447
Ph: 612-551-3100

    Robert Olson ....Vice President

Cassette Productions
4910 Amelia Earhart Dr.
Salt Lake City, UT 84116
Ph: 801-531-7555

Cenna Technology (CenTech)
1375 W. 8040 S
West Jordan, UT 84088
Ph: 801-255-3999

Appendix

Cinram, Inc.
660 White Plains Rd.
Tarrytown, NY 10591
Ph: 914-631-2800

Commercial Documentation Services
2661 S. Pacific Hwy.
Medford, OR 97501
Ph: 503-773-7575

Coptech West
249 Humbolt Ct.
Sunnyvale, CA 94089-1300
Ph: 408-727-6427

Creative Digital Research
7291 Coronado Dr.
San Jose, CA 95129
Ph: 408-255-0999
    Paul Ling .... President

Creative Sound Corp.
25429 Malibu Rd.
Malibu, Ca 90265
Ph: 310-456-5482

Crest National
1000 N. Highland Avenue
Hollywood, CA 90038
Ph: 800-309-DISC

cyberdisk
69 Brunswick Exit
Moosup, CT 06354
Ph: 860-564-6610

Data NW Seattle
120 Belmont Ave. E
Seattle, WA 98102-5603
Ph: 206-633-0524

dataDisc
Route 3, Box 1108
Gainesville, VA 22065
Ph: 703-347-2111

Denon Digital Industries
1380 Monticello Rd.
Madison, GA 30650
Ph: 706-342-3032

Design To Distribution
5429 LBJ Freeway
Dallas, TX 75218
Ph: 800-336-6066

Digital Audio Disc Corp
1800 N. Fruit Ave.
Terre Haute, IN 47804
Ph: 812-462-8100

Digital Magnetics Inc.
801 Jupiter Rd.
Suite 102
Plano, TX 75074
Ph: 214-578-7664

Digitech Inc.
P.O. Box 25177
Greenville, SC 29616
Ph: 803-676-9917

Disc Makers
7905 N. Rt. 130
Pennsauken, NJ 08110
Ph: 800-468-9353
    Larry Ballen .... President

Disc Manufacturing Inc.
1409 Foulk Rd.
Wilmington, DE 19803
Ph: 302-479-2500]
    Rusty Capers .... Vice President

Replication & Packaging Firms

Disctronics
2800 Summit Ave.
Plano, TX 75074
Ph: 214-881-8800
    David K. Williamson.............VP, CD-ROM Sales

Dolphin Computer
532 Great Rd.
Acton, MA 01720
Ph: 508-635-5308

Douglas Electronics Inc.
9777 Alvarado St.
San Leandro, CA 94577
Ph: 510-483-8770

Echo Data Services Inc.
560 Trestle Pl.
Downingtown, PA 19335
Ph: 610-873-6000
    John Latz ....Account Manager

EDSCO
PO Box 2250
West Peabody, MA 90068
Ph: 508-535-8500

EMI Manufacturing (USA)
1 Capitol Way
Jacksonville, IL 62650
Ph: 217-245-9631

Encryption Technology Corp.
171 Lock Dr.
Marlborough, MA 01752
Ph: 508-229-8500
    Kevin Moriarity.........................VP, Sales & Marketing

Eternal Archives Solutions Inc.
61 Holmes Ave
Suite B
Waterbury, CT 06710

Ph: 203-759-0574
    Jeff Weiss ....President

Eva-Tone
4801 Ulmerton Rd.
Clearwater, FL 34618
Ph: 813-572-7000

GRA Packaging Services Inc.
3800 Monroe Ave.
Pittsford, NY 14534
Ph: 716-385-2060
    Donna Jones ....Production Manager

Hauppauge Manufacturing Group
15 Gilpin Ave.
Hauppauge, NY 11788
Ph: 516-234-0200

Image Management Systems
239 W. 15 St.
New York, NY 10011
Ph: 212-741-8765

Image Source Inc.
36 Pond St.
Suite 104
Franklin, MA 02038
Ph: 508-520-4202

IMPAC Technology Inc.
180 Gordon Dr.
Suite 107
Exton, PA 19342
Ph: 610-594-8500
    James Freed..........................President

JVC Information Products
17811 Mitchell Ave.
Irvine, CA 92714
Ph: 714-261-1292

Appendix

JVC Disc America
2 JVC Rd.
Tuscaloosa, AL 35405
Ph: 800-677-5518

Kao Infosystems Co.
40 Grisson Rd.
Plymouth, MA 02360
Ph: 508-747-5520

    John Brush...........................Executive VP

KAO Optical Products
128 Warren St.
Lowell, MA 01852
Ph: 508-458-9788

Klarity Kassette
Post Office Square Main St.
Waterville, ME 04901
Ph: 800-458-6405

Magnetech Corp.
3941 SW 47 Ave.
Ft. Lauderdale, FL 33314
Ph: 317-870-5700

Memcon Corp.
2430 S. 156 Cir.
Omaha, NE 68130
Ph: 402-333-3100

Metatec Corp.
7001 Metatec Blvd.
Dublin, OH 43017
Ph: 800-637-3472
Ph: 614-766-3104

    Dawn H. Powell ....Marketing Manager

Microboards Inc.
P.O. Box 846
Chanhassen, MN 55317-0846
Ph: 612-448-9800

National Data Conversion Institute
5 E 16th St.
New York, NY 10003
Ph: 212-463-7511

    Michael Daniec ....President

National Tape & Disc Corp.
1105 16 Ave. S.
Nashville, TN 37212
Ph: 615-320-9025

National Video Industries, Inc.
15 West 17th St.
New York, NY 10011
Ph: 212-691-1300

Nimbus CD International
State Route 629, Guilford Farm
Ruckersville, VA 22968
Ph: 804-985-1100

    Lyndon Faulkner ....CEO

Noble House
21704 Devonshire
Suite 330
Chatsworth, CA 91311
Ph: 818-709-5053

Northeastern Digital
2 Hidden Meadow Lane
Southboro, MA 01772
Ph: 508-481-9322

NSPAN Corp.
16038 Vickery
Suite 280
Houston, TX 77032
Ph: 713-985-3111

    Leland Costley..........................General Manager

Replication & Packaging Firms

OMNI Resources Corp.
50 Howe Ave.
Millbury, MA 01527
Ph: 508-865-4451

    C.J. Anand ....Vice President- Sales

OneSource, Inc.
8-10 W. 19th St.
New York, NY 10011
Ph: 212-727-1010
Fax: 212-727-2104

Optical Media International
180 Knowles Dr.
Los Gatos, CA 95030
Ph: 800-347-2664
Fx: 408-376-3519

Optimax Disc Inc.
3420 Pomona Blvd.
Pomona, CA 91768
Ph: 909-598-3887

Pacific Coast Sound Works
8455 Beverly Blvd.
Suite 500
West Hollywood, CA 90048
Ph: 213-655-4771

Pilz America
54 Conchester Rd.
Concordville, PA 19331
Ph: 610-459-5035

Pinnacle Micro
19 Technology
Irvine, CA 92718
Ph: 800-553-7070
Ph: 714-727-3300

Polygram Mfg. and Disc
PO Box 400
Grover, NC 28073
Ph: 704-734-4265

Princeton Diskette
1101 Richmond Ave.
Point Pleasant Beach, NJ 08742
Ph: 800-426-9800

Print NW/Six Sigma
4918 20th St. E
P.O. Box 1418
Tacoma, WA 98401
Ph: 206-922-9393

PSI Industries
135 Ludlow Ave.
Northvale, NJ 07647
Ph: 201-768-8007

Publishers Data Service
1 Lower Ragsdale Dr.
Monterey, CA 93940
Ph: 408-372-2812

Quality Data Systems Inc.
2450 Central Ave.
Suite B-2
Boulder, CO 80301
Ph: 303-444-1257

Revelation Products Corp.
1220 Valley Forge Rd.
P.O. Box 2225
Valley Forge, PA 19482
Ph: 610-933-5875

Ricoh Corp.
5 Dedrick Pl.
West Caldwell, NJ 07006
Ph: 201-882-2000

    Claudia Jones ....Public Relations Manager

Rimage Corp.
7725 Washington Ave. S
Minneapolis, MN 55439
Ph: 612-944-8144

Appendix

Seattle Support Group
20420 84 Ave. S.
Kent, WA 98032
Ph: 206-395-1484

Software Services Group
1218 East Hartman Ave.
Omaha, NE 68110
Ph: 402-453-1699

Sonopress
1540 Broadway
New York, NY 10019
Ph: 212-418-9439

Sony Electronic Publishing
9 W. 57 St.
New York, NY 10019
Ph: 212-418-9439

Speciality Records Corp.
1400 E. Lackawann Ave.
Olyphant, PA 18447
Ph:717-383-3535

Spectra Tek
1508 Cotner Ave.
Los Angeles, CA 90025
Ph: 310-473-4966

Star-Byte Inc.
2880 Bergey Rd.
Hatfield, PA 19440
Ph: 215-997-2470

Walter Friedrick........................Vice President

Starpak Inc.
237 22nd St.
Greeley, CO 80631
Ph: 303-352-6800

Brent Cox ....Sales Manager

Tapette Corp.
15702 Producer Ln.
Huntington Beach, CA 92649
Ph: 714-638-7960

Technicolor Optical Media Services
3301 E. Mission Oaks Blvd.
Camarillo, CA 93012
Ph: 805-445-3047

Ram Nomula ....President

TechniDisc
2250 Meijer Dr.
Troy, MI 48084
Ph: 810-352-5353

20251 Sealpoint Circle
Suite 104
Huntington Beach, CA 92646
Ph: 714-536-0025

Ron Balousek ....President

Todd Enterprises
31 Water Mill Ln.
Great Neck, NY 11021
Ph: 718-343-1040

Jay Singer

UNIK Micros
P.O. Box 204491
Austin, TX 78720-4491
Ph: 512-251-8181

Unisys Corp., Custom Software Manufacturing
13250 Haggerty Rd. N
Building 4
Plymouth, MI 48170
Ph: 313-451-4888

US Optical Disc
1 Eagle Dr.
Sanford, ME 04073
Ph: 207-324-1124

Replication & Packaging Firms

Vertical Development Corp.
One Vertical Dr.
Canonsburg, PA 15317

Ph: 412-746-4247

    Chuck Kellar ....Regional Sales Manager

Video West
1065 W. North Temple
Salt Lake City, UT 84116

Ph: 801-575-4400

WEA Manufacturing
278 Fulton St.
North Babylon, NY 11704

Ph: 516-253-0337

3601 W. Olive Ave.
Suite 210
Burbank, CA 91505

Ph: 818-953-2941

Windsor New Media
8 W. 38th St.
New York, NY 10018

Ph: 212-944-9090
Fax: 212-840-0217

WRS Motion Picture Lab
1000 Napor Blvd.
Pittsburgh, PA 15205

Ph: 412-937-7700

ALSO AVAILABLE FROM THE CARRONADE GROUP

Interactive Music Handbook— the essential guide for musicians, artists, developers & audio technicians interested in producing interactive music CD-ROMs, creating Enhanced CDs, or learning more about the online music scene. The book includes case studies and interviews with over 30 top artists and executives in the music industry.

Interactive Music Handbook
320 pages   1-885452-08-x   **$24.95** plus S/H

Interactive Writers Handbook— the writer's bible for everything you need to know about the emerging craft of interactive writing— from character and story issues to compensation and design paradigms. Learn how to create documents such as design proposals, interactive screenplays, and flow modules that will meet the rigid standards of colleagues and industry professionals. Includes interaviews with top interactive writers in the industry.

Interactive Writers Handbook
368 pages   1-885452-11-x   **$24.95** plus S/H

The Multimedia Directory - 6th Edition— the authorative, reference resources used by interactive media professionals. 1,450 detailed company profiles, 6,000+ personnel, indexed by 14 major categories. Need a job? Looking for sales leads? Want to form co-production deals? The Directory is ideal for novices and seasoned pro's who need the latest interactive media data at their fingertips.

The Multimedia Directory - 6th Edition
430 pages   1-885452-12-8   **$59.95** plus S/H

Visit our website:
http://www.carronade.com
To order, call:
1-800-529-3501

BE HEARD ABOVE THE NOISE

Masters of Media

Apple Computer® has always enjoyed a special relationship with communicators of information around the world. In fact, the Macintosh® dominates the media industry.

Apple is now introducing a comprehensive program for artists, designers, musicians, publishers, webmasters, service bureaus, advertising agencies, animators, Hollywood entertainment companies and corporate communicators— Macintosh users for the new millenium.

The **"Masters of Media"** Program shows Macintosh users how to make and save money by leveraging their content or original property. For a corporation, intellectual property is their brand. For the creative talent and publisher, equity lies in their creative content or visual ideas. For the production and press company, color production and color fidelity is their equity. Make equity pay to its fullest potential through **"Masters of Media."**

The opportunity Apple provides is a means for the Macintosh professional to move and expand their content from one to all media. The **cross media authoring** capability means that communications no longer have to be media-specific, (i.e. print media, multimedia, or new media), now they can become Media Universal.

1-800-776-2333

ANIMATION
RUNNING YOUR OWN MEDIA BUSINESS
CREATING ENHANCED CDS
BUILDING A REALLY COOL WEBSITE
USING THE WEB FOR COMMERCE
INTERACTIVE STORYTELLING
CUSTOMIZED MARKETING MATERIAL
FROM SCRIPT TO SCREEN
MODELING
NONLINEAR DIGITAL EDITING
BUDGETING
HOLLYWOOD SPECIAL EFFECTS
MASTERING & BURNING

Use the Power **Macintosh**™ and **Mac**™**OS** technologies to re-express your creativity.

Master the Media.
www.masters.media.apple.com
www.apple.com

Benefits of Membership Include:

Multimedia Guidebooks

Market Research Reports & White Papers

Co-marketing Opportunities

Networking Events

Seminars

Conferences

Special Discounts

Seeding Opportunities

Apple Media Program

Designed to help creative professionals make and save money, network, expand their area of expertise, generate market demand for their products and services, and gain a better understanding of the evolving new media marketplace.

When it comes to multimedia in business, there are two questions we hear over and over: "What are my competitors doing?" and "What's it take to get started?"

The Apple Media Program (AMP) is the online media information source for technology, tools, resources and market trends impacting digital media authors. AMP is designed for new media developers, title publishers, information and content providers, designers, interactive musicians, desktop video professionals, educators, marketers, and in-house corporate developers. AMP provides a breadth of resources and information to keep creative professionals up-to-date on Apple's offerings for authoring and playback. Check out the complete membership benefits on our website.

For an application or worldwide program information, go to www.amp.apple.com, or call 408/974-4897.

www.amp.apple.com
The ultimate source for creative professionals.

©1996 Apple Computer, Inc. All rights reserved. Apple, the Apple logo and Macintosh are registered trademarks of Apple Computer, Inc. This ad was created using Macintosh personal computers.